From the Temple Mount to the New Jerusalem

From the Temple Mount to the New Jerusalem

A Biblical Theology of Zion Symbolism

JARED M. BLAIR

WIPF & STOCK · Eugene, Oregon

FROM THE TEMPLE MOUNT TO THE NEW JERUSALEM
A Biblical Theology of Zion Symbolism

Wipf & Stock
An Imprint of Wipf and Stock Publishers
199 W. 8th Ave., Suite 3
Eugene, OR 97401

www.wipfandstock.com

PAPERBACK ISBN: 979-8-3852-5466-8
HARDCOVER ISBN: 979-8-3852-5467-5
EBOOK ISBN: 979-8-3852-5468-2

VERSION NUMBER 021926

To Beth
for always believing, always hoping, always loving

Contents

Introduction

The presence of God among his people is a biblical theological theme that spans the entirety of the canon of Scripture, and one of the central symbols attached to this theme is Zion. The term "Zion" appears in several forms and is utilized by the authors of the Bible in various ways: Zion can refer to a physical location, the people of God, or the place of God's promised restoration in the future. Thus, the Zion symbol cannot be confined to a singular meaning, but rather its function as a theological motif in Scripture is developed throughout the canon and changes depending on the context and historical situation of the passage.

From the time of King David until John's Revelation of Jesus Christ, Zion appears in various contexts and carries unique meanings depending on whether it appears in the Psalms, Prophets, or the New Testament. However, there is a primary meaning that unifies the various uses of Zion symbolism as it is expanded and reshaped through the canon: the presence of God among his people. Whether in times of peace or judgment, Zion was chosen by God as his eternal dwelling as Ps 132 exclaims, "For the Lord has chosen Zion; he has desired it for his dwelling place: this is my resting place forever; here I will dwell, for I have desired it" (vv. 13–14). What the Israelites, during David and Solomon's reign, witnessed in a physical sense, what the prophets longed for, and what New Testament Christians experience in an already-not-yet way is the presence of God. Therefore, Zion is a powerful biblical motif that intertwines multiple eras of God's redemptive plans into a beautiful tapestry with an inscribed message: God desires to dwell among his beloved creation. Beginning with Eden and ending with a restored, perfected new creation, God desires to be present among his people in joyful communion, and ultimately, this could not be fulfilled without the sacrificial death and resurrection of Christ. Christ himself became the fulfillment of Zion because, through him, those who believe in faith eternally rest in the presence of God. Because of Christ, the thematic hopes of a restored kingdom of God in Zion were transformed, allowing all believers in Christ to experience the eschatological reality of this new Zion in the present with confident expectation of a final salvation in the new Jerusalem. Zion symbolism in Scripture is a theological theme that not only connects Old Testament longing with a New Testament reality but also displays the Father's desire to dwell among his beloved creation forever.

In Psalms, Zion is multivalent, often appearing as a symbol of God's kingship and rule over the nations from Jerusalem but also as a symbol of God's promises for a future restored kingdom.[1] There is an emotional and theological weight to the concept of Zion in Psalms, and depending on the context surrounding a psalm, Zion may bring forth jubilation, mourning, or a confident expectation in God's future restoration of Israel. As God's redemptive plans in times of flourishing and judgment unfold, the application of Zion symbolism embodies new forms.

In the Prophets, Zion likewise is a term with many symbolic functions: Isaiah frequently uses the term to refer to God's majesty and kingship in Jerusalem, yet in Isaiah 40–66, the writer's mood shifts to a more reflective, hopeful, or even somber attitude toward the future of Zion, not only as the physical home of Yahweh's presence but as an eternal symbol of God's divine presence among a redeemed people. The prophet exclaimed, "For out of Zion shall go forth the law, and the word of the Lord from Jerusalem . . . and they shall beat their swords into plowshares, and their spears into pruning hooks" (Isa 2:3–4). On the other hand, the Zion symbol appears in reference to the people of Judah in the context of judgment. "Daughter Zion" becomes a personification of the city to represent God's disappointment and imminent judgment upon the land through the invasion of foreign nations.

As a theological symbol, Zion points forward to God's future redemptive plans: in the Minor Prophets, Zion appears in the context of both judgment and salvation, and it is broadened beyond Israel alone.[2] Under the protection of Yahweh, all the nations will come to Zion to seek wisdom, teaching, and salvation, pointing to the rise of a new king who will lead Israel into a new era of peace in Zion. Joel 2:23–27 paints a vivid image of this time, when the children of Zion will rejoice, and a time when "you shall know that I am in the midst of Israel . . . and my people shall never again be put to shame" (Joel 2:23, 27). This is evidence that the theological symbol of Zion continued to expand through the Prophets, ultimately leading to its transformation in Jesus Christ. In the time of the later prophets, Zion remained the primary symbol for God's future restoration as Zechariah

1. Ollenburger, *Zion, the City*, 19.

2. Boda, *Dictionary of the Old Testament*, 1948.

prophesied, "Sing and rejoice, O daughter of Zion, for behold, I come and I will dwell in your midst, declares the Lord" (Zech 2:10). The promise is not that Israel would have a glorious kingdom for its own sake but that the Lord would dwell among his people once again.

In the New Testament, a new direction is taken regarding the theological symbolism of Zion, for the reign of God in Zion becomes interpreted through a christological lens. The Gospels reveal that Zion itself is built on the Messiah, Jesus, for he is the true cornerstone upon which the spiritual house of God is built. Therefore, the Zion symbol is transformed in the New Testament: texts such as Rom 9:33 and 1 Pet 2:6 reflect upon the imagery of Isa 28:16 and reveal how the prophet's hope for Zion was fulfilled in Christ because he is the "tested stone" upon which God's salvation is built (Isa 28:16). The New Testament also reveals the endpoint for the Zion symbol, for in Christ's eschatological kingdom, the new Jerusalem described in Rev 21 reveals a perfect city where true Israel, the faithful saints of God, dwells eternally in the presence of "the Lord God the Almighty and the Lamb" (Rev 21:22). Built upon Isaiah's vision of the new heavens and earth, Revelation completes the painting by describing Christ as the final king who makes all things new. Through each of these biblical passages, the Zion symbol is transformed, now representing God's holy people redeemed in Christ, for through him the saints find eternal rest in the presence of God.

Zion symbolism developed through the canon of Scripture primarily as a reflection of God's presence among his people and was transformed in Jesus Christ as the church becomes a reflection of the heavenly Zion on earth. The canon of Scripture itself is the primary guide for this process, therefore, additional studies on the dating and authorship of certain texts will be subordinate to the purpose of tracing the changing nature of the Zion symbol through the Bible. By showing the relationship between key texts and the various ways in which Zion represents theological themes, there emerges a movement from expectation to fulfillment as God's redemptive plans unfold. It is also necessary to connect the New Testament implications of the Zion symbol with their basis in the theology of the Old Testament, which will underpin the argument that Zion symbolism was transformed through Jesus Christ as he inaugurated a new era when God dwells among his people in an already-not-yet way. Applying canonical awareness and sensitivity to the theological themes woven throughout Scripture reveals the symbolic movement of Zion toward its fulfillment in the new Jerusalem, which is made possible because of Jesus.

The Hebrew term for Zion (*ṣîyôn*) appears first in 2 Sam 5:7 as reference to the name of the Jebusite fortress that David captured and renamed as "the city of David."[3] While the theological concept of the city of God is closely linked to Zion, other terminology directly associated with the physical city of Jerusalem, the temple, or collective terms to describe the Israelites is not the primary focus of this study. Inevitably, there are overlaps between some of the concepts, but this study is not primarily on the city or the temple but rather on the developing symbolism surrounding the use of Zion and its transformation as a theological symbol denoting God's presence.

The most common descriptor attached to Zion is "Mount," which not only signifies the hilltop location of the city of David and the temple but also the religious connotation associated with God's dwelling place being a cosmic mountain. In most instances, "Mount Zion" and "Zion" do not usually bear unique meanings from one another; however, in certain passages where it may be deemed appropriate, the addition of "Mount" will be addressed. Also, the concept of a "Zion tradition" has been developed in reference to a possible cultic system in Jerusalem, which was built upon existing Jebusite (Canaanite) religious traditions. The theological tradition based upon the Zion symbol that appears throughout Scripture is the focus; thus, the temple cult and its associated traditions are not the primary purpose of the phrase "Zion symbolism," nor is there always a consistent, precise physical referent in focus (such as a temple or physical hill). Rather, Zion will be studied primarily within its theological and canonical meanings in Scripture.

Zion's symbolic journey does not begin with its first mention in 2 Samuel, for the term is immediately imbued with symbolism stretching back to the Garden of Eden, the original place where God's presence rested among the first people. In Exodus, Israel's experience at Mount Sinai also sets an important backdrop for the development of Zion symbolism. Psalm 68 says, "The Lord is among them; Sinai is now in the sanctuary" (Ps 68:17). The presence of God was physically present at Sinai in the clouds and thundering voice, and the instructions given by God there led to the construction of the tabernacle and the ark of the covenant. What began at Sinai transformed into a theology that stretched far beyond the temple or the ark, reminding the people that Yahweh makes himself known through his presence and power among them. The final pieces of the background to Zion symbolism involve David and Solomon, who initiated and developed the temple mount as the primary place for God's rule over Israel and the nations. David captured the Jebusite stronghold and established the area as the primary religious site for the people, yet it was not until the ark was moved from Shiloh that the cult in Jerusalem exploded with zeal for God's reign in Zion.

3. Harris, *Theological Wordbook*, 764.

This important moment marked a new era for the Israelites and ushered in a new fervor for the worship of Yahweh and the belief that God's rule over the nations of earth was centered upon Mount Zion.

In each era of Israel's history, the presence of God remains a central theme that progresses God's redemptive plans and reminds the people of his previous gracious actions toward his chosen people. Through the Prophets, Zion becomes a symbol that anticipates Yahweh's return, envisioning a glorious future where the reign of God will not only protect Israel but draw the nations toward the presence of God, which brings peace. Isaiah saw a time when "out of Zion shall go forth law," leading to a time of peace when the nations of earth would "beat their swords into plowshares, and their spears into pruning hooks" (Isa 2:3–4). Because of the Lord's presence in Zion, weapons of warfare will be transformed into farming tools, for the peoples of earth will live in peace in the presence of God. Isaiah's vision points forward to a new Zion, where the presence of God is accessed by the nations of earth. As Israel's prophets continue to proclaim the word of the Lord, an emerging image of a coming Messiah builds anticipation that this new Zion may become reality one day.

While the term "Zion" is rare in the New Testament, there are nonetheless significant passages that contribute to the development of Zion symbolism and show that, because of Christ, the expectations expressed in the Psalms and Prophets were fulfilled. Paul understood the prophetic hope for a restored kingdom in Jerusalem, and he drew upon elements of the Zion tradition through his plea for the Jews to be saved by faith in Christ. Passages such as Rom 11 and Gal 4:21–31 represent Paul's belief that a "Jerusalem above" was the hope of the believer and that an enduring city was the reward for those in Christ. The promises regarding Zion were not erased in Christ, but rather Christ paved the way for those promises to be fulfilled and offered to both Jews and gentiles through faith. Another significant text regarding the role of Zion appears in Heb 12:18–24 as the author dramatically contrasts Israel's experience at Sinai with the Christian experience of Mount Zion, the heavenly Jerusalem. In this passage, Zion is not a future home for the faithful but is already a present experience, or an already-not-yet reality, for those who belong to Christ.

Finally, Revelation depicts Zion as the place where the Lamb stands victorious with his faithful saints in Rev 14:1–5. By using the Zion symbol, John is drawing from Old Testament prophecy and showing that Zion's eternal king is Jesus Christ, the slain Lamb. Furthermore, Revelation portrays the new city of God descending from heaven as the eternal home of the saints, and its most striking feature is that the center of the city contains the very presence of God and the Lamb. Through an examination of these key texts, Revelation reveals that the symbolism of Zion that supported the prophetic vision of the new heavens and earth was fulfilled because of Jesus. The final reward for God's chosen people is to live in peace forever in the presence of God as inhabitants of the eternal, unshakable city.

Zion symbolism has significant applications for the modern church: if the people of God already belong to the new Zion, then their worship, fellowship, and service in the world arise from that identity. Justice for the oppressed is no longer a concern for the government or advocacy groups; rather, a distinct marker of the local church is its care and defense of those most vulnerable. In Isa 1, the prophet relays the word from God concerning this: "Zion shall be redeemed by justice, and those in her who repent, by righteousness" (Isa 1:27). The picture painted of a redeemed Zion was based upon the city's renewed sense of justice, specifically the widows and orphans (Isa 1:17, 23). In a similar vein, the church's identity as this redeemed Zion is fully realized as local churches become what Isaiah describes as the "city of righteousness, the faithful city" (Isa 1:26). Zion's symbolic journey, beginning with the first sanctuary, Eden, and ending in the new Jerusalem, rests in the promise that God himself would do this transforming work. The church, as God's witness on earth, points the world toward the presence of God through their love, worship, and pursuit of justice.

1

The Forerunners of Zion Symbolism

The developing nature of Zion symbolism did not begin on the Temple Mount; rather, the biblical characters' journey from Eden to Sinai and eventually into the promised land had a significant impact on the ways in which the biblical authors expressed their ideas of God's presence among his people. It is no coincidence that the tabernacle and the temple contained numerous visual allusions to the garden of Eden, each representing a unique aspect of God's presence. While the term "Zion" itself has an unknown origin, the theological concepts built into the term are imbued with Israel's experience beginning in the garden and leading up to Solomon's dedication of the temple. Reflecting on God's actions toward Israel, Asaph wrote, "My flesh and my heart may fail, but God is the strength of my heart, my portion forever . . . but as for me, God's presence is my good. I have made the Lord God my refuge" (Ps 73:26, 28 CSB). The unifying feature that led Asaph to his conclusion was that God's presence, when he "entered the sanctuary," brought him the wisdom he needed to understand God's plans through history (Ps 73:17). Perhaps as the psalmist stood in awe of the temple and its ornate reminders of the presence of God through Israel's history, he was overwhelmed with a sense of peace and understanding about his current situation. The following provides the major background components to Zion symbolism and explains why the symbol expanded and developed through Scripture, especially as the people longed for a greater, final fulfillment where God's presence would be accessible to his people forever.

THE ZION TERM'S USAGE AND FUNCTION

The proper noun צִיּוֹן for "Zion" occurs 154 times in the Old Testament, and the Greek Σιών occurs seven times in the New Testament, but its usage and function within those occurrences is varied and unevenly distributed.[1] In nearly a third of the occurrences of the term, "Zion" stands alone without any descriptors or parallel terms, but in most cases, there are terms such as "Mount," "daughter," or other parallel names such as "Jerusalem" nearby to provide context to its usage.[2] The etymology of the term is uncertain, but several theories suggest the original nature of the term. It is possibly related to the Arabic *ṣâna* which means "protect" or "defend"; thus, Zion would refer to a place of defense or a fortress.[3] The term could also be derived from a similar term *ṣāhâ*, which means "be bald" because the Syriac spelling *ṣehyôn* bears a close resemblance to the Hebrew term. Franz Delitzsch proposed that "Zion" derived from a Syrian parallel to the Hebrew *tsiwah*, which means "set up" or "erect," suggesting that Zion was a place that was built up, as in the Temple Mount.[4] Another view from the *Theological Dictionary of the Old Testament* proposes the name is connected with a theoretical Hebrew verb *tsayay* for "dry up," since the common Hebrew adjective for "dry" occurs frequently in the Old Testament, as in Isaiah, which reads, "The wilderness and the dry land will be glad" (Isa 35:1).[5] Zion may also be derived from the Hebrew *sîyûn* for "signpost" or "monument," which may indicate its role as a mountain crossroads or as a key landmark site for travelers passing through the Judean hill country.[6] While several Hebrew words provide clues to the term's origin, Zion became identified most narrowly with the southeast hill in Jerusalem that was fortified by the Jebusites and, more broadly, in reference to the entire city, its inhabitants, or even its future status as the center of God's activity.

Despite the uncertain nature of the term's origin, it nonetheless became attached to an expanding theological symbol in Jerusalem and eventually became a term denoting the city of Jerusalem, the people of God, and God's eternal dwelling place. The difficulty in determining the exact etymology for the term is partly because the biblical text seems to indicate it was

1. Lohse and Fohrer, "Σιών," in *TDNT* 7:294. "Zion" occurs in the ESV OT 156 times: "to Zion" is added onto Ps 84:5, even though the original Hebrew is lacking, and it is likewise added for clarification in Isa 33:6.

2. Lohse and Fohrer, "Σιών," in *TDNT* 7:294.

3. Harris, *Theological Wordbook*, 764.

4. Delitzsch, *Commentary on the Psalms*, 2:103.

5. Botterweck, *Theological Dictionary*, 12:333.

6. Sweeney, *1–2 Samuel*, 212.

used before it appears in 2 Sam 5:7, likely by the Jebusites who lived there. Since the term predates Israel's occupation of Jerusalem, the term's origin is left to speculation as noted above. While the term referred primarily to the southeast hill in Jerusalem at first, over time, the term took on various symbolic meanings, especially through the Psalms and Prophets. From these symbolic meanings emerges a theological emphasis on the presence of God in Zion which expands through the Old Testament and points forward to God's desire to eternally dwell among his people.

Zion in a Symbolic Tradition

The theological function of the Zion term in the Bible, then, is as a symbol, and symbols typically cannot be reduced to a singular meaning: they are multivalent and serve as a vehicle to convey an often layered meaning.[7] Zion serves as an iconic vehicle in the Bible and is associated with both denotations, or primary meanings, as well as a set of connotations that portray various aspects of the symbol.[8] While Zion does refer to a hill in Jerusalem, the term also takes on various symbolic meanings throughout the Bible because it becomes the place of God's presence. Furthermore, religious symbols have a depth and a power that evoke a moral obligation and a reverence within the hearts of people, so as the psalmists or prophets wrote about Zion, the meaning conveyed is much deeper than merely the name of a place. Symbols evoke memories that often impose a sense of moral obligation: to this, Ben Ollenburger said, "They have the power to impose such obligations because they convey most concretely and with the most force the true nature of reality, the way the world really is."[9] Zion may be a reference to the physical city of Jerusalem or the eastern hill area, but within that sacred space exists a compounding collective memory and a theological system imbued with many connotations. Zion points to a deeper reality behind the physical presence of the city or the temple: it describes and evokes imagery associated with both God's election of Zion and his holy presence dwelling within it.

7. Ollenburger, *Zion, the City*, 19.

8. Ollenburger notes that symbols exist within a system, which means a symbol must be interpreted within a "symbolic design" in which they are located. There is a network of relationships surrounding the use of a multivalent symbol such as Zion, thus Zion is not restricted to Jerusalem or to a primary meaning but must be understood considering the various related ways in which the term is used. Ollenburger, *Zion, the City*, 19.

9. Ollenburger, *Zion, the City*, 21.

The origin of the Zion tradition has been debated but generally falls into one of two basic conclusions: it is either an adoption of Canaanite (Jebusite) traditions already present in Jerusalem, or it developed during the kingships of David and Solomon. Many scholars have traced the development of the Zion tradition to the pre-Israelite inhabitants of Jerusalem, as evidenced by some of the central motifs associated with pagan ideas.[10] In a foundational work on the issue, Edzard Rohland suggested four primary symbolic motifs for Zion: Zion as the peak of Zaphon, the highest mountain; the river of paradise flowing from it; God having defeated the waters of chaos there; and God having defeated foreign kings and their people there.[11] A fifth motif added by Hans Wildberger includes the pilgrimage of the nations to Jerusalem.[12]

J. J. M. Roberts argues that the presumption that the Zion tradition in Jerusalem was primarily based upon preexisting Jebusite traditions is improbable and lacks evidence that such traditions were simply adopted by David and the Israelites in Jerusalem.[13] For instance, since David appeared to have conquered Jerusalem with minimal bloodshed, and men such as Uriah the Hittite and, presumably, Zadok the priest were Canaanites serving in David's administration, it has been argued that certain Jebusite traditions were adopted during David's reign. These are plausible conclusions, but the lack of evidence suggests that the origin of the Zion symbol cannot simply be assumed as a preexisting Jebusite tradition the Israelites integrated into their unique monotheism.[14] Furthermore, 2 Sam 5:6 indicates that the Jebusites arrogantly viewed their stronghold as impenetrable, especially against David's small army.[15] In response to his quick capture of the fortress, David renames it after himself, implying that "the stronghold of Zion" had been replaced by the "city of David" (2 Sam 5:7). This motif of Zion's defensibility against foreign invasion would later become an important aspect of the burgeoning Zion symbolism in Jerusalem.

Little evidence exists regarding Jebusite religion or cultic practices that may have influenced the early Zion tradition. While the city of Jerusalem

10. Roberts, "Davidic Origin," 330.

11. Rohland, "Bedeutung der Erwählungstraditionen," 142.

12. Wildberger, "Die Völkerwallfahrt zum Zion," 62.

13. Roberts, "Davidic Origin," 333.

14. Evidence to support identifying Zadok as a Jebusite priest or Nathan as a Jebusite cult prophet is inadequate. The narrative of David purchasing the threshing floor of Araunah the Jebusite in 2 Sam 24:18–24 suggests David spared at least part of the Jebusite population, but this does not provide evidence for an assimilation of Israelite and Jebusite cultic practices. Roberts, "Davidic Origin," 331.

15. Anderson, *2 Samuel*, 124.

is referenced in several ancient documents, such as the Ebla archives, the Egyptian Execration Texts, and the Amarna Letters, information on Jebusite culture and religion is scarce.[16] Mount Zion as a significant abode for the Canaanite gods such as El or Baal is at best secondary, for the much more prominent mountain Zaphon dwarfs the hill of Zion. From the text of 2 Sam 5:7, it can be concluded that the southeast hill of Jerusalem was called "Mount Zion" with mythical implications attached, but the term "Zion" does not appear to imply the abode of a specific Canaanite deity.

Two of the aforementioned motifs connected with Zion are topographical in nature but express a deeper theological reality: Zion as "the summit of Zaphon" in Ps 48:1 and Zion's river in Ps 46 are not based upon actual topography but suggest a theological expression of God's greatness in Zion.[17] Psalms 46 and 48 may depict preexilic theologies of Zion and indicate the earlier foundational belief that Zion's impenetrability was due to the presence of God.[18] The mythical descriptions of Zion in poetry are designed to convey the expanding symbolic tradition surrounding Zion, especially as it was connected to God's presence. The usage of such imagery in Psalms does resemble descriptions of the Canaanite god El, whose home was atop a mountain from which two rivers proceed; however, it is also plausible that the psalmists used such terminology as a polemic, proving Yahweh to be the only true creator God who had defeated chaos and deserved to be worshiped.[19]

Mount Zion's connection with God's victory over chaos and his rule over the nations also expresses the ancient Near Eastern belief of connecting deities with mountains. One of the earliest names for God, El Shaddai, is typically translated as "God Almighty" or "God Most High," but it could be understood to mean "God of the mountain."[20] While some scholars conclude these characteristics of Yahweh suggest he was a syncretistic creation, it is more likely that the psalmists and prophets used the familiar descriptions of a deity in order to prove their God as the true God over all creation. Therefore, the Zion symbol, though influenced by the beliefs of the neighboring Canaanites, was more than a mere reconstruction or blending of other beliefs; rather, the Israelites developed a Zion tradition that elevated Yahweh above the false gods of their neighbors and drew the people toward

16. Anderson, *2 Samuel*, 123.

17. See also Isa 2:2; Mic 4:1; Ezek 40:2; and Zech 14:10 as expressions of Zion-Jerusalem as the highest mountain in the region.

18. Steiner, "Spatial Theory and Theology," 67.

19. Currid, *Against the Gods*, 133.

20. Currid, *Against the Gods*, 138.

worship of him alone. Psalm 82 serves as an important example of this: "God has taken his place in the divine council; in the midst of the gods he holds judgment" (Ps 82:1). This verse is not intended to place God among the Canaanite pantheon; rather, God is depicted as casting judgment upon them because he is the only ruler of earth, as Ps 82:8 contends.[21] The symbolism within the Zion tradition invokes a sense of superiority or strength against other nations and their gods, and this indicates the expanding nature of the Zion symbol in Jerusalem as the people established the capital and constructed a temple at the site of God's own choosing. Zion's symbolic tradition is deeper and broader than syncretism, for it is based upon God's divine election of his permanent residence and the witness of the Israelites' history with God from Eden, to Sinai, and into the promised land.

Zion's Symbolic Function in the Old Testament

The term "Zion" occurs most frequently in the Major Prophets (seventy-nine times) with most of the remaining occurrences in Psalms (thirty-eight times) and the Minor Prophets (thirty times), but it only appears six times in the historical narrative portions of the Old Testament.[22] In the narrative sections, Zion was initially a pre-David stronghold of the Jebusite people, as indicated in 2 Sam 5:7, but it was renamed to the "city of David" after David captured the fortress.[23] Thus, Zion was likely a topographical term for the southeast hill of Jerusalem during the time of David; but after the time of Solomon, it rarely occurs in a topographical sense and only reappears in the later monarchy as a title for the whole eastern hill of Jerusalem, or even for the entire city.[24] In other narrative passages such as 2 Kgs 19, Isaiah offers a prophetic message regarding the fate of Assyria and the Judean remnant, saying, "For out of Jerusalem shall go a remnant, and out of Mount Zion a band of survivors. The zeal of the Lord will do this" (2 Kgs 19:31). Often in the poetic texts, Jerusalem and Mount Zion are parallel terms, with Zion remaining connected to God's plans for the people occurring in the present and future.[25]

21. Currid, *Against the Gods*, 139.

22. In the Major Prophets, "Zion" occurs in Isaiah (48), Jeremiah (17), and Lamentations (15). In the Minor Prophets, it occurs in Joel (7), Amos (2), Obadiah (2), Micah (9), Zephaniah (2), and Zechariah (8). "Zion" also occurs once in Song of Solomon.

23. C. E. Shepherd, "Zion," in Barry et al., *Lexham Bible Dictionary*.

24. Lohse and Fohrer, "Σιών," in *TDNT* 7:295.

25. "Jerusalem" occurs in the Old Testament (ESV) 643 times as compared to the 156 occurrences of "Zion."

In the poetic works of Psalms and Lamentations, Zion occurs frequently in reference to the political capital of Judah, which has become the primary location of Yahweh's activity on earth.[26] In contrast to Zion's shifting and expanding meanings, "Jerusalem" occurs well over six hundred times in the Old Testament, yet its meaning remains the same even as the city itself grew and changed shape over time. Therefore, while Jerusalem's meaning as the physical city remains constant, the usage and meaning of Zion, though closely related to Jerusalem, is flexible, taking on a sacred or mythical role as compared to Jerusalem.[27] For example, Ps 48 speaks of "Mount Zion, in the far north," as the mythical abode of Yahweh, "the great King." Beyond the capital of Judah, in passages such as Ps 48, Zion is associated with Yahweh's cosmic reign and his defeat over the chaotic forces of the world. Chapter 2 will discuss in detail the various uses of Zion in Psalms and provide contextual evidence for its expanding meaning through Israel's history.

Lamentations, reflecting Jeremiah's language, personifies Zion with the feminine language of a daughter. "Daughter Zion" frequently occurs as an emotional term, treating the people like a woman who brought shame upon her family by her actions.[28] Zion primarily functions as a term of memory and reflection in Lamentations, for it designates the once protected, adored people of God who have fallen into ruin by God's wrath. The use of Zion causes the people not only to weep but to reflect upon Jerusalem's plight.[29] Lamentations provides a deeper perspective into Zion's function as a much broader concept than an affectionate term for Jerusalem or its people: through the chaos of exile and defeat, Zion became both the place of judgment and the place of God's future promises of restoration. The physical city was ruined, but the God who had blessed the people would not forget the people; thus, poetic language in Lamentations serves as a mediator between the grief of that period and the hope of a glorious future.

Perhaps the widest range of meanings and functions for the Zion term can be found in the Prophets. The symbol in the Prophets can represent several key concepts: the people of God; the city of God or the temple city; the city of judgment; the city of the eschatological age of salvation; the city of theocracy; and the place of blessing and life.[30] All of these themes appear in the prophets' use of the Zion term and reflect the expanding nature of

26. Harris, *Theological Wordbook*, 764.

27. Lohse and Fohrer, "Σιών," in *TDNT* 7:299.

28. Mandolfo, *Daughter Zion Talks Back*, 29.

29. Webb, *Five Festal Garments*, 63.

30. Lohse and Fohrer, "Σιών," in *TDNT* 7:315–18.

Zion as Israel's history progressed through times of prosperity, judgment, and exile.

Isaiah utilizes Zion throughout his oracles, and depending on the historical situation, Zion serves as both a symbol of God's protection and presence in Jerusalem and as a symbol of hope for God's future restoration and salvation. However, even within the first chapter of the book, Isaiah presents two unique motifs regarding "Daughter Zion" as a description for the people under judgment, and "Zion" by itself as the place of God's future activity. Isaiah 1:8 says, "Daughter Zion is abandoned," and then Isa 1:27 says, "Zion will be redeemed by justice, those who repent, by righteousness." Isaiah uses the Zion symbol to indicate a remnant of the larger nation and "Mount Zion" to designate Yahweh's throne, the place where worshipers came to offer praises to God.[31] "Zion" occurs forty-seven times in Isaiah, often symbolic of the people, and within those "Mount Zion" occurs twenty-four times, typically with Yahweh's presence and activity in view.[32] Isaiah received visions that correspond to the Assyrian and Babylonian eras, through wars and exile. Thus, the Zion symbol is an important feature of Isaiah's oracles, which both reminds the people of God's presence and current activity while also pointing forward to a time when God would reestablish Zion as the center of his activity on earth.

In Jeremiah, the Zion symbol functions primarily as the place of sin and judgment, often bearing the attached term "daughter." Jeremiah says, "Though she is beautiful and delicate, I will destroy Daughter Zion" (Jer 6:2 CSB). Jeremiah is convinced he cannot find a single upright person in Jerusalem (Jer 5:1), for Zion's once glorious status had been lowered to the level of the harlot.[33] Despite the tragedy unfolding, Jeremiah maintained a hope for the future, seeing a time when the people would say, "Arise, and let us go up to Zion, to the Lord our God" (Jer 31:6). As God brought about the new covenant among his people, the result would be a united people worshiping the Lord in Jerusalem.[34]

The Minor Prophets utilize Zion in a variety of ways as well, depending on the historical situation of their day and their purpose for writing. The term "Zion" only occurs in Joel, Amos, Obadiah, Micah, Zephaniah, and Zechariah for a total of thirty times. The motifs of "Daughter Zion" and Zion as the place of both God's judgment and God's future restoration occur among the Minor Prophets in similar ways as in Isaiah and Jeremiah.

31. Watts, *Isaiah 1–33*, 11.

32. Watts, *Isaiah 1–33*, 10.

33. Lohse and Fohrer, "Σιών," in *TDNT* 7:311.

34. Thompson, *Book of Jeremiah*, 387.

Zechariah presents a unique angle, writing after the exile with great expectation of the return of Zion's past glory. Zion is used as both a symbol of God's protection and as a symbol of God's postexilic restoration of the desolate city.[35] Though still having a multivalent presence in the Prophets, an expanding focus on Zion as the future eschatological city of God points to the coming of the Messiah and the drawing of the nations toward God's holy mountain.

Symbolic Function in the New Testament

In the New Testament, the theological focus on Christ transforms the function of the Zion symbol and its related imagery regarding the temple, the city, and the presence of God. Not only does Christ fulfill what the temple and its prophecies represent, but he also unpacks the very meaning for which the temple existed, which is the presence of God among his people.[36] Therefore, the Zion symbol continues into the New Testament, but it is transformed through the personal salvation offered in Christ. However, the hope of a future, worldwide temple in which God's presence is the center of reality persists through the New Testament, ultimately being revealed in the final chapters of Revelation.

Zion functions in the New Testament as the expanding symbol of God's presence among his people in that all believers have become the eschatological temple.[37] The essence of this new temple, the church, remains as the glory of God, yet the way in which it is expanded is no longer confined to a physical temple structure. This concept develops within an already-not-yet theological emphasis, in that the individual believer experiences the presence of God through salvation and the Holy Spirit, but his salvation is not complete until Christ returns.[38]

Zion reaches its symbolic destination in Revelation, as Zion appears as the mount upon which Christ is victorious with the saints (Rev 14:1) and as the new Jerusalem, which descends from heaven, transforming the new earth into a worldwide temple. Zion both recalls the compounded memory of the Old Testament Psalms and Prophets and envisions a time when the hope of a restored kingdom becomes reality for true Israel, those who have faith in Christ. The original hope of God's presence filling the city becomes

35. Poulson, *Representing Zion*, 93.

36. Beale, *New Testament Biblical Theology*, 642.

37. Beale, *New Testament Biblical Theology*, 644.

38. Gladd, *Making All Things New*, 9.

an eternal reward for the saints.[39] Ultimately, the New Testament reveals that Christ himself fulfills the hope of a restored Zion, for through him the nations have access to the presence of God, and they are eternally safe and experience everlasting peace.

EDEN, THE FIRST TEMPLE

The theological theme of God's presence among his people begins in the garden of Eden as the first humans were given the privilege of walking with God uninhibited by the shame created by sin. As creatures made in the image of God, Adam and Eve were designed to reflect God's glory and then fill the earth with that glory.[40] Even within the framework of the seven-day creation, Genesis communicates that God's rest on the seventh day implicates that the cosmos was not only created for people but it was created for God as a temple. John Walton says, "God does not set up the cosmos so that only people will have a place. He also sets up the cosmos to serve as his temple in which he will find rest in the order and equilibrium that he has established."[41] Thus, Eden, and creation itself, is established with the intent that God would reside among creation, bringing peace, rest, and flourishing. The garden, functioning in the role of a sacred mountain like Sinai or Zion, represents the presence and activity of God, or the place where God's creation comes and receives wisdom. Zion, like Eden, was depicted as the highest mountain because it was the place where people received wisdom, leading to peace and justice.[42]

Eden was more than a lush forest or productive farmland: it serves as an archetype of the temple, where God resides and where mankind worships him and enjoys his presence. This is evidenced by the tabernacle and Jerusalem Temple, which both bear imagery and symbols that reflect the Garden of Eden.[43] As the Zion symbol begins to emerge during the time of the Jerusalem temple, it carries with it many of the features of the first temple, Eden. For example, Eden and the later sanctuaries were guarded by cherubim and were entered from the east; the gold and onyx mentioned in Gen 2:11–12 are used to decorate the priestly garments and temple structures; the Levites are given the same instructions in terms of keeping or

39. deSilva, *Discovering Revelation*, 256.

40. Beale, *We Become*, 128.

41. John Walton, "Creation," in *Dictionary of the Old Testament: Pentateuch*, 161.

42. Moberly, *Old Testament Theology*, 164. See also Isa 2:2–4.

43. Alexander, *From Eden*, 13.

guarding the tabernacle with the same word (*šamar*) by which Adam was commanded "to keep" the garden (Gen 2:15).[44]

In Gen 2:15, Adam was commissioned to care for Eden, "to work it and keep it." The concept of an image that reflects the glory of a deity is common in ancient Near Eastern religion, yet Adam was a living image of the true God who was placed in the Eden temple as a reflection of God's glory and character.[45] Adam's role in keeping the garden sanctuary involved not permitting any unclean thing into the garden, which he failed to do as the serpent brought in temptation and sin. Eden, followed later by the tabernacle and temple, was a special location where God chose to dwell among his people, resulting in the flourishing of mankind and the extension of God's glory throughout creation.

Genesis 3:8 states, "They heard the sound of the Lord God walking in the garden in the cool of the day, and the man and his wife hid themselves from the presence of the Lord God among the trees of the garden." It is plausible that, within this theophanic context, the verse is presenting an anthropomorphic idea of God's presence moving through the garden during the "cool" or "wind" of the day: either way, the emphasis is on the sudden change in Adam and Eve's behavior because they knew the Lord's presence was near.[46] The implication from this verse is that the Lord enjoyed fellowship with his most cherished creation: even though such fellowship was soon undone, God's presence among the first people represents the harmony and relationship intended among people and their God.[47] Eden served as a temple because it was there that God dwelled among his people, and people in turn had the privilege of enjoying him. Furthermore, the concept of people who "walked with God" is attributed to several heroes of Genesis, including Enoch, Noah, and Abraham.[48] The language of "walking" suggests a continuous, intimate connection between God and man, as these heroes of the faith did not merely obey God but enjoyed a personal relationship with him, which defined their lives. In Leviticus, God says, "I will walk among you and will be your God, and you shall be my people," and in Deut 23, the Lord commands the Israelites to keep their camp holy because he "walks in the midst of your camp" (Lev 26:12; Deut 23:14). These

44. Beale, *We Become*, 130.

45. Beale, *We Become*, 132.

46. The Hebrew term for "cool" in Gen 3:8 is רוּחַ (*ruah*), which is typically translated as "wind," "breath," or "spirit." Harris, *Theological Wordbook*, 216.

47. Mathews, *Genesis 1–11:26*, 239.

48. Mathews, *Genesis 1–11:26*, 239.

verses are reminiscent of God's original desire to dwell among his people in Eden, leading to their ultimate satisfaction and flourishing.

Ezekiel calls Eden a temple, speaking of it as "the garden of God," containing a priestly figure adorned with bejeweled clothing (Ezek 28:13–14).[49] However, this priest-like character's sin causes him to be expelled from the sanctuary. This imagery in Ezekiel describes Eden with temple imagery and connects Eden with both the tabernacle and the future glorious temple. Furthermore, the imagery in Ezekiel suggests that Eden was the place where the desires of people should have been completely satisfied and where Adam was intended to fulfill his priestly duties by taking care of the garden.[50]

Two features of Eden are significant pieces in the foundation of Zion symbolism: the tree of life and the river of life. The tree stood in the center of the garden, and its fruit provided eternal life, which is compared to wisdom in Prov 3:18 and is modeled by the lampstand in the temple.[51] As a symbol, the tree represents wisdom, which in turn brings flourishing for those who partake of it: this mythical imagery helps develop the imagery associated with what is lost in Eden and the longing to regain it.[52] With the two trees in the middle of the garden, they represent the destiny of mankind: Adam was given permission to partake of the tree of life and of any other he desired except for the tree of knowledge. This pairing of permission and prohibition relates to the tabernacle and temple as well, for while God desired for his presence to be among the people, there were restrictions placed upon them.[53] John Calvin described the trees as a sacrament, for within them God extended his hand toward mankind, since man was unable to ascend to him; as the first people ate from the tree of life, they were constantly reminded of the blessing of life given from God.[54] Adam's true blessing in the garden was not necessarily enduring life by eating from the tree; rather, he was the perfect image-bearer of God with an unhindered relationship with his creator.

The combination of these images depicts the presence of God shining a light to direct the paths of his people. In the tabernacle, the tree-shaped lampstand with flowering almond blossoms was a visual reminder that God's presence provides flourishing to the people who draw near. In the new Jerusalem, the tree of life is depicted as "on each side of the river,

49. Beale, *God Dwells Among Us*, 18.

50. Beale, *God Dwells Among Us*, 19.

51. Beale, *God Dwells Among Us*, 19.

52. Blenkinsopp, *Creation, Un-Creation, Re-Creation*, 57.

53. Hughes, *Genesis: Beginning and Blessing*, 64.

54. Thompson, *Genesis 1–11*, 252. Calvin, *Commentaries*, 67.

bearing twelve kinds of fruit, producing its fruit every month" (Rev 22:2). As the saints from all nations are welcomed into eternity, they will receive healing and abundant life from the tree and the river, which is "flowing from the throne of God and of the Lamb" (Rev 22:1).

In Gen 2, the picture of abundant life seeping out of the ground of Eden and a flowing river that supports the lush vegetation is later recaptured in Solomon's temple, which contained many such images. Therefore, the Zion imagery that developed around the temple recaptured much of the symbolism first expressed in Eden, which is based upon the theological belief that God's presence among his people brings forth abundant life.[55] Likewise, the tree of life anticipates the final joy humans will experience in fully knowing God in an eternal paradise as described in Rev 22:2.[56] As a temple-garden, Eden served as a prototype for future sanctuaries and temples where people and the divine connected. In this sense, Adam and Eve were given priestly roles over creation.[57] Through their obedience to the command not to eat of the tree of knowledge, they serve as examples of submission to God: their rule over creation was subject to God's will, and this, too, serves as a prototype for the way in which God would make a covenant with his people at Mount Sinai.[58]

The river of life described in Gen 2:10–14 flows outward from the garden and nourishes life on the rest of the earth, where many nations would reside. The very name "Eden" may mean "well-watered place," suggesting that the central imagery of the place is that it is teeming with life.[59] The symbolism depicts the river flowing from the innermost place of God's presence outward to the rest of creation. Similarly, in the temple, God's presence radiated outward from the Holy of Holies to bring teaching and blessing to the Israelites and to all the earth.[60] Psalm 46 exclaims, "There is a river whose streams make glad the city of God, the holy habitation of the Most High" (Ps 46:4). Zion's invulnerability to the chaos of the world is supported by a life-giving river that flows through the city. Since Jerusalem does not have a physical river running through it, this reference symbolizes God's blessing, which is poured out to the people because of his presence in Zion. In other words, God's presence in Zion has led to a spiritually Edenic state in Jerusalem because he has defeated the chaotic waters, bringing tranquility

55. Beale, *God Dwells Among Us*, 19.

56. Schreiner, *King in His Beauty*, 27.

57. Alexander, *From Eden*, 14.

58. Schreiner, *King in His Beauty*, 27.

59. Wenham and Dunn, *Genesis*, 41.

60. Beale, *God Dwells Among Us*, 21.

and peace for the city's inhabitants.[61] In essence, Zion symbolism recaptures some of what was lost when the first people were expelled from the Garden of Eden: the life-giving fruit and river are recurring themes within Zion symbolism, which seek to reclaim the abundance of life left behind in Eden.

Eden, as a place of God's presence, is a place from where the worship of God is expanded outward to all creation. This, too, is an important element of Zion symbolism, for Isaiah exclaims, "Behold, I will extend peace to her like a river, and the glory of the nations like an overflowing stream" (Isa 66:12), and, "For the Lord comforts Zion; he comforts all her waste places and makes her wilderness like Eden, her desert like the garden of the Lord" (Isa 51:3). The flowing river represents final peace, or a time when *shalom* is fully realized: all that was lost by sin will be recovered, resulting in everlasting peace for Zion.[62] The beauty of Isa 66:12 is that the nations will participate in Zion's glory, indicating that Zion has been transformed into a worldwide temple as initially intended in Eden.[63] While Adam's sin disrupted the expansion of the garden, God sought to restore his dwelling place on earth as the location where the people of God would be comforted and where the nations would enter in and glorify him. These hopes were born in Eden, where the garden served as a temple and where God and man existed in harmony. Even through sin and separation, God's plans would continue to bring both physical and spiritual flourishing to the people who draw near to him.[64]

ISRAEL'S EXPERIENCE AT MOUNT SINAI

Although the exact origin of Zion symbolism is uncertain, Zion inherits some of its theological symbolism from the events at Sinai. However, as Sinai remained a memory of the past, Zion symbolism developed and expanded to express Israel's religious idealism from the time of David and beyond.[65] Thus, there are elements of continuity and discontinuity with Sinai and Zion, for in the giving of the Law and the establishment of the Tabernacle and priesthood, Israel entered into a new era of their relationship with God as he instructed them on how to approach his divine presence. As God had revealed his personal name to Moses, he now is moving the people away from slavery and revealing his desire for them to be "my own possession"

61. Craigie, *Psalms 1–50*, 344.
62. Motyer, *Isaiah*, 455.
63. Smith, *Isaiah 40–66*, 669.
64. Martin, *Bound*, 106.
65. Son, *Zion Symbolism in Hebrews*, 41.

and a "holy people" (Deut 7:6 CSB).[66] At the same time, the move from Sinai to Zion would be permanent and irreversible: God was no longer seen dwelling in a remote territory; rather, he permanently established his presence in Zion.[67] Sinai was not the goal of the exodus, but as it stood between Egypt and the promised land, it represented God's sovereignty over both realms.[68]

The Presence of God on Mount Sinai

The narrative of Israel's experience at Mount Sinai provides a significant background for the development of Zion symbolism because it served as an enduring reminder of the power and holiness of God's presence. While the meetings between God and Moses resulted in instructions for righteous living and the construction of the tabernacle, the terrifying imagery associated with Sinai serves as an important contrast to the later Zion symbolism that emerged in Jerusalem. In Exod 19:9–15, God warns the Israelites of the severity of coming into his presence and the penalty for doing so, but also so that the people would hear Moses's instruction and "believe you forever" (Exod 19:9). At this moment, God's presence descended as a thick cloud and was accompanied by thunderous sounds, to the point that the people exclaimed, "Do not let God speak to us, lest we die" (Exod 20:19). The nearness of God's presence in this moment was horrifying to the people because they had not yet received God's Law or the instruction needed to approach him with reverence and faith.[69] The people stood far off as Moses drew near to God's presence, but after the Law was given and the tabernacle consecrated, the people began to draw near. In Ps 132, the author praises God for choosing Zion, yet consequently, "His enemies I will clothe with shame, but on him his crown will shine" (Ps 132:18). The presence of God in Zion, like Sinai, brings blessing to God's chosen faithful but shame and judgment on those who rebel. John Goldingay said, "Yhwh wants to discover not only whether they will respond to the phenomena with the appropriate fear, but whether they will respond to the declaration of Yhwh's expectations with the appropriate revering."[70]

The thunder and lightning on Sinai express God's anger against the Israelites for their constant complaints against Moses and himself, and

66. Dumbrell, *Covenant and Creation*, 114.

67. Levenson, *Sinai and Zion*, 91.

68. Levenson, *Sinai and Zion*, 23.

69. Hamilton, *Exodus*, 440.

70. Goldingay, *Israel's Life*, 79.

the people's fearful response to God as "a consuming fire" in Exod 24:17 is evidence of the severity of the elements. Thomas Mann argues that the primary purpose of this theophanic experience was to legitimate Moses as Israel's leader and Yahweh as their only God, yet this end was only achieved by the realization that the people would be punished if they failed to heed Moses's word.[71] Ironically, the people failed to heed the warning, and despite being terrified, they quickly turned to Aaron to forge an idol in order to divert their attention away from the fearful sight of Sinai. The other primary image, the cloud, represents divine sovereignty and concealment: this is most clearly seen in Exod 24 as Moses ascends the mountain and disappears into the thick cloud for forty days and nights.[72] The significance of this moment for the Zion symbol is that, under Moses's leadership, the people were unacceptable in Yahweh's presence, yet within the Zion symbol, the people of God are welcomed to draw near. Even though Moses mediated for the people imperfectly, this foreshadows a future priestly figure who would enter God's presence and mediate for the people perfectly.[73]

The theological message of the Sinai story centers on the need for a mediator: Moses ascended the mountain to represent the people before God, then he descended to represent God to the people.[74] Even Aaron and the elders of the people were prohibited from drawing near to God's presence, for the text says, "Moses alone shall come near to the Lord . . . and the people shall not come up with him" (Exod 24:2). The presence of God among his people is the core of Zion symbolism, yet in this narrative, a mediator between God and the people was required. Therefore, the Sinai narrative provides both symbolic and theological backgrounds to Zion symbolism: God desired to dwell among his people, yet they first must be consecrated and cleansed of their sin. God chose Moses as an intermediary and Aaron's line as priests, and the tabernacle was then constructed as a way into God's presence. The goal was not for God to make a way to come down to the people, for he had already done that through the cloud and through many miracles; rather, this moment signified the way for people to come into God's presence.[75]

Two important features of God's character from Exod 34 are that "he is a jealous God" and that he is "a compassionate and gracious God" (Exod 34:6, 14). These characteristics of God develop Israel's understanding of

71. Mann, *Divine Presence and Guidance*, 138.

72. Son, *Zion Symbolism in Hebrews*, 35.

73. Son, *Zion Symbolism in Hebrews*, 35.

74. Morales, *Who Shall Ascend the Mountain*, 109.

75. Morales, *Who Shall Ascend the Mountain*, 108.

who God is and remind the people of his desire to forgive and dwell among them, while at the same time maintaining his holiness before them.[76] The prohibition against bowing down to a graven image and the subsequent transgenerational punishment also point to God's desire to be the only source of worship and life for his chosen people.[77] The call for holy living was an invitation into God's presence, and this continues as a permanent theme surrounding the presence of God and the people's response to him.

Psalm 68:8 calls God "the One of Sinai . . . the God of Israel," indicating the unique relationship God has with the mountains, the city, and the people. Goldingay remarks, "While there was no natural link between Yhwh and this people, this land, this mountain and this city, Yhwh entered into a link that inextricably bound Yhwh to them."[78] From Sinai to Canaan, it would have been seemingly more appropriate for God to claim Mount Hermon, the highest peak in the region's Bashan range, yet the Lord chose Zion. Theologically, Zion towers over all the other mountains because it is there that God's ways are taught.[79] Thus, the connection between Sinai and Zion centers on God's teaching going forth and God's election of that place, not the physical location or daunting size of the mountain.

The Tabernacle

The theological function of the tabernacle was to provide the Israelites with a way to a holy God. As God had made clear on Mount Sinai, no one was allowed near his presence except his chosen mediator, Moses. Thus, God gave Moses instructions to create a sanctuary, filled with symbolism relating to Eden and God's holy character, which would provide a pathway for the Israelites to draw near to his presence. Throughout Genesis, altars and shrines were depicted as sacred spaces where men such as Abraham and Jacob communed with God and offered sacrifices, and these serve as precursors to the tabernacle. Such sacred spaces symbolized God's choice to draw his presence near to chosen individuals who were a part of his covenant blessings among humanity.[80] The same idea, but to a much larger degree, is expressed in Exodus as God says, "And let them make me a sanctuary, that I may dwell in their midst" (Exod 25:8). The goal of the tabernacle was for the people of Israel to experience the blessing of God's presence. The tabernacle

76. Schnittjer, *Old Testament Use*, 24.

77. Schnittjer, *Old Testament Use*, 25.

78. Goldingay, *Israel's Faith*, 198.

79. Goldingay, *Israel's Faith*, 198.

80. Merrill, *Everlasting Dominion*, 306.

perpetuated Israel's experience with God at Sinai in the sense that the essence of the new covenant was the Lord's dwelling among the people.[81]

Furthermore, the tabernacle was designed as a symbol of a return to Eden, mediated by the priests and the rituals performed at the tent. The cherubim stitched into the curtain, with the menorah behind the first curtain, was a reminder of the first people's expulsion from Eden and from the tree that represents God's life-giving presence.[82] The precious metals, ornate fabrics, and carefully arranged furniture suggested that the people were entering the presence of a king, and that, in order to approach the presence of God, strict purification and consecration must occur. The tabernacle points forward to a time when access to the presence of God would become increasingly more available to the people. Exodus 29:45 states, "I will dwell among the people of Israel and will be their God," which shows that the Lord's intent was to create a space for the people to draw near to his presence. However, the instructions regarding the tabernacle end with a dilemma: "Moses was not able to enter the tent of meeting because the cloud settled on it, and the glory of the Lord filled the tabernacle" (Exod 40:35).[83]

Part of the story of Exodus includes God "moving" the people from obedience to worship, which resulted in the need for a place where God would be able to meet with them. The goal of the Israelite's true worship was that God would dwell among them; the divinely given laws opened the door for divine presence.[84] In order to move toward the divine presence, the people needed the constant visual reminder of God's holiness: despite the experience at Sinai, the ornate and beautiful structure of the tabernacle served as a visual aid in approaching God's holiness.[85] The entrance faced east, and the holy place contained the lampstand, the table of showbread, and the incense altar. As a sacred space, the layered construction of the tabernacle points to the increasing holiness as the priests entered the presence of God.[86] This also connects the tabernacle to God's greater plans for earth, that ultimately, he was planning to restore earth so that he could once again dwell among his people. During this time of Israel's history, the tabernacle became the dwelling place of God on earth; however, it is important to note the tabernacle was constructed specifically according to God's design. Also, God's presence was not restricted to a tent, for the ark's design as a footstool

81. Morales, *Who Shall Ascend*, 119.

82. Morales, *Who Shall Ascend*, 126.

83. Morales, *Who Shall Ascend*, 132.

84. Hamilton, *Exodus*, 29.

85. Blackburn, *God Who Makes Himself Known*, 142.

86. Alexander, *From Eden*, 19.

points to God's heavenly throne, not his confinement to the tent.[87] This reality is developed further with Zion symbolism: God's presence was never limited to a particular location, but instead, he chose to dwell among his people in a way that allowed people to draw near to him. Whether in the tabernacle or temple, God's desire for the whole earth to be his dwelling place is communicated.[88]

DAVID'S CAPTURE OF MOUNT ZION

Mount Zion: God's Chosen Dwelling

The term "Zion" appears for the first time in the Bible in 2 Sam 5:7 when David captured the Jebusite stronghold and claimed the small hilltop as his own. Customary for that time, David renamed the area "the City of David" and then fortified it using a stepped terrace of stone and earth.[89] In its original context, Zion appears to be primarily a reference to the small acropolis which had been fortified by the Jebusites, yet, as the tradition grew, Zion became associated with the city of Jerusalem, its inhabitants, and even the eternal dwelling place of Yahweh. Geographically, the city is strategically set along a major road that runs east and west from the Jordan River to the coastal highway, and it also is near a prominent road that runs north and south through the surrounding valley.[90] The location was desirable because it had deep valleys on either side and a reliable water source with the Gihon Spring. David's choice of Jerusalem as his capital gave him the ideal location along the border between the southern region of Judah and the northern area of Israel, allowing him to effectively rule over both parts of the recently united kingdom.[91] The geographical features of the hilltop fortress are significant because, as the Zion tradition develops in Jerusalem, the descriptions in passages such as Ps 48 speak of a "holy mountain, beautiful in elevation . . . the joy of all the earth. Mount Zion, in the far north, the city of the great King" (Ps 48:1–2). Mount Zion is neither the highest peak in the region nor is it "far north," so these descriptions often point to the theological symbolism developing around Zion as God's chosen dwelling place.

In the pre-Israelite era, Jerusalem was one of the many Canaanite city-states in Palestine, and it was inhabited by the Jebusites who were listed

87. Alexander, *From Eden*, 21.

88. Alexander, *From Eden*, 22.

89. Matthews et al., "2 Samuel" in *IVP Bible Background Commentary*.

90. Matthews et al., "2 Samuel" in *IVP Bible Background Commentary*.

91. Sweeney, *1–2 Samuel*, 213.

among the people groups of Canaan in Exod 3:8, Deut 7:1, and Judges 3:5.[92] Kings of this city mentioned in Scripture include Melchizedek, who served in a priestly role with Abraham in Gen 14:18, and Adoni-Zedek, who is named as king during Joshua's conquest of Canaan. According to Josh 15:8, the tribe of Benjamin was given the land around the hilltop city, yet Judg 1:21 indicates that Benjamin failed to drive out the Jebusites completely, allowing them to persist as neighbors of the Israelites until the time of David.[93] The text of 2 Sam 5 seems to indicate that, while David captured the hill called Zion, the Jebusites were not completely expelled from the city and continued to live among the Israelites there. Even with no earlier mention of the name "Zion," it is assumed that the stronghold was thus named before the time of David. The Jebusite belief that "David cannot come in here," expressed in 2 Sam 5:6, may indicate that the Jebusite inhabitants considered their hilltop stronghold to be impenetrable. This theme of confidence in Zion's strength against attack is one that dominates the thought surrounding the Zion tradition.[94]

The Hebrew term *har*, for "mountain," occurs frequently in the Bible and can refer to either a mountainous area or a specific mountain; ironically, Jerusalem is outflanked by many nearby mountains, yet it appears in the text as a foreboding, even "cosmic" mountain.[95] Thus, David's capture of the hilltop fortress marks a significant turning point in the theological progression of Israel's faith: while they had experienced Mount Sinai's terror from a distance, the people were now able to inhabit the mountain God delivered to his chosen king, David. Psalm 104 speaks to the significance of mountains by saying, "You covered it with the deep as with a garment; the waters stood above the mountains. At your rebuke they fled; at the sound of your thunder they took to flight. The mountains rose, the valleys sank down to the place that you appointed for them" (Ps 104:5–8). The presence of the mountains affirms God's defeat over the chaotic waters and speaks to the theological significance of mountains for ancient Near Eastern cultures. Furthermore, Yahweh himself is described in mountainous terms in Ps 18: "The Lord is my rock (*ṣûr*) and my fortress and my deliverer" (Ps 18:2). The Hebrew *ṣûr*, for "cliff" or "rocky wall," speaks to Yahweh as an unbreakable cliff in which his people find refuge from the chaos of the world.[96] As David conquered the Jebusite fortress and began to fortify the area and construct

92. Lohse and Fohrer, "Σιών," in *TDNT* 7:301.

93. Lohse and Fohrer, "Σιών," in *TDNT* 7:301.

94. Levenson, *Sinai and Zion*, 94.

95. Cohn, "Mountains and Mount Zion," 98.

96. Brown, *Hebrew and English Lexicon*, 849.

a royal residence, the theological significance of Mount Zion began to swell, not because of Zion's impressive height but because it was the place God had established his people and installed his king.

The political situation surrounding David's capture of Jerusalem is significant for the formation of the Zion tradition as well, for as David was anointed king over all Israel in 2 Sam 5:3, he needed to remove the Canaanite barrier between the north and the south and choose a royal residence acceptable to both sides. Thus, the problem was solved by his surprise capture of Jerusalem and by naming it "the city of David." Through this move, David originally did not incorporate his city into the north or south but maintained that it be the possession of the kings.[97]

David's ascension upon Mount Zion also relates to the Israelite's unique monotheism, which stood against the prevailing Canaanite religion and the worship of Baal and other gods. Baal dwelled upon Mount Zaphon, yet Israel's defeat over the Canaanites placed Mount Zion atop Zaphon to symbolically express Yahweh's defeat of Baal.[98] The retelling of David's conquest in Ps 48:1 identifies Zion as "in the far north" or, perhaps more literally, "in the extremities of Zaphon."[99] The theological connection is implicit, but it speaks to a concept that exalts Mount Zion as a superior mountain, not because of its topographical features but because of its association with Yahweh's divine election of the location and his anointing of King David. At Sinai, God chose the place where he would meet with the people, yet on Mount Zion, David determined to build a house for God there. However, God refuses the offer from David and instead lists how he will "make for you a great name," and "appoint a place for my people Israel," and "give you rest from all your enemies" (2 Sam 7:9–10). God had not previously desired to reside in one location, but because he established his people Israel in Jerusalem, he would choose David's son to build for him a house. In other words, the first person to embody the covenant promises God gave David in 2 Sam 7 would be the one to build a house for the Lord.[100] God's remembrance of his covenant promises is a key factor in Zion symbolism, especially in the Psalms and Prophets as the people reflect on the promises God made amid the chaos of invasion and exile.

God's election of Zion is a fundamental aspect of interpreting the faith of the Old Testament, especially in terms of the way in which the Psalms and

97. Lohse and Fohrer, "Σιών," in *TDNT* 7:302.

98. Cohn, "Mountains and Mount Zion," 110.

99. Cohn, "Mountains and Mount Zion," 110.

100. Goldingay, *Israel's Gospel*, 716.

Prophets use the word.[101] Zion's election is not understood in the same way as the mythical beliefs of Israel's neighbors regarding temples and cities, but rather God's historical action in choosing Mount Zion serves as the basis of Israel's faith in God's presence there.[102] Because of this belief, the resulting psalms and prophecies that reflect on Zion maintain a confident hope in God due to his choice of Zion. For instance, Ps 125 says, "Those who trust in the Lord are like Mount Zion. It cannot be shaken" (Ps 125:1). Even after the exile, Zechariah maintains the confidence that the city will be the place the nations will come for counsel: "Many peoples and strong nations come to seek the Lord of Armies in Jerusalem and to plead for the Lord's favor" (Zech 8:22). Thus, a key component to Zion symbolism's expansion and depth among the people was God's election of the mountain as his dwelling, from which his presence emanated toward the people.

The Ark of the Covenant

The ark of the covenant is an important factor in the development of Zion symbolism as well, for 2 Sam 6 describes a celebratory moment as David had the ark moved from the house of Obed-Edom up to the city of David. Within this narrative, the power and purity of God's presence is displayed when Uzzah braces the ark and loses his life. Despite the fatal mistake of Uzzah (2 Sam 6:6) and David's reluctance to move the ark at that time, David eventually moved the ark to Jerusalem with dancing and great celebration, knowing that wherever the ark rested, blessing and abundance came with it. The ark, as a symbol of God's presence, is a key element to the developing Zion symbolism during David's reign, but it was not until it was installed in Solomon's temple that the full effect of the ark's presence was felt by the people of Jerusalem. Because the ark was there, the city became more strongly identified as the place of God's dwelling, and the term Zion became a reference to Yahweh's chosen dwelling place.[103]

In the ancient Near East, markers of the divine presence were usually a cult image such as a statue, but the construction of the ark was intentionally designed as non-iconic, as the footstool for God's presence instead of a representation of God himself.[104] The ark is intentionally not representative of a throne but is rather a chest containing the divine covenant between God and the people; this symbolism possibly relates historically to a covenant

101. Preuss, *Old Testament Theology*, 2:39.

102. Preuss, *Old Testament Theology*, 2:40.

103. Balz, *Exegetical Dictionary*, 247.

104. Eichler, *Ark and the Cherubim*, 137.

signed between Rameses II and the Hittite king, which was placed under the feet of Egypt's sun god.[105] Such symbolism reminded the people of God's relationship to them and his sovereignty in defending his name from that place. There are various interpretations for the ark's function during this period, and it may be intentional that the biblical text leaves it undefined; however, the central symbolic function of the ark was a sign of God's presence with his people, characterized by a container that held the items given to the people that signify God's relationship to them.[106]

The ark, representing God's presence, in no way limited his presence to a tabernacle or temple; rather, it served as a marker for the place of God's choosing, the place where God chose to draw near to the people and the place where the people were invited to draw near to him. By the time of Solomon's temple dedication, the ark is described as containing only the two tablets of the covenant; this is likely inserted into 1 Kgs 8:9 to draw an intentional connection between the ark's presence and the continuation of God's covenant with the people passed down from Moses, through David, and now Solomon.[107] This is a central element for the Zion symbol: even though the ark's influence diminishes greatly in the Prophets, Zion itself becomes like the footstool of God, or the place where his covenant promises would be fulfilled. The ark ultimately points to Jesus, the perfect image of God, who became the physical presence of God on earth, and who himself became the way to enter the new covenant with God by grace, through faith.

The Jerusalem Temple

First Kings 6–9 chronicles the events surrounding the construction and dedication of the Jerusalem temple, and there is perhaps no other historical occasion more important to Zion symbolism. David established Jerusalem and the Temple Mount as a sacred place of God's choosing, yet under Solomon's leadership, the temple was built and established as the central place for Israelite worship. The temple became symbolic of the Lord's heavenly residence, his holiness, and his creation, and the imagery and design of the temple all point to God's presence among the people.[108] While God is capable of being worshiped from any location, the sacred space of the temple combined with the permanence of the place created a unique setting for the people to draw near to God in a specific location, which created the feeling

105. Eichler, *Ark and the Cherubim*, 141.

106. Eichler, *Ark and the Cherubim*, 148.

107. DeVries, *1 Kings*, 209.

108. "Temple, Solomon's," in Barry et al., *Lexham Bible Dictionary*.

of a meeting place between God and man.[109] Deuteronomy 12:4–7 gave the Israelites clear instructions on worshiping God at "the place that the Lord your God will choose," indicating God's election of Zion and the need for a permanent place where the people would come and bring their offerings in worship and obedience to their God. In relation to the Zion symbol, the temple combined the need for sacred space and a sense of permanence that allowed the people to focus their attention on the temple and be confident in God's protection over his chosen people. Permanence establishes remembrance, a core component of the Israelites' worship, and remembrance enhances the feeling that worship involves meeting a person, namely God himself.[110]

The Dedication of the Temple

Yahweh had chosen Zion according to Ps 132:13, and it was a place God loved, as indicated by his presence filling the area with a cloud in 1 Kgs 8:11. In Exod 40, Moses could not enter the tabernacle due to the cloud of God's presence, and in the temple dedication scene in 1 Kgs 8, the priests "could not stand to minister because of the cloud, for the glory of the Lord filled the house of the Lord" (1 Kgs 8:11). This moment is best understood as a visit of the presence of God, not a permanent dwelling, otherwise the priests would never be able to minister within the temple.[111] However, in a broader sense, the Lord has now agreed to relocate his home on Mount Zion; the mobile tabernacle and pillar of cloud or fire would now be settled atop Mount Zion as the center of God's blessing upon his people and his sovereign plans for the nations.

The climactic dedication of the temple marked the beginning of a new era for the Israelites, one where the glory of God would be witnessed from a single location, a permanent home for Yahweh and for his chosen people. First Kings 8:1 describes a similar scene to the tabernacle's construction where all the elders and leaders of Israel gathered to witness the glory of the Lord and celebrate the temple. The purpose for their gathering was "to bring up the ark of the covenant of the Lord out of the city of David, which is Zion" (1 Kgs 8:1). The movement of the ark signifies the fulfillment of God's promise to David, that David's kingdom would be established forever.[112] It is also significant that this occasion occurred during the Feast of Booths, as a

109. Pierce, *Enthroned on Our Praise*, 60.

110. Pierce, *Enthroned on Our Praise*, 60.

111. Goldingay, *Israel's Gospel*, 717.

112. Woodhouse, *1 Kings*, 246.

celebration of God's blessing and protection on the people; Zechariah would later describe this feast as a moment when the nations gather to worship the Lord as a fulfillment of God's promises to David (Zech 14:16).[113]

Furthermore, the annual Feast of Booths was a moment where all of Israel was to gather and hear the Law, thus celebrating the presence of God, which in turn brought blessing to obedient people. Leviticus 23 describes this feast as a time where the people "shall rejoice before the Lord your God seven days" (Lev 23:40). Therefore, Solomon's dedication of the temple was planned at a time where the people were already gathering to celebrate the Lord's presence among his people and the blessings that flowed from God's covenant promises toward them. The cloud of his presence confirms God's approval of this occasion and his desire to dwell among the people in the newly established temple. Solomon's lofty prayer that praises God and celebrates the Davidic covenant points to the blessing the people receive by drawing near to the temple and offering their prayers and worship. Solomon admits that no temple can house the fullness of God but that the temple will serve as a focal point toward which the people can pray and be heard.[114] This is significant especially as Solomon depicts a time when the people may be in exile (1 Kgs 8:46–53), but their prayers of repentance and obedience will be heard as they pray "toward their land . . . and the house that I have built for your name" (1 Kgs 8:48). This prayer reminds the Lord of not only his election of the people but his choice of Zion as the permanent dwelling place of his presence.

Temple Imagery

The most common belief about a temple in the ancient world was that it was a home for the gods, or a place in which a god descended to dwell among humans.[115] In other words, a temple was a place of access to the divine; thus, temples were often ornate and carefully crafted with symbols and structures to demonstrate loyalty and worship of the deity. A unique feature for the Jerusalem temple was the lack of icons or statues depicting Yahweh; as the Lord had commanded, the Israelites were prohibited from any attempts to capture God's essence in the form of a statue or man-made image. However, the furniture and the décor of the temple served as important visual reminders of God's blessing in the past, his current presence among the people, and the people's confidence in his continued blessing by virtue of his

113. Woodhouse, *1 Kings*, 247.

114. DeVries, *1 Kings*, 210.

115. Stevenson, *Power and Place*, 42.

presence in the temple. The Zion symbolism that developed in the Psalms and Prophets often recounts the imagery of the temple, celebrating the locus of power at the temple and anticipating God's blessing and protection from that central location.

For example, wood panels overlaid with gold and carvings of trees, flowers, fruit, animals, and heavenly beings all point toward a deeper reality that the temple represents. The temple is on earth but heavenly in its symbolism.[116] The costly blue and purple fabrics resembled the sky, and the embroidered cherubim are reminiscent of Eden and God's heavenly throne room.[117] Solomon spared no expense, for 1 Kings indicates that the inner sanctuary "he overlaid . . . with pure gold," as over one hundred thousand talents of gold were prepared for use in the temple (1 Kgs 6:20–21). The presence of such luxurious, costly materials reflects the Israelites' attitude toward the temple and their God: the temple was designed as a sacred space where heaven and earth intersected.

The symbolism of the temple is an important aspect of Zion symbolism, for in key passages such as Isa 28:16, the centrality of the temple as a theological symbol is expressed. What Isaiah calls a "precious cornerstone . . . a sure foundation" reflects the strength, beauty, and majesty of the temple, yet Isaiah is far more concerned with the people turning their affection toward God, not a cultic system. Furthermore, Isaiah repeatedly refers to God in terms of brightness and beauty, reflecting the ornate jewels and precious metals seen in the temple and the priestly garments. Those luminescent materials were visual reminders of the brightness of God's presence and the need for the people to draw near to him. Isaiah's Zion theology builds onto the existing theology surrounding the temple: in his vision of the Lord, the seraphim say, "Holy, holy, holy is the Lord of hosts: the whole earth is full of his glory" (Isa 6:3). The glory that had previously filled the temple in a heavenly cloud was expanding outward to fill the whole earth.[118] Thus, the imagery within the temple served as a foundation for the developing and expanding theological concept that, from Zion, God's presence and glory would fill the earth. It is possible to read Isa 6:3 as "the fullness of the whole earth is his glory," suggesting that the entire world has become like the temple of God.[119] In this sense, the temple imagery reflects the hopes of Eden, that the whole earth would be God's temple, in which he dwelled among his people. Thus, the brightness, luminescence, and reflective nature

116. Goldingay, *Israel's Gospel*, 719.

117. Beale, *Temple and the Church's Mission*, 51.

118. Beale, *Temple and the Church's Mission*, 59.

119. Beale, *Temple and the Church's Mission*, 59.

of all the precious metals, jewels, and décor in the Jerusalem temple were persistent reminders of God's power and presence in Zion, and ultimately, his desire to fill the earth with his presence and draw the nations to himself.

SUMMARY

The Zion tradition was not a creation of an unknown cultic influence or a later development within the apocalyptic fantasies of postexilic prophets; Zion symbolism was built upon the multigenerational experience of the Israelites from the beginning of human history through the time of the Jerusalem temple's construction.[120] The symbolism of Eden, and the effects of God's presence there, was included in the imagery of the tabernacle. As the Israelites grew in their knowledge and understanding of the holiness of God's presence at Sinai, they were again reminded of the awesome and fearful nature of approaching his holiness. Amid their journey, God continually reminded them of his presence among them through the cloud that descended upon the tabernacle and through the teaching Moses provided from the Lord. These symbols pointed forward to the land where God would choose a permanent dwelling among his people on Mount Zion, the place where the temple was constructed and the place from which God's teaching and rule was dispersed across the earth. Each of these landmark events in Israel's history make a significant contribution to the Zion symbolism which developed and expanded during David and Solomon's reign and into the era of the prophets. Ultimately, the Zion symbol points to a time where God's presence would again be fully accessible to his people as in Eden, but only through a perfect mediator between God and man would this be accomplished.

120. Roberts, "Davidic Origin," 344.

2

Zion Symbolism in Psalms

THE DEVELOPING NATURE OF Zion symbolism and its varied usage begins to unfold within Psalms. Since the collection of psalms was written and compiled through several eras of Israel's history, it shows a variety of uses for the Zion symbol; and through a careful examination of key texts, the core theological idea of Yahweh's kingship is expressed alongside of other important concepts, such as God's covenant faithfulness and the hope of restoration. Of the term's 154 occurrences in the Old Testament, "Zion" appears in the Psalter thirty-eight times. Within these occurrences, the Zion symbol can refer to the expanded city of David known as "Mount Zion," or it can refer to the entire temple city by a process of metonymy.[1] By a further process of metonymy, the term can refer to the people of Israel beyond the walls of the city. Typically, "Zion" stands out against "Jerusalem" in that it primarily exists in the domain of theology instead of topography: Zion is the true place of Yahweh's presence due to the temple and the ark therein.[2] From this foundation, the concept of sacred space expands outward from the temple to encompass all of creation. Zion is the sacred mountain of God, from which waters of life flow (Ps 46:4) and from which Yahweh arises from his heavenly throne to repel the rebellious nations through his anointed ruler (Ps 2:8–9). Zion, as the center of the world and the home of God's presence, is the permanent abode of righteousness and justice (Ps 9:7–10) and is ultimately the place where God's people are eternally shielded from harm (Ps 125:1–2).

1. Groenewald, "Psalm 69:36," 358.
2. Groenewald, "Psalm 69:36," 359.

The full range of emotion relates to Zion as well; from high praise and confidence in Zion's invincibility in Ps 48 to the tearful lament of the exiles in Ps 137, the Zion symbol produces an emotional response as the psalmists reflect on God's covenant promises and his choice of Zion as his holy dwelling. As Ps 132 exclaims, "For the Lord has chosen Zion; he has desired it for his dwelling: 'This is my resting place forever; here I will dwell, for I have desired it'" (Ps 132:13–14). From this central belief about Zion, the psalmists developed multiple ways of using the Zion symbol to express their theological beliefs as well as their emotional response to the events of their own time.

From this emerges Psalms's core theological beliefs in terms of the Zion symbol: the dwelling place of the King and the hope of future restoration. These two concepts convey the present blessing of God's presence and the future grace God will extend toward the people; both a sense of permanence and sacred space arise from these two theological concepts in Psalms. Zion is forever the abode of God and his rule, and even in exile, somehow God will never completely forsake the promises he made.

The primary vehicle of the Zion symbol is the kingship of Yahweh, and through this theological expression, several theological connotations emerge throughout Psalms.[3] As these connotations develop, one key aspect is that Zion takes on a dual role of being both the inviolable mountain of God and the city of sin and judgment.[4] There are glimpses of this development in Psalms, and the Prophets develop this concept further. Because of this, the Zion symbol takes on multiple roles, depending on the psalmists' situation and their view on God's activity from Zion. The presence of God brings blessing to the faithful but judgment on the wicked, and the people of Israel are not immune to such judgment should they become unfaithful; yet, often the psalmists seek to remind God of his covenant promises toward his people, pleading for restoration and peace amid times of injustice or suffering. In this sense, Zion exists between judgment and salvation, leading the Psalms to portray a range of responses toward the God enthroned on Zion.[5] The following will discuss key psalms which reflect these themes and display the multivalent nature of the Zion symbol and how it was both a symbol of God's kingship and a picture of God's future activity on behalf of his chosen people and city. Through a biblical theological lens, these themes reveal a movement in the Psalter, progressing from the glorious kingship of Yahweh to Israel's downfall and exile, and finally to Israel's restoration and return to

3. Ollenburger, *Zion, the City*, 20.

4. Poulson, *Representing Zion*, 2.

5. Poulson, *Representing Zion*, 2.

Zion. Ultimately, this reveals an undercurrent in the programmatic design of the Psalter that points to the return of a Davidic King, a messiah who will restore Israel and bring the people back into a right relationship with God.[6]

ZION: THE DWELLING PLACE OF THE KING

The Zion symbol in Psalms is most clearly developed as a visual device for connecting the people to the dwelling place of Yahweh, the King on Mount Zion. However, there is no singular meaning for the Zion symbol; Robert Miller states, "Zion is a multivalent symbol. It denotes Yahweh's kingship, within a symbolic system linked with enthronement, and which consequently raises human kingship to symbolic dimensions."[7] God's choice of Zion as his dwelling place is the primary theme from which others flow: Psalm 78 exclaims, "But he chose the tribe of Judah, Mount Zion, which he loves. He built his sanctuary like the high heavens, like the earth that he established forever" (Ps 78:68–69).[8] From this expression of the Zion symbol, other theological themes, such as deliverance from Zion or God's future restoration, emerge. Zion is also described as the center of peace and prayer and as a mythical vehicle for the future utopia where God reigns supreme over the nations forever.[9] While Zion is depicted as an unbreakable stronghold for God's people, it is not the only way in which Zion is described; rather, the perception of Zion is often a reflection of the people's relationship with God and the historical situation in which they lived. However, the primary uniting feature of the various ways in which Zion symbolism appears is the presence of God. Because God's presence is on Zion, the people are secure, can find refuge, and have an obligation to obey the Lord and his anointed king.[10]

The most prominent imagery related to God's dwelling in Zion is the picture of Yahweh as King; thus, the "Enthronement Psalms," such as Ps 47, reflect a theological focus on Yahweh as the reigning king in Zion. From his position of rule, Yahweh is depicted as ruling over all the nations, protecting his people, and administering justice from his throne. God is victorious over the forces of chaos, and he has supreme authority from his seat of power in Zion. Yahweh is a warrior king who fights on behalf of the poor

6. Grogan, *Psalms*, 291.

7. Miller, "Zion Hymns as Instruments," 228.

8. John T. Willis, "David and Zion in the Theology of the Deuteronomistic History," in Batto and Roberts, *David and Zion*, 140.

9. Poulson, *Representing Zion*, 93.

10. Son, *Zion Symbolism in Hebrews*, 44.

and disenfranchised, extending righteous judgment for those who seek his counsel. From this imagery come two important concepts for the Zion symbol: security and refuge. Because God is King in Zion, the people are safe from enemies and external threats. This notion is particularly important as it relates to the need for refuge for the poor and those without the power to secure their own salvation.[11]

Psalm 2: The Lord's Anointed on Zion

Psalm 2 serves as a foundation for the theological emphasis on Yahweh as King in Zion and his installment of the Davidic line of human kings as his representatives. In verses 1 and 2, the nations are described as rebelling against the "Anointed," representing the opposite of the theological ideal expressed in the psalm.[12] The nations' anger toward the Lord is answered by a statement of confidence: "I have set my king on Zion, my holy hill" (Ps 2:6). God does not seek to terrify his opponents with a threat but instead make a declaration confirming his personal involvement in the choice of the human king.[13] Any privileges obtained by the human king in Jerusalem were gifts from God, who, by his own word, installed the king. The use of the Zion symbol in Ps 2 denotes Yahweh's kingship, but the unique feature of this psalm is the connection with God's choice of the king. Despite any appearance of human success, the claim of Ps 2 is that *Māšîaḥ*, the "Anointed," rules only because of his relationship with the ultimate ruler who has given him the iron rod (Ps 2:9).[14] The claim of sonship in verse 7, "You are my Son: today I have begotten you," further shows that God has adopted the king as his own, including his right to rule and represent the Lord from Zion. In other ancient cultures such as Egypt, similar language is used of kings, but with a metaphysical emphasis on a divine sonship between the gods and the king.[15] In Ps 2, the adoption of the king by Yahweh reflects his covenant promises established with David and points forward to the permanence of God's presence in Zion and his blessing of the king. Comparable to a father giving inheritance rights to the son of his choosing, Yahweh chooses his "son" in Zion to be the recipient of the inheritance of the nations.[16]

11. Son, *Zion Symbolism in Hebrews*, 44.
12. Longman, *Psalms*, 60.
13. Craigie, *Psalms 1–50*, 67.
14. Whiting, "Psalms 1 and 2," 254.
15. Lam, "Psalm 2," 35.
16. Lam, "Psalm 2," 44.

Psalm 2's placement within the Psalter is significant, especially in terms of the hope expressed in the coming Davidic king.[17] The royal psalms are spread out in the Psalter, perhaps intentionally to draw attention to them, which is unlike similar collections of royal poetry from other ancient Near Eastern civilizations.[18] Some scholars, such as Norman Whybray, have pointed out that Pss 1 and 2 are placed together as a dual introduction to the Psalter, describing the two paths before all people of either blessing or destruction.[19] The themes of the vindication of the righteous and the end of the wicked are expressed in the introductory psalms, which undergirds the theme of refuge as well.[20] Therefore, not only does Ps 2 provide an introductory lens into the whole Psalter, but it also presents Zion as the focal location from which wisdom, righteousness, and power originate.

God's response to the nations speaks to his choice of Zion, which symbolizes his victory over the forces of chaos in both creation and the redemption of people. Zion is God's "holy hill" because his name is there, and he chose to place his divine presence at the temple, which recalls the events of the temple dedication in Solomon's day.[21] This "holy hill" was chosen by God as the site of his earthly residence so he could communicate the truth about himself to the people using the cultural language of the day; while common for ancient cultures to associate their deity with a mountain, Yahweh's choice of Zion in Ps 2 reflects his holy character as well as the holiness of the temple.[22] Furthermore, the response of the king in verse 7 to "tell of the decree" highlights that Yahweh is the true king on Zion, and the human king rules by that divine authority.[23] This reveals that the assault on the Davidic king by the raging nations is an assault on an eternal decree; God is enthroned in heaven while the king is on earth, yet the two realms are linked.[24] The lower realm is the human manifestation of the higher; thus, Zion represents the inviolability of Yahweh's reign from his sacred mountain.[25] Zion's permanence is reflected here, suggesting that all political efforts apart from those which emanate from Zion are futile because David's

17. Ellison, "Old Testament Hope," 535.

18. Ellison, "Old Testament Hope," 536.

19. Whybray, *Reading the Psalms*, 79.

20. Whybray, *Reading the Psalms*, 79.

21. Waltke, "Ask of Me," 8.

22. Waltke, "Ask of Me," 8.

23. Waltke, "Ask of Me," 9.

24. Levenson, *Sinai and Zion*, 155.

25. Levenson, *Sinai and Zion*, 155.

kingship has a foot in two realms: the sacred, eternal realm of Yahweh and the physical world from which he executes God's plans.[26]

The motif of a nation's god ruling from atop a mountain and anointing the human king was a common feature in the ancient Near East, but passages such as Ps 2 depict Yahweh as supreme over the nations as he enthrones his human representative, despite the rejection from the nations. Even as the kings of earth reject God's rule, the invitation is offered in 2:10–12 to approach Zion "with reverential awe," which will bring refuge and happiness. While Yahweh will "shatter them like pottery," he also welcomes those who approach with humility and worship. Acts 13:32 and Heb 1:5 quote Ps 2:7 in reference to Christ, who, in a similar way, welcomes those who are willing to submit to his lordship, yet one day he will destroy those who persist in rebellion.[27]

The New Testament quotes Ps 2 seven times, and it is alluded to at least five other times.[28] As one of the most quoted psalms in the New Testament, the emphasis on the Messiah's reign in Zion connects the Davidic covenant with its fulfillment in Christ. In the apostle John's vision in Rev 12:5, he depicts the Messiah as bearing the iron rod of Ps 2:9, pointing forward to the final judgment of Christ in Rev 19:15, when Christ "will shepherd them with an iron scepter." The imagery depicts Christ as a shepherd who defends his flock and ultimately leads them to life.[29] While Zion in Ps 2 describes the physical temple area and city, the New Testament portrays the "Anointed" son of Ps 2:2 as Christ who will judge the nations' sin and bless those "who take refuge in him" (Ps 2:12). In the New Testament, Zion in Ps 2 is interpreted through an eschatological lens that portrays Christ as the fulfilment of the psalm's promises regarding the Lord's anointed king.

Psalms 9–10: The Power and Presence of God

Psalm 9 provides a clear example of how Yahweh's enthronement on Zion affects the way in which the people respond to him. Traditionally, Pss 9 and 10 are joined as a unit due to the Hebrew acrostic structure that connects the two, although the acrostic is incomplete in the Masoretic Text, especially in Ps 10.[30] Nevertheless, the occurrence of the acrostic in every second verse throughout both psalms coupled with the lack of a superscription for Ps 10,

26. Levenson, *Sinai and Zion*, 156.

27. Smith, *Wisdom Literature and Psalms*, 217.

28. Gunn, "Psalm 2 and the Reign of the Messiah," 427.

29. Osborne, *Revelation*, 463.

30. Robert Gordis, "Psalm 9–10," 105.

which is rare in book 1, indicates a relationship between the two psalms.[31] This creates an important view of the Zion symbol, since the praise, victory, and salvation of Ps 9 is paired with the lament and injustice expressed in Ps 10. Embedded within these psalms is the concept of a fluid personality, where the individual and the whole nation are represented; the psalmist identifies his enemies as the enemy of the nation, thus the interplay between singular and plural expresses both a personal and corporate feeling.[32]

Psalm 9:11 says, "Sing praises to Lord, who sits enthroned in Zion! Tell among the peoples his deeds." The theological implication is that God, the one who establishes justice and peace, is victorious and will not allow wickedness to thrive in his dwelling place.[33] The psalmist sings testimony of past wonders when the wicked were repelled and destroyed, yet there is a significant emphasis on the plight of the poor and helpless. An important aspect of God's kingship in Zion is his protection and justice given to the poor, weak, and afflicted. Thus, the psalmist offers high praise of God's previous deeds in hopes that the Lord would respond once again.[34] The Zion symbol in Ps 9 reflects God's kingship regarding his strength and invincibility but also his care and provision for those who are afflicted. The psalmist is confident in this, calling on the Lord to "see my affliction . . . that in the gates of the daughter of Zion I may rejoice in your salvation" (Ps 9:14). Because Zion is the sacred home of the Lord's presence, justice, protection, and salvation can be found for those who enter the gates rejoicing in the Lord. The one "enthroned in Zion" speaks of God as enthroned not only in heaven but also on earth in the sense that the ark of the covenant represented God's presence among the people.[35]

The plea for deliverance from the one "enthroned in Zion" is changed to lament in Ps 10, for the prosperity of the wicked leads the psalmist to cry out to God. Despite the weight of oppression, the psalmist is reminded that "The Lord is King forever and ever," and that "O Lord, you hear the desire of the afflicted" (Ps 10:16–17). Because God is King in Zion, the psalmist is encouraged to cry out to him, and his confidence in God's response is marked by his plea, "Arise, O Lord," in verse 12.[36] Throughout Pss 9–10 there is a dichotomy between the righteous, whom Yahweh will vindicate, and the wicked, whom Yahweh will judge; Yahweh is decisive and it is his

31. deClaissé-Walford, *Book of Psalms*, 114.

32. Gordis, "Psalm 9–10," 107.

33. Gordis, "Psalm 9–10," 107.

34. Eaton, *Psalms*, 84.

35. Craigie, *Psalms 1–50*, 119.

36. Craigie, *Psalms 1–50*, 125.

actions that determine the outcome for the two groups.[37] In this sense, Pss 9–10 are an attempt by the righteous to invite God into the reality that the oppressor has gained significant power over the righteous.[38] The prayer and plea of the psalmist is for God, the King enthroned in Zion, to act justly on behalf of those who are righteous in his sight.

Therefore, Pss 9–10 express God's kingship as the foundation for justice and help in a time of need; while the wicked may prosper and oppress the righteous, it is ultimately God who will judge rightly and bring justice. God's presence among the people provides an avenue for the people not only to pray for help but to have confidence that God will arise to vindicate the oppressed. Psalms 9–10 contain one of the largest clusters of terms for the afflicted and needy in the Psalter, and many of these terms appear first within Psalms in this passage.[39] The role of justice for the afflicted is fundamental to the role of Yahweh's kingship in Zion: God's reign and his anointing of the human king are the reasons why the poor and afflicted cry out in confidence. Such justice for those in need is proof that the Lord truly reigns in Zion, for his kingdom is marked not by sheer power but by compassion, wisdom, and righteousness.[40]

Psalm 24: Lift Your Heads to Zion

Psalm 24 is a hymn of praise, celebrating the "King of glory" in what appears to be structured as an interchange between two priests as part of a liturgical procession.[41] The title associates the psalm with David, but the mention of "the hill of the Lord" and "his holy place" are more naturally references to the temple on Zion, which was not built until after David.[42] Yet, the psalm is also associated with the liturgical event surrounding the procession escorting the ark up to the temple. As Ps 24 follows the intimacy of Ps 23, so does the ark's move to the City of David in 2 Sam 6 follow David's capture of Jerusalem in 2 Sam 5.[43] David's capture of Zion represented a religious revolution: the Canaanite stronghold was replaced with the City of David and the site for the future temple to Yahweh was planned. With the ark's

37. Slabbert, "Coping" 3.

38. Slabbert, "Coping," 4.

39. Patrick D. Miller, "Ruler in Zion and the Hope of the Poor," in Batto and Roberts, *David and Zion*, 196.

40. Slabbert, "Coping," 4.

41. Longman, *Psalms*, 138.

42. Longman, *Psalms*, 138.

43. Goulder, "David and Yahweh," 469.

new home on "the hill of the Lord," a new era emerged with Yahweh as the only king on Zion—the Canaanite gods no longer had a home in the city.[44]

It is plausible that the setting for Ps 24 is during the annual autumn festival where Yahweh's kingship was celebrated with a ritual procession of the ark to the temple.[45] The first composition of the psalm likely reflects the time of the dedication of the temple, when Solomon had the ark moved from the City of David into the temple, resulting in an exchange between the priests in this poetic form.[46] The "gates" and "ancient doors" do not reflect the structure of the tent in which the ark rested but rather point to a grand, festive moment in which the people celebrated God's presence entering its home in the newly established temple, as 1 Kgs 8 depicts.

Psalm 24, even though it does not mention the term "Zion," is filled with symbolic language relating to the Zion symbol. The structure of Ps 24 has been debated due to the question-and-answer format alongside the combination of both pilgrims coming to worship and Yahweh himself entering the gates.[47] However, the narrative dimension of the psalm includes the themes of creation, the coming of the Lord, and the ascent to Zion, all of which are important Zion themes in both the Psalms and Prophets.[48] Thus, the psalm may be a compilation of liturgical songs, but with an eschatological lens, the story of the psalm speaks to a greater theological purpose within the Psalter itself—namely, that Yahweh has chosen Zion as his dwelling place, from which flows blessing and salvation. Thus, the people's response to the Lord's entry (through the ark's arrival) represents an important historical moment for Israel as the presence of God came to rest upon the hill the anointed king David established as the home for the Lord's temple. These themes are especially relevant for Isa 40–55, as the prophet persuades a weary people to trust in God's power alone and realize their role as the servant within God's eschatological plans.[49]

Access to the Lord's presence is also expressed in Ps 24, for the question "who shall ascend the hill of the Lord" is answered by the description of one "who has clean hands and a pure heart" (Ps 24:3–4). Such a person "will receive blessing . . . and righteousness" from the Lord (Ps 24:5). The Lord's presence in this psalm is approachable and results in blessing—a contrast to the fear and judgment of Israel's experience at Sinai. Ironically, the Lord is

44. Goulder, "David and Yahweh," 469.

45. Goulder, "David and Yahweh," 472.

46. Adler, "Historical Background," 270.

47. Sumpter, "Coherence of Psalm 24," 32.

48. Sumpter, "Coherence of Psalm 24," 44.

49. Sumpter, "Coherence of Psalm 24," 44.

praised as the king of glory in military terms in verses 7–10, reminding the people that he is "mighty in battle," as in previous victories for Israel.[50] Thus, the people worshiped God as the King in Zion, the one who has entered victorious through the gates and established his eternal presence among the people, bringing blessing for those "who seek him" (Ps 24:6).[51] In this passage, Zion is the focal location of God's activity among his people and is the source of his activity, in which he blesses the people and reminds them of his previous victories over the nation's enemies.

Psalms 46–48: Zion, the City of God

Psalms 46 and 48 are often labeled as "Songs of Zion" or "Zion hymns" because of their focus on the city of God and the strength and protection it provides.[52] Psalm 46, which does not name Jerusalem or Zion, offers high praise to God, who dwells in "the holy habitation of the Most High," and invites hearers to "come, behold the works of the Lord" (Ps 46:4, 8). The historical setting of Ps 46 may reflect the time when Sennacherib was repelled from Judah during Hezekiah's reign.[53] The Zion theology present in the psalm reflects a confidence in God as the only source of refuge during times of crisis. It revels in the reality that Yahweh is present in the city's sanctuary, so the people will find security when they seek refuge in God alone.[54] John Chrysostom noted God's presence is the central feature of the city: "He supports it on all sides; thus not only will the city come to no harm, but it will not even be shaken . . . it enjoys the most prompt assistance, which is ever ready and prepared."[55]

The tone of confidence expressed in this brief psalm is predicated upon the presence of God in the city; God secured the city and made it his stronghold, thereby offering protection to the people from both natural threats and foreign enemies.[56] God is also described as the one who subjugates the chaotic waters and protects his people from the dangers of the natural

50. Craigie, *Psalms 1–50*, 213.

51. Ollenburger notes that Ps 24:7–10 may represent the pilgrimage of the ark in connection with an autumn festival, which celebrated the kingship of Yahweh. Ollenburger, *Zion, the City*, 31.

52. Other "Zion hymns" may include Ps 76, 84, 87, 122, and possibly 132. Longman, *Psalms*, 204.

53. Earwood, "Psalm 46," 80.

54. Goldingay, *Psalms*, 2:96.

55. Blaising, *Psalms 1–50*, 720.

56. Craigie, *Psalms 1–50*, 344.

world. The lack of the name "Zion" may indicate that Ps 46 is from an early period of the Jerusalem-centered form of Hebrew worship, but the psalm nonetheless conveys that the people of Zion are protected because it is the home of the Lord.[57] Furthermore, Ps 46:10 indicates that God's dominion from his holy mountain extends beyond the reach of the city and sends a message to all nations that Yahweh is "exalted among the nations, exalted on the earth" (Ps 46:10). Thus, God's dwelling in Zion is not limited to his holy mountain, for his rule over the nations extends through the whole earth, causing wars to cease and chaotic forces to calm. The confidence in the city's invincibility is not based upon the thickness of walls or the might of a military; rather, the strength of the city comes from the presence of God in Zion.[58] As Martin Luther wrote his famous hymn from Ps 46, he shared the sentiment with the psalmist that those who find refuge in God alone find an eternal, timeless source of strength.[59]

Psalm 47, sandwiched between two hymns that speak of God's city, presents an important perspective into the concept of sacred space in the Psalms. All three songs of Pss 46–48 reflect the Hebrew obsession with space: the land is of paramount concern; Yahweh's role within the land is a central feature; and the narratives of conquest, exile, and restoration are all in view as the psalmists call the people to worship and remembrance of God's power and provision. With Zion as the holy mountain of the Lord, it serves as the center of earth where horizontal and vertical dimensions intersect: the temple, then, is the meeting place of the heavenly and earthly realms and the place where human and divine interact.[60] The temple on Zion was constructed and decorated specifically to be reflective of the original sacred mountain, Eden, pointing to the dwelling of God among the people. Temples were treated like microcosms of the world, and the Jerusalem temple, specifically the holy of holies, was a sacred space set apart from the human space, where the presence of God rested among the people.[61] However, space in the ancient world was not only the concrete, empirical measurements seen with the eye: it also included the cultural, ideological, and social "space" experienced by people.[62] Psalm 47 rests between two

57. Craigie, *Psalms 1–50*, 344.

58. Earwood, "Psalm 46," 83.

59. Weiser, *Psalms*, 367. The hymn "A Mighty Fortress Is Our God" was written by Martin Luther in 1529.

60. Schäder, "Understanding," 136.

61. Schäder, "Understanding," 140.

62. Steiner, "Perceived and Narrated Space," 690.

songs of Zion to emphasize the Lord's reign from Zion, which expands across the breadth of the earth.[63]

God is depicted as ruling over the chaos of nature and the nations in Ps 46, and in Ps 47, the people praise the Lord who "reigns over the nations" from "his holy throne" (Ps 47:8). Psalm 47 brings forth the tradition of how Israel gained the land, reaching back to the covenant made with Abraham; yet now, praise goes forth to God since he rules over all the earth. In this sense, "God has gone up with a shout" speaks to the dual imagery of God's ascension to Zion and his rule from the heights of heaven.[64]

The enthronement hymn of Ps 47 praises God's kingship, possibly in connection with a cultic celebration of God's accession to the throne in light of David's expanding kingdom: Israel had risen from a tribal nation to a powerful empire through God's kingship.[65] Thus, the imagery of God ascending to his heavenly throne and sitting down in majesty signifies his reign as the King of the earth. This, in turn, leads the "princes of the peoples" in verse 9, since "king" only befits God himself, to gather as one people who worship the King.[66] The reference to the Abrahamic covenant provides an eschatological angle on this psalm, for it depicts the various peoples of the earth becoming as one to joyfully worship the God who reigns over the whole earth. In conjunction with the message of Isaiah and Zechariah, Ps 47 provides a brief glimpse into the final hope of Zion, that all the nations of the earth would draw near to the presence of God and receive peace and salvation (Isa 2:4; Zech 9:10).[67] All the peoples of earth are told to "clap your hands" and "shout to God," indicating that, because God is on the throne in Zion, all the nations of earth should respond in paying homage to the King (Ps 47:1).[68]

Psalm 48, often categorized as a "Song of Zion," offers a more emotional response to God's dwelling in Zion, exclaiming that the holy mountain is "rising splendidly" and "is the joy of the whole earth" (Ps 48:1).[69] Psalm 48 serves as a climax of four psalms in book 2, which celebrate the reign of God on earth: Psalm 45 expresses confidence in God's anointed king, who reigns in Jerusalem; Psalm 46 expresses confidence in the city since God is present; Psalm 47 celebrates God as king over all the earth; and Ps 48 calls on the

63. deClaissé-Walford, *Psalms*, 344.

64. Schäder, "Understanding," 148.

65. Craigie, *Psalms 1–50*, 348.

66. Weiser, *Psalms*, 378.

67. Weiser, *Psalms*, 379.

68. Botha, "Enthronement Psalms," 29.

69. Craigie, *Psalms 1–50*, 352.

audience to marvel at Zion, God's great city.[70] In this psalm, offering praise to Zion or the temple is a way of praising God, for having a physical location on which to center one's praise reminded the people of God's majesty and power.[71]

Zion is also equated with Mount Zaphon of Canaanite mythology, which was a sacred mountain and home to Baal.[72] While Ps 48 is not necessarily a polemic against Baal-Zaphon, the mention of the mountain conveys the theological idea that Yahweh's establishment of his kingdom in Zion has brought victory over chaos and peace to the inhabitants of the city. The emphasis is that God is the highest God with greater power than the familiar storm god, and he has control over the winds and seas and offers protection for not only the city but for "Judah's villages," or literally "daughters," under his care (Ps 48:11).[73] Thus, the core component of Zion symbolism in Ps 48 is that Yahweh is king, offering protection from natural or man-made threats to which the people respond in awe and wonder.

The imagery, such as the paradise river, Zaphon, and the mountain of God, gather traditions from before Israel's capture of Jerusalem and reapply them to create a religiously concentrated center of worship at Zion.[74] The phrases "city of our God," "his holy mountain," "reaches of Zaphon," and "the city of the great king" can all be understood in apposition to one another as symbolic expressions that Yahweh rules supreme in Zion (Ps 48:1–2).[75] Some scholars take this to be an example of how Canaanite religious language and tradition was adapted by the Israelites, but in passages such as Ps 48, there is a deeper sense of God's eternal glory extending over the earth in view.[76] Furthermore, one of the significant features unique to Psalms as opposed to Ugaritic texts is that often cosmic upheaval relates to interactions between the gods; but for Israel, there is only one God who is untouchable and who upholds his covenant promises.[77] As an ancient Near Eastern

70. deClaissé-Walford, *Psalms*, 459.

71. Longman, *Psalms*, 212.

72. Miller, "Zion Hymns," 222.

73. deClaissé-Walford, *Psalms*, 348.

74. Eaton, *Psalms*, 33.

75. Clifford, *Cosmic Mountain*, 146.

76. Clifford, *Cosmic Mountain*, 154.

77. Such a celebration of God's kingship has been linked with an autumn festival possibly dating back to the ark's arrival in Shiloh before David. Ollenburger argues that much of the imagery in Ps 48 relates to existing Canaanite traditions involving the divine warrior's victory over chaos and death. In this sense, Ps 48:3 represents Baal's dethronement and Yahweh taking that place, with Zaphon now associated with Zion. Ollenburger, *Zion, the City*, 48.

culture, Israel's poets may have used the imagery of the "extreme north" or "Zaphon" in opposition to the pagan idea that a deity would be found atop the highest mountain; instead, the Lord had chosen Zion for his dwelling and because of his presence, Israel's enemies have been routed.[78] Israel's God did not need a temple for rest or images by which he related to the people: Yahweh was the one true God, invisible and unable to be manipulated as the pagan gods of Israel's neighbors.[79]

Psalm 76: Zion's Enemies Subdued

In Ps 76, God's dwelling place in Zion is described as the place from where he will bring peace by destroying the weapons of war. However, this peace only comes through the total defeat God has brought upon Zion's enemies.[80] God is depicted as a lion, whose "lair" is in Salem, and whose "den" is in Zion.[81] This psalm may have formed originally from a historical event, yet its imagery of celebration reflects a scene of worship by God's people on Mount Zion.[82] There is a high density of words indicating time and space in Ps 76, which also reflects a spatial focus on Zion and calls attention to the specific historical events that are celebrated in the text.[83] Whether a victory in the time of David or Hezekiah, the Zion theology present in the psalm points to a celebration of the security found in Zion because it is the place of God's eternal protection and salvation.[84]

The focus of Ps 76 is not on the presence of human wars but rather God's ability to end conflict through his strength and righteous judgment.[85] Zion is not the place of vengeance or violence as it may appear at first glance; rather, the strength that comes from God's rule in Zion has the ability to stop wars because "even human wrath will praise you" (Ps 76:10). Praise resulting from human anger appears paradoxical, and scholars have theorized many solutions to make sense of verse 10. J. A. Emerton suggests the Hebrew can be construed to mean "surely you crush the wrath of man,"

78. Weiser, *Psalms*, 381.

79. Beale, *Temple and the Church's Mission*, 69.

80. Poulson, *Representing Zion*, 68.

81. "Abode," from *sōk*, in Ps 76:2 can be translated "lair," as in Jer 25:38. "Dwelling place" from *mĕʿōnâ* is often associated with the dens of animals in the OT. deClaissé-Walford, *Psalms*, 465.

82. Tate, *Psalms 51–100*, 263.

83. Rebecca Watson, "Therefore We Will Not Fear," in *City in the Hebrew Bible*, 202.

84. Tate, *Psalms 51–100*, 263.

85. deClaissé-Walford, *Psalms*, 615.

supporting the beginning of the psalm where God brings peace through dismantling the weapons of the enemy.[86] Yet, the original Hebrew likely suggests that the wrath of God's enemies will be transformed into praise because of their defeat, or that, through the display of God's glory, his rebellious enemies will be humbled and give praise.[87] While such a verse proves difficult in translation, the emphasis remains that from Zion God will bring peace; Zion's enemies will fail because "who can stand before you when once your anger is roused?" (Ps 76:7).

Instead of a king fighting a battle, the elements of Zion theology in Ps 76 reflect God as a supreme king who receives tribute from foreign kings who have been humbled. The forces of evil on earth will be turned toward praise, and even the lowly and poor of earth will receive aid because of the king's presence in Zion. Therefore, Zion serves as both a fortress for humbling powerful kings of earth and as a refuge for the poor to find justice and salvation. When the people draw near to the sanctuary, they find rescue from enemies, and their fear is turned to thanksgiving because the weapons of the enemy have been shattered.[88] God's wrath has resulted in judgment, but this judgment brings salvation and justice for the afflicted, which leads the people to respond by keeping their vows and offering tribute, as expressed in verses 11 and 12.[89]

Psalms 122 and 132: Zion in the Songs of Ascents

Psalms 120–34 are bound together by their common heading of "a song of ascents," indicating a group of psalms that may have existed as a separate collection before becoming part of the Psalter.[90] As "pilgrimage psalms," these songs represent the prayers of travelers and sojourners approaching Zion, likely from different eras of Israel's history and compiled after the exile.[91] The collection of songs mostly reflects the time period when the temple was rebuilt, likely between 515 and 300 BC as the Psalter was being developed into its final shape.[92] Commentator Erich Zenger suggested the collection is "a document of Jewish identity that holds fast to Zion/Jerusalem as the

86. Emerton, "Neglected Solution," 145.

87. Tate, *Psalms 51–100*, 262.

88. Eaton, *Psalms*, 275.

89. Grogan, *Psalms*, 24.

90. Rohde, "Observations on the Songs," 24.

91. Rohde, "Observations on the Songs," 24.

92. Berlin, *Psalms 120–150*, 183.

center of Israel."[93] There is a thematic unity centered on three theological emphases in this collection: Yahweh's presence on Zion, Yahweh's blessing from Zion, and Israel as a community around Zion.[94]

Sigmund Mowinckel argued that these psalms are not indicative of a pilgrimage or festival journey, but rather they represent the "solemn festival procession that took place every year on YHWH's enthronement during the New Year's festival in the month of Tishri."[95] Psalm 132, for example, may have been sung during a celebration within the temple court as part of the liturgy involved with that festival. The superscription for "ascent" would then denote the New Year's festivities and the enthronement festival, which both took place on the way to the temple and within it.[96] In contrast, Ollenburger argues that no such festival exists explicitly in the biblical text, and the existence of such a festival cannot be reconstructed from historical material unless it is already assumed to have existed.[97] Despite the lack of evidence regarding such a festival of God's enthronement, texts such as Ps 132 indicate how the Israelites celebrated the kingship of Yahweh in conjunction with his anointing of the Davidic king. It is important to note that in terms of the Zion symbol, the notion of Yahweh's kingship predates the monarchy, thus any connection to the earthly king flows downward from the theological ideology surrounding Yahweh as king.[98]

Alastair Hunter proposed five major themes across the songs of ascents: Judah's formal institutions; family and farm; the quest for Yahweh; enemies of the faithful; blessings and joy.[99] These themes comprise a framework of interpreting this collection in light of a festival gathering, ensuring the prosperity of the people and the kingly dynasty as long as the Lord is faithful to his chosen dwelling place, Zion.[100] The songs of ascents combine to express a high interest in an important development in the Zion symbol: God will remember Zion and from there will emerge a future ideal king. The combination of the references to David and Solomon as well as the emphasis upon the spiritual significance of Zion in the life of the people creates an anticipation, or a "messianism," which looks forward to a future king

93. Hossfeld and Zenger, *Commentary on Psalms 101–150*, 298.

94. Rohde, "Observations on the Songs," 24.

95. Mowinckel, *Psalm Studies*, 2:604.

96. Mowinckel, *Psalm Studies*, 2:604.

97. Ollenburger, *Zion, the City*, 27.

98. Ollenburger, *Zion, the City*, 30.

99. Hunter, *Psalms*, 121.

100. Hunter, *Psalms*, 121.

who will once again rule with an iron rod and establish peace and justice from atop the Lord's holy mountain.[101]

While the songs of ascents represent several thematic elements tied to Zion symbolism, the primary hope found within this collection is that blessing and security come from Yahweh, whose home is in Zion. Psalm 125 exclaims, "Those who trust in the Lord are like Mount Zion, which cannot be moved, but abides forever. As the mountains surround Jerusalem, so the Lord surrounds his people" (Ps 125:1–2). Mount Zion, certainly not the highest peak in the region, is surrounded by mountains, but this is a reminder of how Yahweh surrounds and protects his chosen city. Yet, despite its diminutive stature, the people flock to Zion because it is there that God's ways can be known.[102] Isaiah adds to this notion, including the nations joining the pilgrimage to Zion, saying, "All the nations shall flow to it . . . that he may teach us his ways and that we may walk in his paths" (Isa 2:1, 3). Ultimately, Zion is the place of God's eschatological kingdom, where all the nations cease their wars and find peace through following God's ways, taught to them on Zion.[103]

Psalm 122

Psalm 122 does not mention the term "Zion," but it is often associated with other "songs of Zion," such as Pss 46, 48, 76, and 84.[104] However, more akin to Ps 84, this psalm regards Jerusalem with spiritual emotion and enthusiasm instead of wisdom and teaching coming from Zion.[105] It is also the psalm most explicitly connected with pilgrimage to the city from the songs of ascents and may have been composed in such a context. The psalm remembers a time when a family or community, in obedience to the Torah, sought to travel to Jerusalem to celebrate one of the major festivals.[106] However, the psalm could also be understood as a "theology of the city of Jerusalem" with its unique focus on the city itself.[107] While Jerusalem and Zion can have a similar reference, Jerusalem typically refers to the earthly city and Zion typically points to the religious entity of the city, the temple, and the abode of God.

101. Hunter, *Psalms*, 121.

102. Goldingay, *Israel's Faith*, 298.

103. Preuss, *Old Testament Theology*, 2:288.

104. Goldingay, *Psalms*, 3:462.

105. Allen, *Psalms 101–150*, 212.

106. Goldingay, *Psalms*, 3:464.

107. Allen, *Psalms 101–150*, 212.

The significance of the cult in Ps 122 is not only about the piety of the pilgrims or the city; rather, it points to the administering of justice for all people.[108] Verse 5 indicates that equitable justice is closely linked to the "thrones of the house of David," reminding the audience that the law and order within the city are extensions of God's covenant with David. Even if this describes a governmental court instead of the temple, this points to the close connection between Zion theology and the royal ideology depicted in such psalms: just as the palace and temple were in the same vicinity, the royal courts were infused with spiritual significance.[109] Robert Miller describes it this way: "Reification, or making the human situation divinely or naturally authorized, often by saying that it reflects the divine or natural situation, gives institutions of power status independent of human activity and signification."[110] This is significant in terms of the Zion symbol, for both the kingship of God and the human king are elevated within the social spheres of everyday life for Zion's inhabitants. Blessing, justice, and mercy for the afflicted are results of the anointing from the heavenly King upon the earthly king. Miller also says, "These symbolic universes are sheltering canopies over the institutional order, delimiting what is relevant."[111] Through a shared collective memory, the people generate a sense of permanence regarding Zion's role in their life: even if Ps 122 was primarily sung in the postexilic period, the ideological realities that defined David's kingship continue as generations of pilgrims approach Zion.[112] Furthermore, the sense of *shalom* desired by the pilgrims is not a vain wish; rather, it is based upon the reality that Jerusalem houses the temple of Yahweh, and from there come peace and prosperity, not only for the city but for all the people of Israel.[113] In Ps 122, the emphasis as expressed in the opening line is "the house of the Lord" (Ps 122:1). Thus, this psalm recalls the promises made to David, leading the pilgrims to approach Zion with joy and thanksgiving to the Lord. From the perspective of a pilgrim entering the great city, the city's walls and foundations are a marvel, leading the pilgrim to offer prayers on behalf of the city for peace and security. The impassioned plea of the psalmist is God-centered and reflects the importance of the theocratic institutions surrounding the temple and monarchy.[114] These aspects show that this psalm

108. Miller, "Zion Hymns," 230.

109. Allen, *Psalms 101–150*, 214.

110. Miller, "Zion Hymns," 230.

111. Miller, "Zion Hymns," 230.

112. Miller, "Zion Hymns," 231.

113. Wilk, "Pilgrimage to Jerusalem," 297.

114. Allen, *Psalms 101–150*, 215.

describes a more communal setting for the temple, since verse 8 implies a fellowship with "brothers and friends" (Ps 122:8). The peace of Jerusalem affects not just the pilgrim but the entire community of worshipers.[115] Thus, Ps 122 portrays an abiding belief that Zion is a sacred space for pilgrims and citizens alike: by drawing near to the presence of God, the people celebrate with worship and thanksgiving, knowing that God's covenant promises will persist throughout generations. This is especially potent for a postexilic audience as they reestablished the temple and regained their national and spiritual identity based upon the presence of God on Mount Zion.

Psalm 132

Psalm 132 is an important example of the developing nature of the Zion symbol, for it contains an unusual arrangement of symbols, historical events, intercessions, and promises. As one of the "songs of ascents," the psalm may relate to the festival surrounding the dedication of the temple, which points to a preexilic origin.[116] The rare mention of the ark in verse 8 also recaptures the celebration of the dedication of the temple in 1 Kgs 8, or possibly the moment David brought the ark into Jerusalem from Kiriath-Jearim in 2 Sam 6. Either way, the sentiment in verse 8 recalls the theme of Yahweh as the divine warrior who will march against Israel's foes from his resting place in Zion.[117] The psalm favors the righteousness of David and connects God's covenant promises with his "desire" for Zion: the prosperity of the king and the blessing on the people is contingent on God's choice of Zion as the place of his presence among the people. Under Solomon, the temple became the home of the ark, the place where God makes his presence known. As King, the temple was his palace, and the holy of holies was his throne room.[118] Thus, the attention and blessing given to the poor and to Zion's leaders come from God's presence in Zion.

The Zion symbol in the psalm is expressed in four distinct ways: the particular emphasis on the physical place of Zion; the link between the place and the Davidic covenant; the blessings for the righteous; and Zion's significance for the community.[119] All of these are effects from the belief that God

115. Rohde, "Observations on the Songs," 32.

116. Some scholars, such as Herman Gunkel, identified Ps 132 among the "Zion songs" with Pss 46, 48, 76, 84, 87, and 122, but Ps 132 is usually designated as a "Royal Psalm." Weiser, *Psalms*, 780.

117. Laato, "Psalm 132," 63.

118. Longman, *Psalms*, 439.

119. Rohde, "Observations on the Songs," 42.

had chosen Zion as verse 13 explains, "For the Lord has chosen Zion; he has desired it for his dwelling place" (Ps 132:13). This conveys an intensely personal attitude from God, compared to the Lord's love for Zion expressed in Ps 78:68: "But he chose the tribe of Judah, Mount Zion, which he loves."[120] This uniquely warm and personal tone in Ps 132 toward David and Zion reflects God's desire to dwell among the people forever, based upon his own divine election of both the Temple Mount and the ideal king, David.[121]

The blessings received from Zion are not based upon the faithfulness of men but rather on God's choice of Zion, which comes from his incomprehensible grace.[122] The people's need for food (132:15) is satisfied and the priests are anointed with blessing because the sovereign God will provide them with prosperous lands, children, and food for the needy.[123] Zion, then, is deeper than a religious site, for God's presence in Zion results in material and spiritual blessings for the people. As the people are fed and the priests minister well, God reminds the people that Zion is "my resting place forever" (Ps 132:14).

Psalm 132 is a royal psalm and a plea for God to remember the current king because of his covenant promises made to David. Since God desired Zion as his dwelling, it is the place where his manifest presence is made known to the people, and it is the source of blessing for the anointed king.[124] As a climax to the songs of ascents, Ps 132 expresses the goal of the collection: David and Jerusalem will once again be the center of Jewish life, and of the whole world, because of God's presence and blessing on Zion.[125] The second half of Ps 132 is also the first time Yahweh's voice is heard in the songs of ascents, and in climactic fashion, he affirms his own choice of Zion and David as the heir of his covenant promises with the nation. In the last of the songs of ascents, Ps 134 reaffirms this notion, for if the temple is worthy of the people's focus and loyalty, it is only because Yahweh, "he who made heaven and earth," dwells eternally within his chosen house.[126]

120. Allen, *Psalms 101–150*, 274.

121. Allen, *Psalms 101–150*, 275.

122. Weiser, *Psalms*, 782.

123. deClaissé-Walford, *Psalms*, 727.

124. Longman, *Psalms*, 434.

125. Phillip E. Satterthwaite, "Zion in the Songs," in Hess and Wenham, *Zion: City of Our God*, 126.

126. Phillip E. Satterthwaite, "Zion in the Songs," in Hess and Wenham, *Zion: City of Our God*, 126.

ZION, THE HOPE OF RESTORATION

Intertwined with the psalmists' hope that God will remember his people through war and exile remains the belief that God will restore the people and their capital because he is a God of the future and a God who would rebuild his kingdom.[127] The Psalter portrays a hope, especially in the parts written during and after the exile, that Zion's history has not ended. Many of the psalms that convey a deep sense of repentance and the need for cleansing among the people undergird the notion that Zion would be rebuilt and that once again the people would worship the Lord at his temple.[128] These psalms reveal the eschatological nature of Zion as the symbol developed: while still an imagery-rich depiction of the temple and God's chosen city, the psalms focused on restoration point to a deeper, eternal reality based upon the character of God himself and the covenant promises he had made with his chosen people. During times of exile, suffering, and lament, the psalmists fixed their gaze toward Zion, even if it had been abandoned, with the hope that God would remember his chosen city and renew it through his divine presence.

From the following selection of psalms, which is not exhaustive, it is important to note that Zion as a symbol of God's presence should not be understood in the same way as other ancient Near Eastern temples where the deity is directly tied to his temple.[129] From the beginning, the Zion symbol reflects the fact that God's true temple is heavenly: the holy of holies and the ark therein were not the true abode of the king but rather represented God's heavenly throne, of which the ark was a footstool. Furthermore, as Ps 132 indicates, God chose to dwell in Zion, and it was his own choice, not the actions of men, that caused him to dwell among the people in Zion. All the subsequent blessings and promises flow from God's sovereign choice of Zion as well as the teaching, wisdom, and blessing he chooses to pour out upon the people, including the hope of a future return of the city's glory. Even as Zion is personified to express God's judgment on an unfaithful people, it opens the door for restoration and an end to suffering.[130]

127. The themes of Yahweh's kingship and future restoration are not mutually exclusive in the Psalms; rather, it is the foundational belief in the return of God's presence to Zion that generates the belief in God's future restoration. Grogan, *Psalms*, 244.

128. Grogan, *Psalms*, 244.

129. Son, *Zion Symbolism*, 43.

130. Son, *Zion Symbolism*, 47.

Psalm 69: From Lament to Thanksgiving

Psalm 69 is written as an individual lament that transforms into thanksgiving and was probably recited in public settings. The historical setting is difficult to discern, for although the poet is consumed with "zeal for your house," he has suffered through severe trials.[131] Although the superscription attributes this psalm to David, the reference to Zion's restoration at the end is usually associated with the period after the Babylonian exile.[132] Therefore, it likely functioned as an individual lament in the preexilic period but through the crisis of exile became a more corporate lament, which personified the "I" to represent the nation. The ending of the psalm may be a postexilic addition, which provides an important characteristic for how Zion symbolism was utilized as a picture of God's promises for restoration.[133] However, it is also possible that "build up," as the ESV translates verse 35, could be understood as "make strong," indicating God's desire to strengthen the afflicted and bless the people throughout the generations.[134] Structurally, the psalm opens and closes with divine salvation: it begins with an individual appeal but ends with a call for universal praise focused on the great work of God to restore the place of his covenant promises.[135]

The full lament in verses 1 through 29 expresses the suffering the Israelites felt in exile, but in response to their suffering, their hearts were gladdened because of Zion. God's faithfulness toward the suffering individual is expanded to reflect God's restoration of Zion and the cities of Judah, creating the hope that Zion will experience the abundance of God's love despite the suffering incurred.[136] By reflecting on Zion, the psalm's ending transcends an individual's suffering and imagines a time where the entire nation will live at peace in God's eternal kingdom.[137] This movement from individual lament to communal confession highlights the way in which the Zion symbol expresses the communal identity of the people; by placing their hope in the God who would restore, their individual needs were seen through the lens of not only other afflicted individuals but through the nation's identity

131. Weiser, *Psalms*, 494.

132. Groenewald, "Psalm 69:36," 359.

133. Longman, *Psalms*, 267.

134. Eaton, *Psalms*, 256.

135. Allen, "Value of Rhetorical Criticism," 598.

136. Groenewald, "Psalm 69:36," 361.

137. deClaissé-Walford, *Psalms*, 434.

as a whole.[138] Zion was a theological symbol that represented God's presence for both the individual and the collective nation.

As one of the most frequently quoted psalms in the New Testament, Ps 69 represents the prayer of a royal leader who has fallen into a time of overwhelming suffering. The zeal for God's house, the mockery, bitter drink, and judgment on enemies all relate to Christ's experiences in the Gospels, and thus the building up of Zion reflects God's building of the church through the testimony of Jesus, leading "all those who love his name" to "dwell in it" (Ps 69:36).[139] The belief that God would "build up" Zion for New Testament Christians was transformed through Christ, who not only fulfilled the prayer of Ps 69 but who, in himself, ushered in the eternal kingdom of peace imagined in the hopes of the psalmist. Furthermore, since the psalm was often sung in a national, communal sense, it points to the future restoration of Israel beyond the physical city of Jerusalem to a time when all of creation sings praise to God for his salvation. Artur Weiser notes, "Even the cult community's concern for the future of its native country, whose cities lie in ruins, is transformed in the light of such an experience into confident hope in God."[140]

Psalm 87: Zion, the Spiritual Mother of the Nations

Another important aspect of God's restoration in Zion is expressed in Ps 87: Zion will become the city of all peoples because of the Lord's presence there. In other words, since Zion is the place where God makes his presence known, the natural result is that all the peoples of the world will find their spiritual home in Zion, the home of Yahweh.[141] The psalm opens by describing God's love for the city "he founded," and then it opens into a momentous oracle concerning the nations.[142]

The listing of hostile nations being "born there" signifies a future time where even Israel's enemies will find wisdom and spiritual life from Zion. Rahab (possibly Egypt) and Babylon were massive, mythically evil empires known for their oppression of God's people.[143] Then the list moves toward smaller, regional hostile nations such as Tyre and Philistia, and finally, far

138. Gerstenberger, "Psalm 69," 12.

139. Eaton, *Psalms*, 257.

140. Weiser, *Psalms*, 495.

141. Longman, *Psalms*, 317.

142. Eaton, *Psalms*, 311.

143. Bos, "Psalm 87," 283.

away people such as Cush, which typically represents Ethiopia or Nubia.[144] In connection with God's love for the city of Zion, this presents a unique angle on the Zion symbol. The Lord's presence there, fueled by his own love for his chosen city, results not only in the protection and prosperity of Israel but brings all the nations near as they find a spiritual home in the place of God's presence. A celebration of an ethnically diverse group of people in Zion foresees a time when peace has come, and all are welcomed into the presence of God. While it may have been common for there to be a mixture of peoples among the Israelites, this psalm envisions a vast array of peoples all gathering to be registered as citizens of Zion.[145]

In verse 7, the worshipers exclaim that "all my springs are in you," indicating that the fountains of God, or his salvation, can only be found in Zion.[146] Wisdom, teaching, and righteousness are not found in Egypt, Tyre, or Philistia; when read in light of other Scripture, it becomes clear that only in Zion can one be born anew.[147] Thus, Ps 87 maintains a hopeful perspective on Zion beyond the security it may have provided to the people of God. It looks forward to a time when the enemies of Zion will find refuge and salvation in the city and even become citizens. This psalm relates to Isaiah's vision of the city "in the last days" when "many peoples will come" and "walk in his paths" (Isa 2:3). Weapons of war will be broken down into farming tools, for the Lord's wisdom and teaching has shown them the proper way to live.

The Zion symbolism of Ps 87 reflects the transforming power of the presence of God: God is not only the King enthroned in Zion, but he is the source of wisdom and righteousness that draws the nations toward himself, not for war but for peace and salvation. This points to the ultimate purpose of the temple as well, for through it the Israelites had the opportunity to reveal God's glory to the nations and welcome the outsider into his presence. To this future hope, God says to Ezekiel, "My dwelling place shall be with them, and I will be their God, and they shall be my people. Then the nations will know that I am the Lord who sanctifies Israel, when my sanctuary is in their midst forevermore" (Ezek 37:27–28). Thanks to the springs of life in Zion, the nations will bear witness to God's presence in Zion and the blessings attached to his nearness to the people.[148] From the perspective of the New Testament, it is in Zion that the Messiah is crucified, buried, and

144. Bos, "Psalm 87," 283.

145. Allen, "Psalm 87," 139.

146. Allen, "Psalm 87," 140.

147. Allen, "Psalm 87," 140.

148. Beale, *Temple and the Church's Mission*, 122.

resurrected; and through faith in the Son of God, all nations are welcomed into the presence of God and declared to be citizens of his kingdom.[149]

Psalm 102: Hope in the God Who Will Restore Zion

Psalm 102 bears a unique superscription, which identifies it with the specific situation of "one afflicted" as he "pours out his complaint before the Lord." The psalm is also unassociated with a leader, such as David or Korah, so it may have been used as a model prayer for a person in deep need.[150] Despite the personal nature of the plea, the psalmist speaks of Zion three times, indicating how his personal trouble is connected with the broader good of the city and the people as a whole. Structurally, the psalm is a typical lament with the statement of a lament (2–3), the complaint (4–12), a statement of trust (13–18), and a vow of praise (19–23).[151] The final section includes another complaint, petition, and motivation for praise, but the unique interpretive issue within the structure is how the communal expression regarding Zion in the middle relates to the individual's lament over his affliction. Yet, this is where an important aspect of Zion symbolism appears in the psalm: an individual's lament is shaped through the lens of God's presence and promises in Zion.

It is plausible that verse 13 shows how an individual petitioner cannot comfort himself with God's activity in the past, so he focuses on the future. In other words, his fate is embedded in God's future activity toward Zion.[152] Verse 13 expresses trust, not that the individual's affliction will be healed but rather that the Lord's love for Zion will result in the city's restoration and the people's praise.[153] The verse also speaks with great confidence, giving no basis for "the appointed time" but rather asking God to rise up from his royal throne and act on behalf of Zion. God is expected to show pity upon the city; thus, the psalmist is confident God will rebuild the city and hear his cry for help.[154] Furthermore, Yahweh's compassion toward Zion will result in a time when the nations of the earth "fear the name of the Lord," and "all the kings of the earth will fear your glory" (Ps 102:15). Zion is the place of

149. Allen, "Psalm 87," 140.
150. deClaissé-Walford, *Psalms*, 567.
151. Witt, "Hearing Psalm 102," 583.
152. Witt, "Hearing Psalm 102," 587.
153. Eaton, *Psalms*, 355.
154. Goldingay, *Psalms*, 3:155.

Yahweh's name, the earthly counterpart to the heavenly temple, where one day the nations will offer the praise due to the King of all creation.[155]

In verse 16, the phrase "for the Lord builds up Zion" can be understood as either an assurance that God will rebuild Zion in the near future or it may reflect the psalmist's view of a reconstructed Zion, as if it had already happened.[156] The latter view is favorable, for the contrasts in the psalm highlight the theological emphases regarding God's faithfulness toward Zion. The fate of the individual is left unresolved, yet he expresses great confidence in Zion's future glory; the petitioner is frail, yet God is eternal, and Zion will be exalted among all other nations and kings.[157] These contrasts point to the importance of the Zion symbol in Ps 102: Zion reflects the eternal presence of God, so in times of great suffering, the community around Zion finds comfort in the symbol of hope and restoration. The vertical perspectives from the ones suffering and how such affliction is viewed from an ultimate, cosmological perspective combines with the horizontal perspective on God's activity regarding Zion and the community leading to an understanding that Zion represents the community of faith in times of victory, suffering, and restoration.[158]

Zion in Ps 102 reaches beyond the confines of the temple and becomes a symbol whose destiny is connected to the individual members of the community. As the psalmist is withering, so, too, is Zion, or the community of God, hence the plea for God not to alleviate the individual's pain but rather rebuild Zion and return its glory.[159] Leslie Allen states, "This psalm is a fine example of spirituality at work, if spirituality is defined as the intersection of theology and real human life."[160] Such an intersection relates to New Testament theology and the belief that Christians are present members of the heavenly Jerusalem, or the eschatological Zion. As 1 Peter speaks to the role of suffering, it reads, "Let those who suffer according to God's will entrust themselves to a faithful Creator while doing what is good" (1 Pet 4:19 CSB). As the psalm expresses clearly, the hope for restoration is not that the present suffering will simply end but that God will act with compassion and restore the whole community of faith. For the Christian, this hope is ultimately realized in the presence of God in the new Jerusalem, where God and man dwell permanently together in peace.

155. Allen, *Psalms 101–150*, 22.
156. van Wolde, "Psalm 102:12–23," 214.
157. van Wolde, "Psalm 102:12–23," 218.
158. Culley, "Psalm 102," 33.
159. Longman, *Psalms*, 354.
160. Allen, *Psalms 101–150*, 23.

Psalm 126: From Tears to Joy

Psalm 126 is a brief, joyful song of praise to God for the great things he has done in restoring Zion. Weiser remarks, "At the very beginning of the psalm the faith of the cult community spreads the wings of its thoughts in a bold flight into the future, and looks into the smiling fields of blissful hope as through a widely opened gate."[161] The hope of the people is not found in their agricultural success nor political power; rather, it is found in the Lord. The transformation of their circumstances has nothing to do with their own works, for it is God alone who has restored Zion's fortunes and turned sorrow into shouts of joy. However, this hope is based upon previous experiences of God's restoration, providing support to the community's prayer and invigorating their praise.[162]

The usage of the Zion symbol in Ps 126 provides a clue to the theme of restoration, for the syntax may prevent the term from being the indirect object of the verb. Thus, it could be read, "When the Lord returned Zion," emphasizing Zion itself being returned to a former state.[163] The closest parallels to this function occur in Isa 49–52 where the exiles in Babylon are labeled as "Zion" or "captive daughter of Zion" (Isa 49:14; 51:3). Thus, the symbol has been transferred from the holy mountain of God onto the devoted people of God, even if far away from the temple.[164] Zion, as a theological symbol of God's presence, is not confined to the temple, for God's devoted people are identified in a communal sense as "Zion." This points to a time of restoration when the people of God will worship him in harmony and when the presence of God will extend across the earth. Isaiah 51:3 predicts this time, saying, "For the Lord comforts Zion; he comforts all her waste places and makes her wilderness like Eden." Through the Lord's restoration of Zion, the "dreamers" worship in awe of what God has done, praising him for all the great things he did for Israel. The fear and distress of exile has been transformed into shouts of praise through God's eschatological work in restoring Zion.

In the same vein, Zion is a sacred place, the holy mountain of the Lord, and the people experience laughter and joy as "dreamers" who have envisioned a moment when redemption comes: visions that were, at one time, a hope have become reality.[165] A secondary aspect to the sacred space of Zion

161. Weiser, *Psalms*, 760.

162. Weiser, *Psalms*, 760.

163. Harman, "Setting and Interpretation," 75.

164. Harman, "Setting and Interpretation," 76.

165. Segal, "Psalm 126," 53.

is referenced in verses 2 and 3, with the mention that the redeemed people will say "among the nations" that "the Lord has done great things for them" (Ps 126:2). While many psalms denoting the kingship of Yahweh speak of Zion's enemies being repulsed by God's holy presence, here, the notion is one of praise that reaches the ears of the nations, implicitly inviting them to come near to Zion. Such a momentous event has happened in Zion that the people respond with jubilant praise that extends to their neighbors, turns tears into joy and scarcity into abundance. In the New Testament, such an event relates to salvation in Christ, for the redemptive work has begun in one's transferal from spiritual death to life, yet the fullness of joy will not be complete until the final resurrection. Thus, rejoicing in God's restoration is an ongoing process as the people of God have their sorrow turned to joy through drawing near to God's presence.[166]

Psalm 137: We Remembered Zion

Psalm 137 provides a unique perspective on Zion as both a postexilic lament from Babylon and as one of the imprecatory psalms. Its placement in book 5 is somewhat perplexing since most of book 5 celebrates the return from exile and the rebuilding of the temple; yet Psalm 137 may serve as an example of the importance of remembering the pain of the past in order to celebrate present blessing.[167] The song opens by identifying the setting as "by the waters of Babylon," indicating a time in which the captives have little left of Zion other than a distant memory. Zion, the place of God's presence, only existed as a memory in the hearts of the captives because it was ruined.[168] The Babylonian captors mock Yahweh, provoking the exiles to sing "one of the songs of Zion," yet the exiles refuse and mourn the condition of their beloved temple city. Zion was central to the people's identity and survival, and songs such as Ps 48 express the inviolability of the city: as God's holy mountain, Zion was the place of his kingly reign, the place from which rivers of life flow (Ps 46:4) and from where Yahweh will guide his people forever (Ps 48:13–14). Zion lay in ruins but was not forgotten, for in remembering Zion, there is a renewed devotion to the Lord.[169]

Verses 5 and 6 indicate that love for Zion is linked with a love for God: as the temple represented God's heavenly rule on earth, the love for

166. Longman, *Psalms*, 425.

167. deClaissé-Walford, *Psalms*, 741.

168. Simango, "Comprehensive Reading," 223.

169. Simango, "Comprehensive Reading," 225.

the temple and for God are intertwined.[170] The word "remember," occurring in verses 1, 6, and 7, holds the psalm together, calling on those passionate about Zion never to forget the blessing of God's presence and what was lost in its destruction.[171] Such remembrance of Zion stirs the psalmist toward a passionate appeal to Yahweh regarding the fate of Babylon and Edom. Weiser describes such passion as "blind hate" or "vulgar rage," yet the imprecation against Babylon and Edom in verses 7 and 8 speaks to a deeper theological reality.[172] Origen allegorized the psalm, describing such violence in terms of one's "troublesome sinful thoughts that arise in the soul," yet this, too, avoids the passion of the psalm in a way that detracts from the centrality of the Zion theology upon which such imprecation is based.[173]

Zion, as Yahweh's sacred space upon earth, was a reflection of his glory and rule over the whole earth: the ultimate purpose of Zion was to fill the earth with the glory of the Lord. This promise was not completely lost, but nonetheless, the ferocity of Babylon and the betrayal of Edom had left the city in ruins and the people in exile. The imprecation against Zion's enemies is founded upon the former promises concerning Zion, that the nations who rage against it will be crushed (Ps 2:9–12). Erich Zenger said the psalm is "an attempt . . . to suppress the primitive human lust for violence in one's own heart by surrendering everything to God—a God whose word of judgment is presumed to be so universally just that even those who pray the psalm submit themselves to it."[174] Thus, imprecation, while passionate or even furious in tone, is deeper than raw emotion and exists as an outlet for the people of God to cry out in faith, knowing that God's promises are unbroken. Edom and Babylon are the antithesis of Zion; they are the ones who should be repulsed from God's holy mountain, yet they appear victorious over God's people. From this, Ps 137 shows how the Zion symbol not only stirred passion in the souls of the exiles but it created a hopeful confidence that God would restore Zion and once again establish his reign over the nations. Exile must be temporary, for God's promises to the people of Zion are everlasting (Ps 48:8).

170. Simango, "Comprehensive Reading," 223.

171. Gillingham, "Jewish and Christian Approaches," 446.

172. Weiser, *Psalms*, 796.

173. Wesselschmidt, *Psalms 51–150*, 682.

174. Allen, *Psalms 101–150*, 309.

ZION AND THE MESSIANIC HOPE IN PSALMS

One of the most encouraging aspects of the Psalter is that, despite the apostasies of the monarchy and the failure of the people to uphold their covenant obligations before God, the hope of a coming Messiah perseveres. Built upon, or at least heavily influenced by, the covenant given to David in 2 Sam 7, the hope of a coming Messiah emerges as a programmatic, intentional feature of the Psalter.[175] *Māšîaḥ*, for "anointed one," appears ten times in the Psalter, but it is important for the term not to be understood only through a New Testament lens as "Christ," for the term refers to a broader concept that is narrowed through the Prophets and then specified in the New Testament through Jesus Christ. Understanding the concept of "Messiah" in the Old Testament involves a multidimensional approach that includes the contexts in which the term is used, the range of meaning, the time involved in such meanings, as well as the transcendent quality behind the theological purpose of this concept.[176] As early as Ps 2, there is an undercurrent in the shape of the Psalter that points to a future Messiah who will ultimately fulfill the promise given to David and reign with righteousness and justice from atop Zion. Because Zion is God's holy mountain, the rebellious nations are vanquished, but those who seek justice and wisdom from the Lord will be welcomed into the city. These themes are not only reflective of David's reign but point forward to God's eschatological kingdom which extends over the whole earth from Zion.

The arrangement and structure of the Psalter points to this undercurrent of a coming King. In Ps 2, the kings of the earth are depicted as raging against the Lord and his *Māšîaḥ*, but the Lord speaks from heaven to confirm "I have set my King on Zion." The authority given to "my Son" is based upon God's choice of both Zion and his anointed king.[177] Along with Ps 1, the opening psalms provide a clear path for Israel to live righteously and receive divine instruction and justice, but within this there is an emphasis on God's purpose for the Davidic dynasty.[178] The first psalm calls for the individual to follow the path toward life, and the second urges the nations to make the same choice, which broadens the scope of Ps 2 beyond the coronation of a king to a more universal appeal for God's reign through the king.[179] However, the kings over Israel were largely a failure, and some completely

175. Grogan, *Psalms*, 290.

176. Durham, "King as 'Messiah,'" 426.

177. Durham, "King as 'Messiah,'" 427.

178. Grogan, *Psalms*, 294.

179. Lee, *From Messiah*, 243.

apostate: 2 Samuel describes David's moral failure, and even Isaiah's messianic prophecies occur in the context of Hezekiah, who also was unable to meet the ideal of a truly godly king.[180] Thus, the perspective of Ps 2 is that God's Messiah will ultimately triumph and reign from God's holy mountain, Zion.[181] In the New Testament, Rev 14 describes Christ the Lamb standing victorious on Mount Zion with the saints, confirming the imagery of Ps 2 and fulfilling the psalm's promise that the Messiah will have "the ends of the earth" as "your possession" and that "all who take refuge in him" will be blessed (Ps 2:8, 12). The New Testament interprets Ps 2 through this eschatological lens: Acts 13:33 quotes Ps 2:7, connecting the Davidic sonship with Christ's resurrection. This Davidic ruler will not only sit on David's throne but on the throne of the Lord, from where he will rule with an iron rod.[182]

In Ps 45, the bridegroom king is depicted as coming to daughter Zion in terms of a beautiful wedding ceremony, and this imagery highlights how the Davidic kingship reflects God's kingship. Thus, it anticipates the Messiah, David's greater Son and the ultimate fulfillment of God's covenant that David would have a son on the throne forever.[183] In other words, God's enduring love for Zion results in the coming of a final Messiah who will reign with justice and peace forever. The king, called "God" in Ps 45:6, points to the transcendent role of the king, that his throne is everlasting and that he is God's representative on earth.[184]

Book 3 of the Psalms, as it laments the fall of Israel, closes in Ps 89 with an emphatic and energetic affirmation of God's covenant promises to David, yet with a sense of disappointment that God appears to have turned away from Zion.[185] The psalm may reflect the events surrounding Jerusalem's downfall in 587–86 BC, but more generally, it speaks to the hope that God will not forget his covenant promises to David.[186] By its placement at the end of book 3, Ps 89 contemplates the fulfillment of the Davidic covenant, describing one coming whom God will make "the firstborn, the highest of the kings of earth" (Ps 89:27). This future king's "offspring shall endure forever, his throne as long as the sun before me" (Ps 89:36). In book 5, the promise of 2 Samuel 7 is quoted in Ps 132, saying, "One of the sons of your body I will set on your throne . . . their sons also forever shall sit on your throne" (Ps

180. Grogan, *Psalms*, 295.
181. Mitchell, *Message of the Psalter*, 245.
182. Merrill, *Everlasting Dominion*, 482.
183. Longman, *Psalms*, 204.
184. Merrill, *Everlasting Dominion*, 482.
185. Grogan, *Psalms*, 295.
186. Goldingay, *Psalms*, 2:988.

132:11–12). With its location in the songs of ascents, Ps 132 indicates that, amid exile, there must be a further fulfillment of God's covenant promises.[187] Thus, Ps 132 reflects on God's election of Zion as his desired dwelling, the place where his covenant promises will be established forever through an anointed Davidic king.

Perhaps the clearest example of the Psalter's movement toward a coming Messiah appears in Ps 110, often quoted in the New Testament in reference to Christ's role as the eschatological King and Priest. This messianic figure is described as sitting at the right hand of the Father (110:1), ruling from Zion (110:2), and as "a priest forever," like Melchizedek (110:4). As part of book 5, the psalm expresses a confident assurance in the Davidic covenant and the everlasting nature of the divine connection between the offices of king and priest.[188] The imagery of God's universal rule extending from Zion over the earth in verse 2 reflects the theological significance of sacred space in the Psalms as well. The reigning king-priest, anointed to extend God's rule over the earth, is himself the intersection between the throne of heaven and its earthly counterpart, Zion. Book 5 presents this theological truth as something to be expected, as a confident hope that God will usher in his Messiah at the right time in order to restore Israel and establish Zion as the center of the earth from which Yahweh's rule is extended. As the Psalms were compiled and shaped into its final form, it becomes clear that an eschatological emphasis was intended, as the people longed for the return of a Davidic king who would rule with an iron scepter, as Ps 2 portrayed. While Pss 2, 110, and 132 may have originally been used in celebration of God's kingship and his presence in Jerusalem in conjunction with the king, the shape of the Psalter points to a messianic hope that continues through the Prophets and ultimately finds fulfilment in the New Testament, as Christ becomes the eschatological king-priest who is himself the remade Zion, the place of God's presence from which all the nations are invited to draw near and receive salvation.[189]

187. Grogan, *Psalms*, 296.

188. Allen, *Psalms 101–150*, 116.

189. Mitchell, *Message of the Psalter*, 198.

3

Zion Symbolism in the Prophets

In the prophetic literature of the Old Testament, Zion continues to develop as a multivalent theological symbol with various connotations depending on the author's context and intent. For example, earlier oracles of Isaiah parallel Psalms' primary theme of Yahweh's kingship in Zion, yet this fades as Zion becomes the place of judgment due to Israel's apostasy. The sacred space of God's holy mountain became polluted with idolatry and disobedience, causing him to respond by driving out the sinful people from his presence. Nevertheless, as Daughter Zion is punished for her disobedience, the prophets maintain a vision of the future rooted in God's promises that an anointed Davidic king would return, ushering in a time of restoration.

Zion appears in Isaiah more than any other book of the Old Testament, and within the forty-eight occurrences of the term, there are various ways in which the theological symbol represents the presence of God.[1] As a symbol of God's sacred mountain, Zion becomes the place of God's kingly dwelling, the place of his judgment upon the wickedness of the city, and the eternal restored home of his faithful servant Israel. One of Isaiah's primary concerns is the holiness of God, and throughout Isa 1–39 God's presence within the temple on Mount Zion is assumed.[2] However, as the Zion symbol denotes God's kingship on his holy mountain, it also refers to God's people, called "Daughter Zion," who are chastised for their apostasy. Thus, for Isaiah, Zion represents the center of reality, or the location of God's presence among his people, which brings forth blessing and judgment because of his

1. Poulson, *Representing Zion*, 25.
2. Duvall, *God's Relational Presence*, 114.

holiness. Isaiah's unique title for God, "The Holy One of Israel," communicates the author's focus on the holiness of God, of which there is no greater symbol than the temple where his presence dwelt.[3] This chapter will discuss the most prominent uses of the Zion symbol in Isaiah and show how the term transforms from the place of God's presence in Jerusalem to the eschatological kingdom of God, which will bless all the world.

For Jeremiah, the destruction of the city of God is a dominant theme, as Daughter Zion is destroyed and left desolate; however, Jeremiah also conveys a message of hope regarding Zion's restoration, according to God's new covenant he will make with the faithful remnant.[4] Jeremiah uses the Zion symbol in similar ways to Isaiah, but he also has a unique vision of the future kingdom of God when Zion is remade through the transformation of its inhabitants. In Lamentations, Zion takes on a host of female roles, such as a widow, a whore, a betrayed lover, or an abandoned wife. Zion in Lamentations is often personified to emphasize the lost relationship of God with his people as the Lord as abandoned her in his holy wrath. This section will focus on the unique aspects of Jeremiah and Lamentations regarding the Zion symbol and how they develop the symbol through the fall of Jerusalem and exile.

The Zion term's absence in Ezekiel provides a unique angle on the transformation of Zion from a symbol denoting God's kingship to a deeper theological concept regarding the true, faithful people of God, who will enjoy his presence forever. Through his visions of a restored people and a new temple, Ezekiel foreshadows a time when God's presence will be the centerpiece of creation. Even though God's glory abandoned the original Temple Mount, the exiles' hope of restoration is depicted through Ezekiel's emphasis on a new, perfected temple with worldwide influence.[5]

The Minor Prophets present Zion through the lens of multiple theological motifs, depending on their historical context. Micah conveys a similar message as Isaiah regarding the fate of Zion, and Joel offers a clear illustration of the typical Zion motif regarding Yahweh's defense of Zion and the repulsion of its enemies.[6] Zion also occurs in Amos, Obadiah, and Zephaniah in terms of both God's defense of Zion and the salvation that comes from the presence of God on Mount Zion. Zion occurs in Zechariah nine times, and he provides a clear picture of how Zion had expanded from

3. Duvall, *God's Relational Presence*, 114.

4. Poulson, *Representing Zion*, 36.

5. Block, *Beyond the River Chebar*, 2.

6. Poulson, *Representing Zion*, 53.

a symbol of God's kingship on Mount Zion to a symbol reflecting God's worldwide dominion from Zion, carried out through the Davidic covenant.[7]

Through an analysis of the key Scriptures reflecting the multivalent nature of the Zion symbol, a future-oriented theology emerges. Even as Zion laid desolate and the people exiled, the prophets, reflecting on God's covenant promises, portray Zion as the eternal place of God's presence among his people. This hope undergirds Zion symbolism in the Prophets and serves as a continual reminder of God's desire to forever dwell among his people.

ZION SYMBOLISM IN ISAIAH

Isaiah is both the longest of the Old Testament Prophets as well as the most quoted in the New Testament; thus, its impact on the theology of both the Old and New Testaments is profound.[8] In spite of this, Isaiah is also known for critical studies that suppose various authors, editors, or time periods involved in the composition of the book. Typically, Isa 1–39 reflects the era in which Isaiah ministered, perhaps as a court prophet for the four kings listed in Isa 1:1. Isaiah 40–66 envisions the future hope for Israel and a glorious restoration of Zion after its desolation, leading many scholars to hold to a later writing of those chapters.[9] Nevertheless, Isaiah's prophecy presents a cohesive theology, centered on God's sovereign activity in Zion and his future glory that will cover the earth. Zion can appear as a theological symbol for the people of Jerusalem or, more broadly, as the place of God's judgment and salvation. The remnant of Israel is saved in Zion (1:8) and it is the place where the nations come to receive instruction (2:3). Zion is left desolate like a wilderness (64:10) but is the place where God's presence will return to dwell among a holy people (62:12).[10] Thus, Zion plays an important role for Isaiah, although the precise meaning of the term is often ambiguous.

7. Poulson, *Representing Zion*, 60.

8. Witherington, *Isaiah Old and New*, 42.

9. Some scholars further divide Isaiah into three parts: Isa 1–39, 40–55, and 56–66. Witherington states, "Discussions about authorship in the traditional sense tend to overlook the activity of the scribal community in Jerusalem who collected, compiled, edited, and augmented all kinds of Hebrew texts including prophetic, wisdom, and legal texts." Thus, for the sake of this research, the emphasis remains on the theological motif of Zion as expressed throughout the entirety of Isaiah as a literary whole. While there may have been later editions and compilations, the theology of Isaiah and its use of the Zion symbol is the primary focus of this study. Witherington, *Isaiah Old and New*, 42.

10. Poulson, *Representing Zion*, 26.

Zion is a major theme throughout Isaiah, and God's holiness that resides in the city is the foundation for many of Isaiah's oracles.[11] The thematic movement through the book from the apostate city toward the new Jerusalem reflects Isaiah's emphasis on Zion as the sacred space of Yahweh, from which he delivers both judgment and restoration.[12] Yahweh's kingship in Zion protects his people, judges the wicked, and will one day invite the nations to enter Zion and receive instruction from the Lord. The following will analyze the ways in which the Zion symbol impacts the theology of Isaiah as well as how the symbol appears in various forms as a symbol of God's protection, judgment, and restoration for Israel. Ultimately, Zion points to a time when the presence of God will be the center of creation as the nations come to receive instruction. Isaiah expects that God will fulfill these promises through a future Davidic king who will reestablish Zion as the focus of worship, not only for Israel but for all the nations of earth.

Zion in Isaiah 1–39: Yahweh's Holy Mountain

The Zion symbol in Isa 1–39 interacts with the major themes of God's judgment upon the wickedness of the city and the external threat from neighboring nations.[13] In order for Zion to reach its goal of becoming the eschatological city of salvation, it must first be purified. Yet, because of Yahweh's divine election of Zion, he protects the city against external threats for his own purposes, even as the people deserve to be disciplined. The major themes surrounding Zion in Isa 1–39 are God's judgment, which prepares the city for salvation and God's sovereign protection of his holy mountain against threats from the nations. Isaiah's prophecies surrounding the events of the Assyrian invasion of Judah through the time of Hezekiah develop these themes through a theocentric lens: Isaiah repeatedly reveals that Yahweh's will is supreme and he acts according to his own purposes, which will ultimately usher in a restored and recreated Zion, which will be a light and a blessing to the nations.[14]

11. Goldingay, *Theology of the Book*, 110.

12. Poulson, *Representing Zion*, 25.

13. Poulson, *Representing Zion*, 25.

14. Goldingay, *Theology of the Book*, 113.

Zion, the Place of Judgment and Salvation

Isaiah's prophecy opens with a broad divine accusation, calling on the heavens and earth to bear witness to God's indictment of his rebellious people, who have lost their way.[15] Isaiah's words in 1:7–9 symbolically communicate a nation that was nearly destroyed through warfare, likely referring to the Assyrian invasion in 701 BC when Judah's major cities were captured except Jerusalem.[16] The "daughter of Zion" was the only city left, like a "booth in a vineyard" or a lonely hut in a field (Isa 1:8). Ironically, Zion in this moment looked more like Sodom and Gomorrah than the glorious city of Yahweh, home of the King.[17] Amid the destruction, Isaiah's words in the opening chapter depict a conversation between the people and God: the Lord addresses the wayward daughter, who has at least recognized the benefit of God's blessing.[18] However, God reveals that the discipline received is due to a lack of justice, not worship. The multitude of temple ceremonies, sacrifices, and offerings had become vain in God's eyes because the people's deeds did not correspond to their worship. Even still, the Lord provides right instruction from Zion, teaching the people to "wash yourselves," "seek justice," and "bring justice to the fatherless, plead the widow's cause" as an invitation to restore the broken relationship (Isa 1:16–17). Although Zion is weak and under discipline, it remains the place from which righteous teaching, and thus righteous living, comes. Furthermore, the distinction between Sodom and Jerusalem in Isa 1 is not the behavior of the people but the grace of God in delivering the city from the Assyrians.[19] This recalls God's election of Zion in Ps 132:13, that it was the place "he has desired" to dwell. Therefore, Zion's protection against Assyria says little about the people within the city but much about the character and grace of God.

In Isa 1–2, the prophet described how God will take the current city of Jerusalem and transform it through judgment into the Zion that will be.[20] For this to be complete, God must allow the place he chose for his presence to be judged: in Isa 5:1–17, his "beloved" vineyard has been abandoned, becoming a "waste." This vineyard, likely referring to Daughter Zion and the people who had become apostate, was planted as a fortress for God's justice and righteousness; instead, it had become a place of "bloodshed" and

15. Childs, *Isaiah*, 17.
16. Smith, *Isaiah 1–39*, 104.
17. Smith, *Isaiah 1–39*, 104.
18. Watts, *Isaiah 1–33*, 22.
19. Smith, *Isaiah 1–39*, 104.
20. Webb, *Message of Isaiah*, 45.

"outcry" (Isa 5:7). The theme of Zion's restoration is fully developed in Isa 40–66, yet already in the opening chapters, Isaiah reveals a glimpse of God's intention for the place of his divine presence.[21]

It is God's will both to punish and restore Zion for his own purposes: Isa 2:1–5 reverses the lament of chapter 1, describing Zion's restoration as an act of God regardless of any effort or repentance by the people.[22] This brief interlude between the court drama of chapter 1 and the description of the "Day of the Lord" in 2:6–22 expresses a condensed theme for Isaiah's entire message.[23] Isaiah 2:1–5 introduces the vision of an ideal Zion (a theme that repeats throughout Isaiah), a place that is the epicenter of God's rule for the whole earth, which leads to worldwide peace.[24] This oracle opens with imagery of "the mountain of the house of the Lord" being established "as the highest of the mountains," indicating Yahweh's royal residency as supreme over any other political or religious entity (Isa 2:2).[25] This imagery echoes Pss 48 and 68, which both speak to the elevated status of God's holy mountain against all other high peaks, despite the topographical reality that Mount Zion was not the highest peak. Thus, Isa 2:2–3 envisions a theological reality that Zion has become the greatest sacred mountain because it is the dwelling place of Yahweh, and from it comes the teaching needed to distribute justice and peace to the nations.[26] In other words, for there to be peace, the nations must come to Zion in order to receive the Torah needed to "beat their swords into plowshares, and their spears into pruning hooks" (Isa 2:4).

In Isa 2:3, Torah will go forth from Zion, leading to righteous judgment from God and a time when weapons of war are no longer needed. In this passage, Zion is presented as the glorious home of the King, a sacred space from which perfect judgment and teaching come; yet this ideal vision of the city cannot be achieved in its present state. Thus, Isaiah offers a harsh contrast between the daughter of Zion, who is disciplined severely for her

21. Webb, *Message of Isaiah*, 45.

22. Groenewald, "Transformation of the City," 2.

23. Watts, *Isaiah 1–33*, 29.

24. Groenewald, "Transformation of the City," 4.

25. Roberts, "End of War," 4.

26. Micah 4:1–5 contains the same oracle as seen in Isa 2:1–5. Roberts argues that neither oracle envisions how the teaching will be issued from Zion: human agency is not ignored, yet the text reads as if God himself will accomplish this. He states, "It is not unusual for biblical texts to focus on God's actions to the exclusion of God's human agents, even when the activity of those human agents is clearly implied." The leaders of Jerusalem had been condemned in 1:4–20, so this likely points to a time when the religious and political leaders of Israel have been restored, perhaps due to the arrival of a new Davidic King as described in Isa 11. Roberts, "End of War," 4.

apostasy, while at the same time portraying a renewed Zion. All of this is accomplished by God as an all-encompassing work to complete his purposes for his people.[27] Within the first two chapters of Isaiah, there is a glimpse of what is to come: Zion represents God's rule over the whole world. As a particularized vision of God's worldwide kingdom, Isaiah envisions both a new creation and a new city, filled with holy people who have come under the teaching of Yahweh.[28] Zion is a symbol pointing to a deeper purpose than a holy site for Israel; it's future destination is a place of pilgrimage for the nations, the highest mountain to which all the peoples of the earth will come. Yet, in the early chapters of Isaiah, the future symbolic function of Zion conflicts with the present condition of the city, thus God must refine his holy mountain and purify the people through judgment in order to reach such a destination. Isaiah's inclusion of the first-person plural in 2:5, "let us walk in the light of the Lord," signifies the cleansing that must take place and invites ancient and modern readers to consider whether their lives attract people far from God toward his presence.[29]

Isaiah 3–4 continues to develop the prophet's major themes as Israel's leadership is condemned and the haughty "daughters of Zion" are judged for their opulence (Isa 3:16). The contrast between the current and future state of Zion develops the prophet's argument, for what appeared to be a city full of wealth and pride would soon be humbled, but through such judgment would come a time of great hope for the city. While chapter 3 emphasizes the failure of Zion and the corruption within it, Isa 4:2–6 reveals that the Lord will bring a cleansing fire, resulting in a society built upon true worship of God on Mount Zion.[30]

The theme of judgment and salvation on Mount Zion is expressed clearly in Isa 4:2–6, for the prophet speaks of a day when the "branch of the Lord" will bring prosperity to Zion (Isa 4:2). Those remaining in the city are described as "holy" because their "filth" has been washed away (Isa 4:3–4). This "branch," used elsewhere to denote a messianic figure, describes a divine leader who will bring abundance to the remnant of Zion; however, because he is connected to the "fruit of the land," his humanity is also in view.[31] The "fruit of the earth" has been interpreted by some scholars to be a reference only to vegetation and future agricultural prosperity, yet throughout prophetic literature, the picture of fertile land refers to a time

27. Roberts, "End of War," 4.

28. Abernethy, *Book of Isaiah*, 175.

29. Berges, "Zion Theology," 177.

30. Motyer, *Isaiah*, 66.

31. Harris, *Theological Wordbook*, 770.

of eschatological salvation for the people.[32] In connection to the vision for Zion in 2:2–4, this abundance and prosperity is a condition created by the Lord himself, which will attract the nations toward Zion so they can receive teaching and live at peace.[33]

This "branch" may also relate to Ps 132:17 where God will make "a horn grow for David," indicating a future messianic king.[34] The promise of Ps 132 is based upon God's love for David and Zion, his chosen dwelling place, so this "branch" in Isa 4:2 indicates that Zion will be purified and once again become the dwelling place of God's presence through the actions of a future messianic king. The result is that the presence of God will once again be manifested in Zion through the cloud and fire like in Moses's time.[35] These images emphasize the protection of God, not only for the holy of holies but for the entire mountain of Zion. Isaiah's theocentric message conveys the idea that history would find its climax as all the peoples of the earth journey into a restored Zion to rejoice in the divine presence of God.[36]

As a symbol of God's presence, Zion must be purged of sin for the glory of God to once again be the centerpiece of Israelite life. However, God reveals to the people that he will accomplish this himself. For the people, described as a purified remnant, to enjoy the fullness of God's presence, he must remove sin from his sacred mountain. John Watts states that Isaiah emphasizes "God's purpose to dwell in Zion and judge the nations from his throne there. The role of his people in the city, be it only a remnant, is secure."[37] The temple does not hold a significant place in Isaiah's vision of a restored city but rather the whole of Mount Zion is enveloped in God's protection, and the people are provided a "booth for shade" and a "shelter from the storm" (Isa 4:6).[38] This indicates that Isaiah uses the Zion symbol to represent the sacred space of God's presence, which cannot be confined to a temple and will one day fill the whole mountain, resulting in a purified community of saints who are "beautiful and glorious" like the "branch" who leads them (Isa 4:2). However, this vision of Zion cannot come to pass until the sin within Zion has been removed, so that the nations can stream to the city to learn from Yahweh's teaching.[39]

32. Williamson, *Isaiah 1–5*, 308.
33. Williamson, *Isaiah 1–5*, 309.
34. Smith, *Isaiah 1–39*, 155.
35. Childs, *Isaiah*, 36.
36. Oswalt, *Book of Isaiah*, 33.
37. Watts, *Isaiah 1–33*, 51.
38. Hoppe, *Isaiah*, 18.
39. Hamilton, *God's Glory in Salvation*, 192.

Another way in which Isaiah communicates the movement from judgment to salvation in Zion is by his use of female personification with terms such as "daughter of Zion."[40] Isaiah 1:8 introduces Daughter Zion as a woman abandoned due to the enemy's attack, and then she is depicted as a whore in need of purification in Isaiah 1:21–27.[41] By attaching "daughter" to the already established imagery with Zion, the prophet personifies the people of God as a wayward child in need of discipline. For her to be pure and suitable for God's holy mountain, she must face the proper punishment for abandoning the Father and forsaking his blessings. Rebecca Hays contends, "The story of Daughter Zion's experience of this process weaves throughout the remainder of Isaiah."[42] These feminine images associating Zion with a daughter, mother, wife, or prostitute occur throughout the Prophets and reflect the dynamic relationship between God and his people.[43] Thus, the visualization of Zion as a wayward daughter develops Isaiah's theme of God's holy mountain by portraying a people in need of discipline and purification in order to become true children of God.

In summary, the mountain of the Lord is a symbol pointing to the coming kingdom of God when Zion has been restored.[44] Through Isaiah, Yahweh reveals his plan for his chosen city to both redeem the people and reestablish the Temple Mount as the holy mountain, which draws in the nations to receive righteous judgment and teaching. The drama of Isa 6:1–13 develops these themes as well, for as the prophet experiences the glory and majesty of God, the Lord's holiness exposes Isaiah's sin. Then, Isaiah confesses his sin, and through the burning coal from the altar, Isaiah's guilt is removed.[45] This movement from glory to judgment to salvation is God's plan for Zion and for the faithful remnant, those who have "been recorded for life in Jerusalem" (Isa 4:3).[46] The presence of God can again be the center of life in the city once he has judged sin and removed the guilt of his faithful remnant, and in the middle of this activity stands the chosen place for his presence, Mount Zion. Thus, as a theological symbol, Zion represents the place where heaven and earth meet, both for judgment and for the purification of the people. God's glory through judgment will bring salvation

40. In the ESV, "daughter of Zion" occurs in the Prophets twenty-four times: Isa (six), Jer (three), Lam (eight), Mic (four), Zeph (one), and Zech (two). Other translations, such as the NIV and CSB, read "Daughter Zion."

41. Hays, "Sing Me a Parable," 744.

42. Hays, "Sing Me a Parable," 745.

43. Hays, "Sing Me a Parable," 756.

44. Webb, *Message of Isaiah*, 46.

45. Hamilton, *God's Glory in Salvation*, 194.

46. Hamilton, *God's Glory in Salvation*, 194.

not only to Israelites who are faithful to Yahweh, but all the nations will be welcomed to Mount Zion to experience God's presence (Isa 66:18). These eschatological promises in the earlier chapters of Isaiah, according to James Hamilton, are "no less extravagant than those in Isaiah 40–66."[47] Thus, Isaiah as a literary whole bears a theological continuity regarding Zion's present condition and future glory.

Zion, the Protected City of God

Another major theme in Isa 1–39 regarding the Zion symbol is God's protection of the city against external threats. Within the vision of a coming king, a subsequent theme is the universal rule of the king; thus, Zion serves as the seat of such an empire, or the place from which the king's rule is extended.[48] While the city must be cleansed of its pride and wickedness internally, God also promises to protect the city from threats imposed by neighboring nations. Much of Isa 9–39 deals with the "burden" of other nations placed upon Israel and God's response to those threats. Isaiah 10:20–26 depicts God's faithful remnant returning to Zion under God's protection against the Assyrian threat: verse 24 says, "O my people, who dwell in Zion, be not afraid of the Assyrians" (Isa 10:24). Zion represents the place of security for God's people, while Assyria is judged.[49] This remnant is not merely those left over, but according to Isaiah 5:25, they are the ones who obey the "Holy One of Israel" and have followed his teaching. The inhabitants of the protected Zion are a purified, holy remnant whom God himself has established for his own glory among the nations.[50]

Isaiah 13–23 contains ten oracles about the "burden" of the gentile nations who have surrounded God's covenant people.[51] Many of the judgments pronounced on the nations were carried out by the Assyrian conquest during Isaiah's day, and often, the pride of the nations is given as a reason for their downfall.[52] Zion, the place of God's presence and the place where God made himself accessible to the Israelites and anyone seeking him, symbolized God's reign over all the earth; yet, the nations often responded to Zion in opposition and even through war. Isaiah 14 provides God's response to

47. Hamilton, *God's Glory in Salvation*, 194.

48. Motyer, *Isaiah*, 20.

49. Motyer, *Isaiah*, 111.

50. Childs, *Isaiah*, 94.

51. Raabe, "Christ and the Nations," 25.

52. See Isa 13:11, 19; 16:6–7; 21:16 in reference to the gentile nations' pride. Raabe, "Christ and the Nations," 27.

this: "As I have planned . . . I will break the Assyrian in my land, and on my mountains trample him underfoot" (Isa 14:24–25).

Zion was threatened by many nations, especially Assyria, yet God had "planned" that Assyria would be drawn into Israel's land and there the Lord would overthrow them (Isa 14:24).[53] Zion is the Lord's holy mountain, so the nations seeking to trample it will in turn be trampled by the Lord. Isaiah 17:13 exclaims that they will be "like chaff on the mountains before the wind," indicating that God will protect his holy mountain against those who oppose Zion.[54] In the gentile oracles, then, Zion is the only place of refuge, the only city standing after the Assyrian invasion into Judah. In Isaiah's Zion theology, this can only be true because Yahweh dwells in Zion, for Isa 14:32 states that "the Lord has founded Zion, and in her the afflicted of his people find refuge." Furthermore, God says he will "sit on the mount of the gods' assembly," referring to Zaphon, which is the place where the Canaanite deities would convene (Isa 14:13). However, the emphasis is that Yahweh rises above the great pride of the nations, and ultimately, their self-deification will be their downfall.[55] Zion rises above the other holy mountains because Yahweh is not only the God on Mount Zion but the creator and King of all creation. For Zion's remnant, the oracles against the gentile nations produce confidence that Yahweh will not forsake his chosen dwelling place.

The historical situation in Isaiah's time regarding the invasion of Assyria into Israel and Judah sets the backdrop for much of Isaiah's prophecy. Often labeled "Isaiah's Apocalypse," Isa 24–27 repeatedly characterizes Zion as God's holy mountain, which will be protected while the whole earth is "stripped away," "punished," and "put to shame" (Isa 24:22–23).[56] Zion, in these chapters, is depicted as the throne room of God where he will "display his glory in the presence of his elders" (Isa 24:23). On this mountain, God will "prepare for all the peoples a feast of choice meat" and describes a time when he "has swallowed up death once and for all" (Isa 25:6–8). In the context of judgment, these images create a beautiful depiction of Mount Zion as God's holy mountain, from which he not only rules the nations but he also provides protection and blessing for his faithful people. God will "swallow up" the curse that has afflicted the people, depicting a time when the evils of the world that "swallow up" the people will themselves be destroyed.[57] Such statements remind Isaiah's audience that every characteristic of Zion derives

53. 2 Kgs 19:20–34 and Isa 37:21–38 record the account of Assyria's defeat in Judah.

54. Raabe, "Christ and the Nations," 29.

55. Webb, *Message of Isaiah*, 83.

56. Hamilton, *God's Glory in Salvation*, 198.

57. Watts, *Isaiah 1–33*, 331.

from God's choice of Zion as his dwelling place: the city is secure, and it is the source of life and wisdom because God desired it to be so.[58]

The inviolability of Zion is also expressed in Isa 28:16, which reads, "Therefore thus says the Lord God, 'Behold, I am the one who has laid as a foundation in Zion, a stone, a tested stone, a precious cornerstone, of a sure foundation: Whoever believes will not be in haste.'" Yahweh speaks, affirming that what he will do in Zion deserves the faith and trust of the people.[59] The people's efforts to establish alliances with Egypt in their rebellion against Assyria were futile, for God had already determined Assyria's fate, and because of the "cornerstone" he placed in Zion, the city would be secure.[60] The meaning of *bōḥan* ("tested") has been noted as a significant interpretive crux in the Old Testament, but elsewhere in the Old Testament, the root term is often associated with determining special qualities or attaining knowledge.[61] This foundational stone is "tested" or "proven" to indicate its permanence and strength, but it has also been interpreted in reference to the particular kind of stone used in the construction of statues and temples to be a visual for the beauty and majesty of Zion's temple.[62] It could also be a term that stresses the theological notion of the verse, which is that Zion is the only viable "fortress" for those who trust in the Lord instead of turning to failed leaders or other nations for help.[63] The specific identity of this stone has also been variously interpreted, for it has been labeled as the coming reign of God, God himself, belief in God, or faith in God's promises.[64] Commentator Paul Wegner argues that a combination of these ideas is sufficient because the primary thrust of Isaiah's prophecy has been that God is building his kingdom in Zion for those who believe in him and follow him alone.[65]

Watts argues that the idea of God affirming the protection of Zion and, at the same time, judging the leadership of Jerusalem through foreign invaders was incomprehensible to the Israelites.[66] However, Isa 28:16 adds an additional layer of meaning by contrasting the dysfunctional society found

58. Morales, *Who Shall Ascend*, 276.

59. Watts, *Isaiah 1–33*, 370.

60. Motyer, *Isaiah*, 210.

61. Harris, *Theological Wordbook*, 100.

62. Other plausible definitions for "tested" are "touchstone," "watchtower," and "graywacke," but most English translations interpret the term as "tested." Noonan, "Zion's Foundation," 318.

63. Roberts, "Yahweh's Foundation in Zion," 32.

64. Wegner, *Isaiah*, 211.

65. Wegner, *Isaiah*, 211.

66. Watts, *Isaiah 1–33*, 372.

in Jerusalem with a new order based on justice and righteousness.[67] In other words, the contrast is the point: because Zion is a symbol of God's holy presence among the people, he must protect the city, not for the sake of the walls and buildings but for the sake of his future plans regarding the place of his presence. Zion, then, serves as a beacon of hope for those who would choose to trust Yahweh, despite the looming threat of invasion—Zion is the only refuge in a world under assault.[68]

Another important passage for developing the Zion symbol as the place of God's protection occurs in Isa 33, where Zion is depicted as the city filled with "justice and peace," and where "the fear of the Lord is Zion's treasure" (Isa 33:5–6). This passage moves from a picture of defeat into a description of a future Zion after the Lord has risen for battle to protect his holy mountain.[69] God himself will be Zion's stability and provision, according to Isa 33:6, and since he has arisen for battle, all of Zion's enemies will be overthrown, not by overwhelming force but rather by hearing and acknowledging the truth.[70] Isaiah 33:13–14 develops the recurring theme in Isaiah that Zion will become the place where the nations will come to receive wisdom and knowledge about the Lord: the city is protected and purified in order to accomplish God's ultimate goal for Zion. Isaiah 33 has multiple speakers and recipients of the message, which can make the passage difficult to understand; but as a reflection of the oral culture of Isaiah's day, it presents a conversation that reflects on Zion's past, present, and future.[71] By presenting Zion and Yahweh in the form of a "literary performance," Isa 33 depicts a back-and-forth conversation between God, the prophet, and the people in anticipation of how God will rescue Zion and deal with its enemies.[72]

Yahweh filling Zion with justice and righteousness may be associated with Jerusalem's salvation from Assyria, but more likely, in the context of salvation yet to come, Isaiah describes a coming Zion that has been judged and purified according to God's divine purpose for the people.[73] Isaiah 33:13–24 presents a metaphorical view of Zion from the perspective of those "far off" and "near," showing them that Zion will be restored to a place of strength and beauty, a "place of broad rivers and streams" (Isa 33:13, 21).

67. Blenkinsopp, *Isaiah 1–39*, 387.

68. Brueggemann, *Isaiah 1–39*, 226.

69. Motyer, *Isaiah*, 235.

70. Motyer, *Isaiah*, 235.

71. Hong, "Isaiah 33," 123.

72. Hong, "Isaiah 33," 123.

73. Balogh, "He Filled Zion," 488.

The residents of such a Zion were not yet there, but through the Lord's own actions, such a place was coming. Even the "majestic ship" will be unable to penetrate this new Zion, for the Lord has chosen it for his dwelling and will both protect and preserve it as his holy mountain.[74] God asks his audience to envision Zion after the Assyrian threat has passed, for it will be a place of peace, only interrupted by the feasts to celebrate God's presence among the people and his blessing upon them.[75] In this light, Walter Brueggemann describes Zion as "an exuberant place of unending festival . . . Zion is one long doxology. The city is now, with the new governance, precisely the place of quietude and well-being."[76]

Zion in Isaiah 40–66: The Eternal Dwelling of Yahweh's Presence

Although the themes regarding Zion as the place of judgment and salvation resonate through the entirety of Isaiah, Isa 40–66 shifts focus to the glorious future of Zion and the return of Yahweh's presence. God's forgiveness of sin and the way out of exile takes center stage, for Yahweh promises to act again to restore the people as they return to Zion.[77] A shift in tone occurs in Isa 40, and although the Babylonian invasion is not mentioned, the movement toward a return from exile likely has such an occasion as its background.[78] The book of Isaiah pictures a new exodus, where God is gently leading his people through the wilderness of exile back into his presence in Zion; thus, Isa 40 serves as a hinge to encourage the people with a deep sense of hope and trust in God's future plans for the nation.[79] In this section of Isaiah, the repeated phrase "I am with you" comforts the people and reminds them that, even in exile, his presence is near.[80] Yet, God maintains his promise

74. Holmyard, "Does Isaiah 33:23 Address Israel," 274.

75. Watts, *Isaiah 1–33*, 428.

76. Brueggemann, *Isaiah 1–39*, 265.

77. Poulson, *Representing Zion*, 29.

78. The structure and dating of "Second Isaiah" are debated, but for the purposes of this study, the theological implications surrounding the Zion symbol are the primary focus. Seitz argues that Isa 36–39 is a proper close to Isa 1–35 because it answers the question regarding Zion's inviolability against the Assyrian threat. If chapter 40 and beyond are later additions, they nonetheless convey a cohesive theological emphasis on Zion as the place of God's presence and the center of his rule. Seitz says, "The rhetorical intensity evidenced in Second Isaiah on the questions of Zion's destiny is best explained against the backdrop of earlier Zion theology," indicating a continuity regarding Zion and its role in Israel's future. Seitz, *Zion's Final Destiny*, 141.

79. Duvall, *God's Relational Presence*, 146.

80. Isa 41:10; 43:2, 5.

that Zion will be restored, and that the people will become a holy remnant, forming a holy city where the presence of God attracts the nations and ends hostility toward Israel. However, God's presence among his people is not only something to be experienced once Zion is fully restored but rather something from which courage can be drawn during exile.[81] The presence of God in Isa 40–66 appears less intense than the powerful, protective presence of God dwelling on Mount Zion, for the "I am with you" statements convey God's guiding, comforting presence as he leads the people toward a restored Zion.[82] There are two major ways, among several, in which the theological symbol of Zion functions in Isa 40–66: it symbolizes the return of God to his holy mountain, and it becomes the final place of restoration for the people of God.

Zion and the Return of the King

Isaiah 40 contains a distinctive style that emphasizes speeches from the heavenly realm regarding comfort for the people and the Lord's promise to restore Zion.[83] The darkness anticipated in Isa 39 fades as Isa 40 shines a bright light on the situation of the Israelites in exile, for the imagery of a transformed wilderness and the return of the Lord to Zion pictures a restored glory to the abandoned city.[84] In the context of the Lord's return, Zion is depicted in Isa 40:9 as a herald of good news for the cities surrounding Jerusalem. The historical setting for this scene is debated, for although many scholars believe this portion of Isaiah was written after the Babylonian invasion, others believe the Assyrian invasion and withdrawal could be the backdrop of Isa 40.[85] Either way, the function of the Zion symbol in Isa 40 maintains the same emphasis on Zion as the herald of good news. The language of Isa 40:9 is puzzling, mostly because of the ambiguity regarding who is sending or receiving the message of good news.[86] However, if the background of this passage is the repulsion of Assyria from the land, it is sensible that Zion, the only city left standing after the Assyrian invasion, would be delivering a message of comfort to its neighboring cities.[87] The im-

81. Duvall, *God's Relational Presence*, 127.
82. Duvall, *God's Relational Presence*, 127.
83. Watts, *Isaiah 34–66*, 72.
84. Wilson, "Yahweh's Consciousness," 648.
85. Seufert, "Reading Isaiah 40:1–11," 271.
86. Watts, *Isaiah 34–66*, 78.
87. Seufert, "Reading Isaiah 40:1–11," 273.

agery suggests a time when Zion itself becomes a messenger of good news that the Lord is returning to be the people's Shepherd-King.

Isaiah 40:9 is structured as A-B-A-B-A, with a command (A) followed by the recipient (B).[88] Ben Witherington argues that the Septuagint makes it clear these good tidings are being delivered to Zion by an anonymous speaker instead of the city delivering a message.[89] In this case, the NIV translates verse 9 more closely in line with the LXX while other major translations indicate that Zion and Jerusalem are the heralds of good news. The NIV reads, "You who bring good news to Zion, go up on a high mountain," while the ESV reads, "Go on up to a high mountain, O Zion, herald of good news" (Isa 40:9). Goldingay follows the NIV, translating verse 9 as "Get yourself onto a high mountain as a herald to Zion."[90] "Herald" is a feminine word, but it is awkward to think of the city climbing a mountain; thus, the term may generally refer to a messenger, but the ambiguity keeps the focus on the message and not the one delivering it.[91] Whether giving or receiving the message, the content of the message is the same: the Lord is returning to his dwelling place in Zion.

Zion in Isa 40 symbolizes the presence of God atop his sacred mountain, and the commissioning of messengers to bring good news to the cities of Judah signals that the old age of the curse is passing away and a new era is dawning.[92] Alec Motyer notes that Isa 40:9 reveals the Lord's return to Zion with language resembling the occasion when Miriam played her tambourine and sang of song of victory in Exod 15, thus picturing singing women coming out of Zion to meet their returning king.[93] Zion is no longer the place of God's judgment but rather it has been waiting patiently for the King to return, so that the people could once again find comfort from his presence. The message of doom from Isa 39 is quickly transformed as Isa 40 speaks of Zion as the place God will once again inhabit. In the face of despair or temptation to trust in idols, Isa 40 declares God's return to the place he had chosen for his name's sake.[94] While God's protection of the city and his purification of sin consumed the theological focus of Isa 1–39, the symbolic nature of Zion shifts toward the future in Isaiah 40, indicating

88. Eddinger, "Analysis of Isaiah 40:1–11," 132.
89. Witherington, *Isaiah Old and New*, 182.
90. Goldingay, *Message of Isaiah 40–55*, 28.
91. Goldingay, *Message of Isaiah 40–55*, 28.
92. Childs, *Isaiah*, 296.
93. Motyer, *Isaiah*, 277.
94. Abernethy, *Book of Isaiah*, 54.

that a new era has opened because the Lord is returning.[95] In a sense, Isa 40 functions as a forerunner to the gospel, pointing to a time when the King's return would bless the people through the forgiveness of sin. Barry Webb states, "The gospel of Jesus Christ is the gospel of Isaiah 40 transposed into a new, higher key . . . It must be shouted from the housetops, not just for the cities of Judah, but for all the world to hear."[96]

In Isa 52:1–2, Zion is personified as "Daughter Zion," and the imagery pictures her seated in the dust with her punishment around her neck, but now called to take a seat of honor.[97] While Zion is experiencing its deepest humiliation, Yahweh enters into the city to lift up his child.[98] The beauty of Zion is visualized as being stripped away in Isa 3:16–26, but here the desolate daughter is summoned to dress in her finest because the King is returning.[99] She is called to "loose the bonds from your neck," which indicates there is no longer fear of being attacked because the Lord is returning and bringing salvation for his beloved people.[100] In another sense, Zion has awakened to a new reality because the ideal priestly people will finally be realized in the new Zion as the Lord's presence returns.[101] Jerusalem is becoming "the holy city" and is commanded to "put on your beautiful garments" in preparation for the King's entry into the purified, holy city (Isa 52:1). The Zion symbol represents both the collective people of God and the physical city, but the emphasis is on the new reality that the city has become holy and that no unclean people will be allowed inside. It is within this purified city that those who were once exploited and oppressed will now know God. Brevard Childs remarks, "The holy city and divine name are indissolubly joined, and this unimpaired unity is constitutive of the new eschatological order about to be realized."[102]

"Zion" occurs seven times in Isa 51:1—52:12, and this frequency undergirds the ongoing comparison of the way things were as opposed to the way things will be in the future in God's chosen dwelling place.[103] In Isa

95. Abernethy, *Book of Isaiah*, 54.

96. Webb, *Message of Isaiah*, 164.

97. Goldingay, *Isaiah 40–55*, 255.

98. Baltzer, among others, contends that Zion and Babylon are switching roles, for the curses originally upon Zion will now be upon Babylon. The imagery of Zion as an enthroned prisoner is a paradoxical idea, which may in fact be Isaiah's intent. Baltzer, *Deutero-Isaiah*, 369.

99. Goldingay, *Isaiah 40–55*, 255.

100. Watts, *Isaiah 34–66*, 213.

101. Motyer, *Isaiah*, 370.

102. Childs, *Isaiah*, 405.

103. Goldingay, *Message of Isaiah 40–55*, 417.

52:7, the imagery of a runner bringing good news to the people also points to the end of God's wrath and the beginning of a new era marked by peace and holiness. The messenger tells Zion, "Your God reigns," indicating that the comfort heralded in Isa 40 has come.[104] Before Isa 52:8, the "return of Yahweh to Zion" is a subject not mentioned since the prologue of the book; this concise expression captures both the restoration of the people and the return of God's presence upon his holy mountain.[105] In a sense, passages such as Isa 52:7–12 display the inseparable nature of the physical space and the people connected to it: these verses show how people are inherently connected to a physical place from which they draw their identity.[106] With the dramatic poetry exclaiming good tidings regarding Yahweh's return to Zion, the heavenly and the physical domains collide with an optimistic outlook regarding the home of God's people. However, Isaiah avoids addressing the temple, for he repeatedly refers to Zion in terms of the entire city or as an intimate term for the inhabitants of Judah.[107]

In Isa 35, the return of Yahweh is described using imagery of a wilderness becoming like a garden and the Lord coming on a highway into the city; then, in Isa 40, the same imagery is used as a voice cries out to "prepare the way of the Lord" as he returns to Zion. The imagery of a highway and the dangerous hills being flattened into a garden uses Edenic language to convey the Lord's return to Zion as a permanent, enduring reality.[108] Joseph Blenkinsopp contends that this pictures God being exiled with his people and returning afterward, an image similar to Cyrus's claim of returning Sumerian and Akkadian gods to their own cities.[109] However, Isaiah does not merely picture Zion as Yahweh's city, which contains his presence; rather, the recreation of the surrounding land and Yahweh's glorious return imply that all the nations will be affected by this event. According to Isa 2:3–5, the ultimate purpose of Zion was to spread the peace of God over the earth, causing the nations to drop their weapons and seek wisdom from God's holy mountain. Thus, the return of the Lord to Zion points to a deeper purpose than a rebuilt Jerusalem: ultimately, Zion would be the place where "my servant" would be pierced for the transgressions of the people and open the door for the nations to enter Zion and receive salvation. This "servant," often interpreted as a personification of Israel, cannot reach the new Zion

104. Motyer, *Isaiah*, 372.
105. Westermann, *Isaiah 40–66*, 251.
106. Tiemeyer, *For the Comfort*, 252.
107. Tiemeyer, *For the Comfort*, 252.
108. Goldingay, *Message of Isaiah 40–55*, 18.
109. Blenkinsopp, *Essays on the Book*, 45.

without first suffering, being purified from sin, and restored through God's own action. Isaiah 52–53 highlights the theme of judgment, which leads to salvation, and ultimately points forward to the Messiah, who himself would be crushed and then exalted according to the Lord's plan.[110]

In Isa 62:11, the "Daughter Zion" symbol appears, but this time, she is personified in a positive context as a once lowly city who has now been elevated because the Lord has brought salvation and "his reward is with him" (Isa 62:11).[111] Daughter Zion now includes all the people whom God has gathered from the earth to become "The Holy People" (Isa 62:12).[112] Throughout Isa 40–66, there is a comparison between "Daughter Zion" and the "servant," and through the various passages containing feminine imagery, "Daughter Zion" progresses from abandonment and fear to fulfillment and joy.[113] In the final chapter of the book, Daughter Zion is described as joyful and full of life, like a tender mother nourishing her children whom she "bounced upon her knees" (Isa 66:12). Such imagery points to the blessing of life given to God's faithful remnant because of his own action toward the people. God's desire to dwell among his people in peace and holiness results in a transformed people who are comforted and free to rejoice in his presence. Isaiah 1–3 had depicted Daughter Zion as a promiscuous harlot who had lost her dignity, yet after God returns to Zion to restore her, she has been transformed into a radiant and joyful woman filled with abundant life.

The focus in Isa 62:11–12 is upon Yahweh's action toward the people: it is his gift of salvation and his guarantee of Zion's complete healing.[114] The imagery of "The Holy People," "Redeemed of the Lord," and "A City Not Forsaken" all resonate with the return of Yahweh into Zion, for it his presence that purifies, protects, and preserves the people (Isa 62:12). These changes in names for the city reflect the personal relationship of Zion to God, signifying that the people are now wholly committed to Yahweh alone, brought out from the bondage that once estranged them, and cared for by God himself.[115] Because of Yahweh's return to Zion, the people's lives can begin anew; thus, the message that Zion is no longer forsaken points to the enduring presence of God among a holy people. The idyllic imagery regarding Zion in Isa 60–62 anticipates God's intervention into the world

110. Brueggemann, *Isaiah 40–66*, 143.

111. The last two lines of Isa 62:11 are identical to the last two lines of Isa 40:10, showing a connection to the prologue of Isa 40–66.

112. Motyer, *Isaiah*, 433.

113. Sawyer, "Daughter of Zion," 99.

114. Brueggemann, *Isaiah 40–66*, 224.

115. Brueggemann, *Isaiah 40–66*, 224.

with Zion as the exalted holy mountain of God's presence, where he has inaugurated a new era not only for the remnant of Israel but for all who draw near to his presence. Simply put, Zion's salvation is the world's salvation.[116]

Zion Restored

Flowing from the return of God's royal presence among the people is the imagery of Zion as the restored city of God. Isaiah's language shifts toward a focus on the hope that God is not finished with Zion, and although the city lies in ruins, God himself will accomplish his purpose in restoring Zion for his own glory.[117] Zion's multivalent usage in Isaiah climaxes with the imagery of a holy city that has been restored and exalted as the place of God's holy presence for his people and for the nations. Coupled with this imagery is the mission of the "servant," who both suffers for the people but also becomes a teacher, instructing the people in the ways of Yahweh even when that brings suffering upon him.[118] Preceding the dramatic description of the servant in Isa 52–53 is an oracle in Isa 51, which says, "For the Lord comforts Zion; he comforts all her waste places and makes her wilderness like Eden, her desert like the garden of the Lord" (Isa 51:3). Like a thread extending from Isa 40, this verse speaks to God's promises to comfort the people through hope in a restored Zion.[119] Isaiah 51:3 depicts Zion as the eternal dwelling place of God, a city restored beyond its original condition: the "waste places" and "desert" of sin and exile have now become lush gardens resulting in the people's joy.[120] However, since Zion is paralleled with the "waste places," Zion is currently ruined and is awaiting a time of restoration, which will amaze the world as a result of the songs of joy and praise coming from the holy city.[121] This new Zion has become a place of joy because it has received new life: the imagery of Eden reminds the people that true life comes from the presence of God, and ultimately, they are dependent upon his action to receive such life.[122] This brief reminder in Isa 51:3 also speaks to the recurring theme of

116. Motyer, *Isaiah*, 433.

117. Abernethy, *Book of Isaiah*, 80.

118. Witherington, *Isaiah Old and New*, 230.

119. Some scholars, such as Watts, believe that the speech in Isa 51 is spoken by Darius to the people of Israel. Darius is the benevolent king who is allowing the Israelites to return to Jerusalem and rebuild their temple, and he reminds the people of their history regarding God's blessing through faithful figures such as Abraham. Watts, *Isaiah 34–66*, 212.

120. Childs, *Isaiah*, 402.

121. Westermann, *Isaiah 40–66*, 237.

122. Brueggemann, *Isaiah 40–66*, 126.

sacred space in Isaiah, for the prophet's theocentric approach to the life of the Israelites shows that it is only through God's presence in Zion and God's own action toward his people that Zion can be restored.

Another picture of the joyous restoration of Zion appears in Isa 51:11, which says, "And the ransomed of the Lord shall return and come to Zion with singing; everlasting joy shall be upon their heads . . . sorrow and sighing shall flee away" (Isa 51:11). "Redeemed," from verse 10, echoes the promises of Exod 6:6, but "ransomed" looks forward to God's future acts in restoring Zion.[123] Because of Isaiah's focus on both the land and God's holy mountain, the imagery of the new people, called "the ransomed of the Lord," envisions a new people living in a new land. The hope that has been kept alive through exile also emboldens the remnant to return in great expectation of God's divine presence as they rebuilt the temple and reestablished themselves as a holy nation.[124] In the following verses, 12 through 16, Yahweh responds by saying he has "put my words in your mouth," and "saying to Zion, 'You are my people'" (Isa 52:16). These words indicate the changing nature of the Zion symbol and the way in which Isaiah develops Zion from a desolate, abandoned people to a joyful, redeemed city filled with God's presence. Zion is a place that once was filled with judgment and fear, but now there is no need for fear, for Yahweh himself has arisen to redeem his beloved people.[125]

Beginning with Isa 2:1–4, Zion, as a symbol of God's presence among the people, journeys toward a time of complete and final restoration. The purpose of Isaiah's emphasis on the restoration of Zion is hope, or a confidence in a tangible, attainable reality in which the people could believe. Zion was depicted as a wasteland, abandoned and forgotten due to her own betrayal of her King, but hope in God's covenant promises remained. The final images of a restored Zion in Isa 66 draw this hope toward a concluding emphasis on Isaiah's earlier visions of both judgment and salvation. God's justice toward Zion's oppressors, envisioned as the undying worm and unquenchable fire (66:24), will cause the people to worship the Lord alone.[126] Isaiah's central theological emphasis on God's glory in salvation through judgment is consistently visualized through the spiritual journey of Zion: as the primary place of his presence, God himself acts to transform his chosen dwelling place into a restored, holy city filled with redeemed people.[127]

123. Motyer, *Isaiah*, 366.

124. Watts, *Isaiah 34–66*, 212.

125. Brueggemann, *Isaiah 40–66*, 132.

126. Hamilton, *God's Glory in Salvation*, 211.

127. Hamilton, *God's Glory in Salvation*, 211.

Isaiah 66 also speaks of Zion as a gathering place for the nations to experience God's glory, for Isaiah highlights the original goal and destination of Zion to encapsulate the purpose of God's presence among the people. Isaiah issues a final warning against ritualism: God is not against the temple and its associated activity, but rather, the point of the temple is to create authentic worship and repentance in the hearts of people.[128] The prophet writes, "The time is coming to gather all nations and tongues. And they shall come and shall see my glory, and I will set a sign among them . . . and they shall declare my glory among the nations" (Isa 66:18–19). These verses depict Yahweh coming to establish supreme authority over the nations, but he does not merely come, he "gathers" the nations. This picture of a worldwide covenant community where the nations see the Lord's glory reaches toward a renewed Eden where God's presence is experienced by all.[129] Zion, as the place of God's presence, does not confine his presence but rather is the intersection between heaven and earth where the glory of God is seen by the nations. Brueggemann calls this the "ultimate imagery of inclusiveness," meaning that the gentile nations will not only be invited into God's presence and washed clean from their sin, but some of them will even be ordained as priests.[130] This departure from the norms of the Torah emphasizes that the nature of worship, namely a "clean vessel," is the focus of worship in Yahweh's new Zion.[131]

In Isaiah, Zion transforms from the royal presence of God in Jerusalem's temple into a glorified, holy mountain filled with all nations and languages. As a theological symbol, Zion bears many meanings and emphases, yet the primary purpose of the symbol is to express the presence of God in a tangible, experiential way for the people who were willing to humble themselves and follow God's commandments. God had promised to ransom his people, to preserve a remnant, and dwell among them in peace; thus, the Zion symbol buttresses the comfort God promises in Isa 40 and envisions a utopic city where the nations glorify God in his presence. Zion also serves as the symbol of Yahweh's sacred mountain, or the place of his victory over the nations, for as his sacred space upon earth, God must repel wickedness and purify those who draw near in humility.[132] From this mountain, God dispenses justice that attracts the nations to come and sit under his righteous

128. Oswalt, *Book of Isaiah*, 591.

129. Brueggemann, *Isaiah 40–66*, 258.

130. Brueggemann, *Isaiah 40–66*, 259.

131. Baer, *When We All Go Home*, 253.

132. Lynch, "Zion's Warrior and the Nations," 261.

teaching.[133] Zion connects the promise to Abraham in Gen 12:3 regarding the nations with a physical, visible symbol of God's presence, teaching, and wisdom as well.[134] Zion reminds the people that Yahweh can be trusted, and as they prayed toward Jerusalem in exile, or made pilgrimage to the temple, the people were reminded of God's presence through Israel's history, and that ultimately, God desired to dwell among all people, which points to a new heavens and a new earth, free from the curse that separated people from his presence.[135]

ZION IN JEREMIAH AND LAMENTATIONS

Regarding the role of Zion in Jeremiah, Gerhard von Rad said, "The Zion tradition which was determinative for the whole of Isaiah's prophecy has no place whatsoever in Jeremiah."[136] Jeremiah maintains a different attitude toward the fate of Zion, yet there remains a hope that God would act on behalf of his chosen city and bring a future restoration. The term "Zion" occurs seventeen times in Jeremiah: twelve times independently and five times as a construct with terms such as "daughter" or "inhabitants."[137] From a theological perspective concerning the future of Zion, Jeremiah maintains a similar posture toward God's faithfulness, despite Daughter Zion's rebellion and abandonment. Although Zion's inviolability has faded from Jeremiah's perspective, Zion symbolism serves an important role as a motif of God's promises for Israel in the face of intense destruction and exile. Similar to Isaiah, Jeremiah describes Daughter Zion as the place of God's discipline upon the people, but Jeremiah extends this to the reality that God had forsaken his temple and hidden his face from the city because his sacred space had been filled with wickedness and idolatry (Jer 33:5). Zion's symbolic function appears to oscillate between the place of God's righteous judgment and the place to which God will restore his people. The backdrop of the Babylonian invasion intensifies the drama between these two versions of Zion, but after the pain of suffering and exile, Zion becomes the home of "an everlasting covenant that will never be forgotten" (Jer 50:5). The concept of a new covenant is unique to Jeremiah, and in the New Testament, Heb 12:22–24 connects the promise of a new covenant in Jer 31:31–34 to

133. Lynch, "Zion's Warrior and the Nations," 262.

134. Lynch, "Zion's Warrior and the Nations," 262.

135. Snook, "Interpreting the Book," 460.

136. von Rad, *Old Testament Theology*, 1:192.

137. Poulson, *Representing Zion*, 36.

the person and work of Jesus Christ in relation to the Zion symbol.[138] Ultimately, then, Jeremiah's vision of a new covenant kingdom is centered upon the one who ratified such a covenant through his own sacrificial blood.

Lamentations provides a unique perspective on Zion, for various feminine images are used to describe the desolate city in both positive and negative ways.[139] Despite Judah's desolation, the writer exclaims, "But you, O Lord, reign forever; your throne endures to all generations" (Lam 5:19). Even though Zion lay in ruins, the hope of Zion had not been built upon stone and wood; rather, it was the enduring presence of God that gave the people hope amid devastation. Lamentations pushes Zion forward in this sense, for within the sorrow for Zion's destruction rested an unshakable hope that God himself would "renew our days as of old" (Lam 5:21).

Zion, The Abandoned Daughter

As Jeremiah becomes the mouthpiece for the Lord amid chaos, judgment, and exile in Jerusalem, his comments about the plight of Jerusalem often personify the people using feminine language. Daughter Zion is beyond a wayward child in need of discipline, for she has become a harlot who is being destroyed for her own wickedness. Nevertheless, Jeremiah frequently uses the term *šûb* for "turn" or "return" in the context of Judah turning away from idolatry and toward Yahweh, or away from captivity and toward Zion.[140] A versatile term such as *šûb* reinforces the message of Jeremiah concerning Zion: the wayward people are being abandoned by God because of their idolatry, yet God will create a new covenant people who will return to Zion by turning back to the Lord.[141] The constant use of *šûb* highlights the chaos and uncertainty in Judah but also points to the Lord as the only one who can restore the people and recapture the original purpose of Zion as a place for the nations to receive wisdom and seek the presence of God.[142]

Jeremiah 4:29–31 laments the fate of Zion, yet the response of Jerusalem to the impending invasion is not to flee to the hills as expected,

138. Son, *Zion Symbolism*, 51.

139. Poulson, *Representing Zion*, 69.

140. Lalleman, *Jeremiah and Lamentations*, 37.

141. Lalleman notes further that *šûb* is used in Jeremiah's earlier ministry as "return" or "repent," but later, the calls for repentance are replaced by God's promises regarding a new people who will return to the land. When God is the subject of *šûb*, repentance has become possible because he is the one making it happen. The same term is also used in the context of restoration, such as in 30:18, 31:18, and 31:23. Lalleman, *Jeremiah and Lamentations*, 38.

142. Harris, *Theological Wordbook*, 909.

but rather Zion is seen as a prostitute who lavishly adorns herself for the occasion.[143] Yet, this would be in vain, for the city can no long cover up her lost beauty: her desired lovers will expose her ugliness and become her murderers.[144] Verse 31 describes Zion as a harlot about to give birth, and in agony, she cries out as she "is fainting before murderers" (Jer 4:31). This horrific imagery regarding Zion shows that the city's sin has reached its limit, for wayward Judah has paid the price for her idolatry.[145] Judah had been warned that disaster was coming, but instead of repenting or even fleeing from harm, the idolatrous people would be overwhelmed by their adversaries and overtaken like a pregnant woman unable to escape the hands of ruthless soldiers. By relating the Zion symbol with such a gruesome image, Jeremiah reveals that the presence of God connected with the temple had become an afterthought due to the idolatry in the city. Jeremiah had begun in 4:5–6 with Zion as a refuge but ends with Daughter Zion pleading for mercy from her killers.[146] Such language is designed to evoke a reaction from the people or to shock the people and penetrate their dulled senses so they would return to Yahweh, but it is perhaps too late.[147] Foolishly, Jerusalem has fallen into the trap of believing the disaster cannot affect her: the inviolability of Zion expressed in passages such as Ps 48 has crumbled and there is no option but defeat.[148]

The theme of Zion as an abandoned daughter continues in Jer 6:1–2 as an announcement is made to "flee for safety" because "the lovely and delicately bred I will destroy, the daughter of Zion" (Jer 6:1–2). Instead of a place of strength because of God's presence, the people are now told to flee south because of the impending invasion from the north. By continuing to portray Zion with feminine language, Jeremiah intensifies the city's weakness and vulnerability: she is exposed due to her idolatry and has no defense left.[149] Even though she is beautiful and "delicately bred," Zion's beauty would not save her. Jeremiah's words appear to conflict with all the previous promises and hopes regarding the future glory of Zion, yet this language opens a window into the heart of God and his purposes for the people he had called to be a light to the nations.[150] Yahweh's sacred space, his holy

143. Craigie, *Jeremiah 1–25*, 84.

144. Craigie, *Jeremiah 1–25*, 84.

145. Thompson, *Book of Jeremiah*, 166.

146. Goldingay, *Book of Jeremiah*, 182.

147. Craigie, *Jeremiah 1–25*, 84.

148. Kaiser, *Walking the Ancient Paths*, 95.

149. Kaiser, *Walking the Ancient Paths*, 108.

150. Dempster, *Dominion and Dynasty*, 188.

mountain, should have been a bright light to the nations surrounding Israel, yet the people's rejection of God and pursuit of meaningless idolatry has left their home in ruins. Furthermore, Jeremiah's emphasis on the people being uprooted from the land and fleeing the place of God's presence enhances the theological theme of God's holy presence. In other words, the people had become so evil that God has rejected any effort by the people to reconcile their relationship with Yahweh until the wickedness is purged.[151]

In the context of Jer 2–6, the prophet calls on the people to remember Israel's exodus from Egypt and the journey the people endured through the wilderness. Israel was Yahweh's bride, and he desired to protect and provide for his people through his presence among them.[152] Zion, the goal of the exodus and permanent place of God's royal presence, had been corrupted because the people had become spiritual adulterers. The temple served as the physical representation of that presence, yet the people in Jeremiah's day were behaving as if they had lost track of the temple's significance.[153] Thus, describing Zion as an abandoned and vulnerable daughter maintains that Yahweh still loves his people, yet due to their choice to abandon him, the temple is no longer the place of the divine presence but a place of emptiness. Brueggemann labels Yahweh as a "scorned spouse" in the early chapters of Jeremiah, for Israel's infidelity toward him has brought about the nation's shame and destruction.[154]

The cry of the people in Jer 8:18–22 further reveals the emptiness of Jerusalem and the removal of God's presence from Zion. It is plausible that, with the autumn New Year festival in the background, the annual celebration of Yahweh's kingship and Zion's inviolability was crumbling due to the threat of the Babylonian invasion.[155] However, God's presence is not what is questioned, for it has become obvious that the people's sin has left them in such a forsaken state. Jeremiah 8:21–22 provides an emotional perspective on God's response to the situation: God's wrath toward sin is typically in view, yet here his own suffering is equally severe.[156] Instead of enjoying the presence of God, the people had sought after "idols," which, in Hebrew, is also the word for "vanity" or "breath."[157] The people chose to bow to meaningless idols instead of experiencing the blessing of the true God's presence

151. Dempster, *Dominion and Dynasty*, 190.

152. Goldingay, *Theology of Jeremiah*, 46.

153. Goldingay, *Theology of Jeremiah*, 50.

154. Brueggemann, *Theology of the Book*, 83.

155. Craigie, *Jeremiah 1–25*, 140.

156. Huey, *Jeremiah, Lamentations*, 117.

157. Allen, *Jeremiah*, 112.

among them, causing the prophet and God himself to mourn the loss of relationship.

Zion had been the symbol of God's intimate presence and power among the people, but by the time Jeremiah spoke for God, hope had been suffocated by the threat of destruction and exile. Leslie Allen notes that the prophet's "retort not only accuses the people of pagan worship in a dismissive, derogatory fashion, but mentions its foreign origin as a damning denial of the community's right to appeal to the indigenous tradition of Zion theology."[158] Zion's original glory as the place of Yahweh's royal presence (Ps 48) was diminished because it was intended to be bound through the relationship of God to his people, and that relationship had been severed by Israel's apostasy. Therefore, Zion's symbolic function in Jeremiah shifts dramatically from Psalms and much of Isaiah; while Isaiah maintained a hope in Zion's restoration, Jeremiah laments the reality that God's presence is no longer the focus of the city, and even the temple has lost its glory.

Another angle on Zion as the abandoned daughter appears in Jer 14:19 which states, "Have you utterly rejected Judah? Does your soul loathe Zion? Why have you struck us down so that there is no healing for us? We looked for peace, but no good came; for a time of healing, but behold, terror" (Jer 14:19). Hetty Lalleman argues the intended meaning of verse 19 is, "We know you have not rejected Judah or despised Zion, but why then are we so wounded?"[159] The answer to the question comes in 15:6, for the people rejected God and believed the council of false prophets who proclaimed peace and victory when Jeremiah prophesied defeat. The fact that the people "looked for peace" implies that the Zion tradition still existed in Jerusalem, yet it had been corrupted through idolatry. The covenant obligations joyfully obeyed when Solomon dedicated the temple (1 Kgs 8) had been forgotten, and any attempt to find peace in Zion had become an exercise in futility. The people appear bewildered at their situation, yet they should not be surprised that God would fulfill the covenant curses spoken clearly to Solomon in 1 Kgs 9:6–10.[160] The theological depth of the Zion symbol in Jeremiah rests in God's covenant promises to the people; in other words, God has done exactly as he had decreed to the people from the time of Moses until Jeremiah's day. Zion, as a collective term for the people of God, had become an abandoned daughter not because of Yahweh's unfaithfulness but because the people neglected to uphold their covenant obligations. Nevertheless, Jeremiah's prophecy would move toward a time of restoration where

158. Allen, *Jeremiah*, 112.

159. Lalleman, *Jeremiah and Lamentations*, 152.

160. Allen, *Jeremiah*, 174.

God himself would act, preserving a remnant and writing a new covenant on the hearts of the people as they returned to Zion.

Zion, the Home of a New Covenant Kingdom

A major theological emphasis in the later chapters of Jeremiah is the new covenant community, which is envisioned as a healed, reconciled people who have returned from exile to become a new community of faith in Zion. The imagery of a healed Zion, continuing the picture of the abandoned and punished daughter, occurs in Jer 30:17, saying, "For I will restore health to you, and your wounds I will heal, declares the Lord, because they have called you an outcast: 'It is Zion, for whom no one cares'" (Jer 30:17). In this moment, Zion has become a weakened, sickly daughter with a deadly wound. Such medical metaphors are common expressions regarding the severity of sin.[161] The dramatic contrast that God himself will heal emphasizes the uselessness of Jerusalem's "lovers" in verse 14 and the current helpless state of the people. Zion has fallen from a position of strength, dignity, and beauty into a pit of suffering and misery. In terms of God's sacred space, Zion's punishment has come due to the sin and idolatry that had filled the city; yet, because of God's love for his chosen dwelling place, he has decided to heal because "they have called you an outcast" (Jer 30:17). Zion does have someone who cares and who has taken notice of the city's wounded condition: it is Yahweh, moved by the pain of his covenant partner, who acts on Zion's behalf.[162]

Known as the "Book of Consolation," Jer 30–31 is a composite text containing six songs alongside other literary components that emphasize the failure of the people to heed the warnings of the Lord.[163] Yet, the theme of reversal emerges, for even though God himself has dealt punishment for Judah's sins, he also will be the one to restore Zion to health. The paradox of a remedy for Israel's incurable condition only heightens the people's pitiful state and utter dependency upon God to save.[164] Therefore, both the judgment and deliverance of Zion demonstrate the Lord's sovereignty: Zion is his to punish and his to heal, according to his plans. The Lord's prophecies neither failed nor were they partially fulfilled; rather, in the ancient Judean context, God has chosen to cancel the full judgment decreed upon the

161. Lalleman, *Jeremiah and Lamentations*, 226.

162. Allen, *Jeremiah*, 338.

163. Shead, *Mouth Full of Fire*, 201.

164. Huey, *Jeremiah, Lamentations*, 265.

nation and replaced it with a new covenant.[165] For Zion's sake, this theme of reversal highlights the enduring quality of Zion as a theological symbol beyond the presence of God in the temple; it represents the presence of God upon the whole earth and his eschatological plans to draw the nations toward his presence as envisioned in Isa 2:2–4.

As a theological symbol, Zion appears in Jer 30–31 like a two-sided coin: the wounded daughter is on her deathbed, yet Yahweh has promised to bring full healing. At the same time, Zion is depicted in a healed state, as the city of God to which pilgrims are traveling to seek the Lord and enjoy his presence. Jeremiah says, "For there shall be a day when watchmen will call in the hill country of Ephraim: 'Arise, and let us go up to Zion, to the Lord our God'" (Jer 31:6). This describes watchmen waiting for the first pilgrims to arrive so they can alert the city to begin a procession to the temple.[166] Jeremiah envisions Zion as the place where a unified Israel will once again join in the worship of Yahweh, for the mention of Ephraim and Samaria in 31:5–6 highlights examples of northerners who are again coming to Zion.[167] Closely connected to this is the announcement that these pilgrims will again enjoy the goodness of the Lord, for verse 12 says, "They shall come and sing aloud on the height of Zion, and they shall be radiant over the goodness of the Lord" (Jer 31:12). Zion represents the place to which all the exiles from across the world will return, and upon such a return, they will enjoy the goodness of God through his provision and protection over them.[168]

In Jer 30–33, the descriptions of the restoration of the land recall some of the dominant themes expressed earlier in Isaiah, such as the return of David to the throne, Yahweh's everlasting love for his people, and God's sovereignty, both in judgment and salvation.[169] Among these themes in Jer 30–33 emerges the powerful word from the Lord that a new covenant community would be created, one in which God "will put my law within them, and I will write on their hearts. And I will be their God, and they shall be my people" (Jer 31:33). God declares this new covenant will be defined by forgiveness, for he will forget the sins of the people as part of the purification of the land. Complete forgiveness points to God's original intent for Israel: that they would be a light to the nations and live in such a way that the nations streamed to Zion in order to receive transformational instruction in the presence of God (Isa 2:3–4). Such forgiveness points to God's

165. Carver, "Biblical Prophecy," 280.

166. Huey, *Jeremiah, Lamentations*, 270.

167. Allen, *Jeremiah*, 346.

168. Keown, *Jeremiah 26–52*, 112.

169. Hamilton, *God's Glory in Salvation*, 220.

covenant faithfulness and ultimately serves as a foreshadowing of a new king who would open the way for the forgiveness of all who draw near to God in faith.[170]

Therefore, Jeremiah's vision of a new covenant community is based upon God's desire to dwell among his people in peace. In order to achieve this, God himself must act to purify the people and prepare them for his return to Mount Zion. This preparation included judgment as promised to Israel in Deuteronomy, for in abandoning their covenant obligations, the people were sent into exile under the rule of Babylon. In Jer 50, Babylon's fall is announced, and the prophet envisions a return of the exiles, saying, "They shall ask the way to Zion, with faces turned toward it, saying, 'Come, let us join ourselves to the Lord in an everlasting covenant that will never be forgotten'" (Jer 50:5). Zion is now the place of reunification, a place where the people of Israel and Judah have been joined together and joined to Yahweh after their time in exile.[171] This verse, with its emphasis on an "everlasting covenant," indicates that God's actions in the new covenant community are spread out over a long period of time, perhaps into the days of the Messiah, when God ushers in a time of ultimate peace for his redeemed community.[172]

The permanence of Zion as a symbol of God's presence among his people also persists through Jeremiah, even though the prophet's earlier oracles foresaw judgment and destruction on Judah. Although a time of exile would come, the prophecies concerning Babylon's ultimate destruction show that God was involved in the whole process: the people had been sufficiently punished and would return to Zion, acknowledging that the Lord was the one who placed them in exile and brought them back.[173] The people will declare, "The Lord has brought about our vindication; come, let us declare in Zion the work of the Lord our God" (Jer 51:10). The result of the exile was not devastation but redemption, leading to the worship of God once again in Zion. Because God himself forgave the people and established a new covenant, Zion would once again be filled with his presence, and he would once again dwell among the people.[174] Zion serves as a consistent, permanent image of God's presence and rule on earth as he divinely acts on behalf of his people to accomplish his purposes in the world.

170. Willis, "I Will Remember," 15.

171. Kaiser, *Walking the Ancient Paths*, 560.

172. Kaiser, *Walking the Ancient Paths*, 561.

173. Huey, *Jeremiah, Lamentations*, 420.

174. Goswell, "Forgiveness," 376.

Zion Forsaken in Lamentations

On the Jewish sacred calendar, the Ninth of Ab commemorates the destruction of the Jerusalem temple in 587 BC and serves as a day of fasting and mourning to remember that pivotal moment in Israel's history.[175] It is possible that some of what is contained in the book of Lamentations was recited as the people gathered to mourn the site of the ruined temple on such an occasion.[176] Lamentations, as the title suggests, serves as a collection of sorrowful reflections on the plight of Jerusalem. Five times in Lamentations, Zion is described as having no one to comfort her, like a "widow," and like a "princess" who has become a "slave" (Lam 1:1).[177] Thus, the primary way in which the Zion symbol appears in Lamentations is as a destitute woman, and the various feminine imagery highlights the weakened state of the city and its temple. As the covenant partner of Yahweh, the city's adultery has left it in a ruined state, as the book reads, "Jerusalem sinned grievously; therefore she became filth; all who honored her despise her" (Lam 1:8).

The personified Zion, pictured as a daughter or widow, draws upon ancient kinship traditions, which emphasize the city's vulnerability and induce empathy toward it.[178] However, passages such as Lam 2:1–9 do not hide from the reality that it was God who unleashed devastation upon Zion. No confession exists in the second chapter, for the withdrawal of God's presence has brought chaos and calamity upon the city.[179] The sacred space of Mount Zion was abandoned, for God could no longer suffer the wickedness and idolatry that had polluted his temple and city. God purged the people from the city and allowed them to be exiled as both the result of his covenant stipulations and because of the rejection of his sacred space. Lamentations 2:1 states that Zion has been covered with "the cloud of his anger," for instead of the cloud of his glory as seen in the temple dedication, the people now face the fierce storm cloud of God's wrath.[180] In other words, God's anger now overshadows all the good he had done for Zion. Furthermore, Zion is "swallowed up," signifying that God has become an adversary of the people instead of their King (Lam 2:2).[181]

175. Webb, *Five Festal Garments*, 59.

176. See Jer 41:5; Zech 7:3, 5; 8:19.

177. Mandolfo, *Daughter Zion Talks Back*, 104.

178. Bosworth, "Daughter Zion and Weeping," 218.

179. Huey, *Jeremiah, Lamentations*, 459.

180. Huey, *Jeremiah, Lamentations*, 460.

181. Lalleman, *Jeremiah and Lamentations*, 344.

Lamentations utilizes several literary techniques to express Zion's devastation and the general mood of the exiles.[182] Beyond personification, the text also uses synecdoche to use the image of a city to represent the collective whole of the people who survived the devastation. The text also uses what Knut Heim calls "topification" to translate the people in a geographic locale as well as impersonation, which translates the people into one spokesperson.[183] Through these literary devices, Zion serves as a theological symbol related both to God's judgment and salvation for the people. For instance, the image of Zion sitting in the dust as a grieving widow was a powerful cultural image in the ancient Near East. This kind of personification helps to conceptualize and verbalize the pain experienced by the people since their homeland and way of life had been shattered. Zion's personification also exists at four distinct levels in Lamentations: the individual, the suffering community, the world outside Jerusalem, and God.[184] Thus, the Zion symbol in Lamentations can be viewed through multiple lenses, allowing the people to mourn and allowing others to empathize with the city's grief.

Lamentations is not without a glimmer of hope in the future restoration of Zion, for even in the depths of despair, the poet cries out for God to restore the people. The poet says, "For Mount Zion which lies desolate; jackals prowl over it. But you, O Lord, reign forever . . . Restore us to yourself, O Lord, that we may be restored" (Lam 5:18–21). Hope is kindled in the reality that the ability to lament itself is a gift from God, for being alive to weep is an object of divine grace.[185] The sorrowful book closes with an open-ended conclusion, believing that God will renew the people as he had in the past. In the center of both the lament and the cry for restoration lies Zion, the symbol of God's presence and reign upon the earth. Although it was desolate and ruined, it nonetheless remained the symbolic place of God's presence. The poet exclaims, "The steadfast love of the Lord never ceases; his mercies never come to an end; they are new every morning; great is your faithfulness" (Lam 3:22–23). Even through the pain of exile, the people were given the opportunity to seek the Lord and worship him. This foreshadows a time when geographic location would become less important than the heart of individuals. As Jer 31 foresaw, God was in the process of creating a new

182. Knut M. Heim, "Personification of Jerusalem and the Drama of Her Bereavement in Lamentations," in Ollenburger, *Zion, the City*, 133.

183. Knut M. Heim, "Personification of Jerusalem and the Drama of Her Bereavement in Lamentations," in Ollenburger, *Zion, the City*, 135.

184. Knut M. Heim, "Personification of Jerusalem and the Drama of Her Bereavement in Lamentations," in Ollenburger, *Zion, the City*, 141.

185. Webb, *Five Festal Garments*, 69.

Zion, a covenant community of forgiven, redeemed people who would fill the city of God with worship.

ZION IN EZEKIEL AND THE MINOR PROPHETS

Zion symbolism remains an important feature through Ezekiel and the Minor Prophets, and many of the theological themes regarding Zion resemble those of Isaiah and Jeremiah.[186] The term "Zion" does not appear in Ezekiel, yet his vision of a restored Israel and a return to an intimate relationship with God relates to the Zion theology present in the Psalms and Prophets. One of the most significant theological themes among the twelve Minor Prophets is the "Day of the Lord," and for several of them, this concept is linked to Zion's role in both the present and in the eschaton.[187]

Zion's Absence in Ezekiel

The term "Zion" does not appear in Ezekiel, but Ezekiel is also lacking certain theological expressions such as the kingship of Yahweh and the role of the monarchy.[188] Since Ezekiel is heavily interested in the temple and the city of Jerusalem, the avoidance of the term "Zion" is striking. This may be in part due to the prophet's lack of interest in the earlier monarchy and the corrupt temple system before the exile, but it may also point to Ezekiel's theology that, even though Jerusalem remains the center of God's future eschatological plans, its new position will not resemble the role Zion played in the previous eras.[189] Daniel Block explains Zion's absence as part of "the theological crisis to which the exilic prophet Ezekiel speaks."[190] Ezekiel's goal was to transform his audience's perception of their relationship with Yahweh by offering a divine understanding of reality. The Zion tradition of the past had assumed Zion's inviolability and protection, so Ezekiel wrote

186. For instance, Micah, a contemporary of Isaiah, uses the Zion symbol in very similar ways to Isaiah. For the purposes of this study, the Minor Prophets that utilize Zion symbolism frequently and in unique ways will be examined. This includes Joel, Obadiah, Micah, and Zechariah. The name "Zion" also appears in Amos two times as a reference to the city of Jerusalem as Yahweh's residence, and it appears twice in Zephaniah in context of Israel's restoration, resembling the language of Isa 40–66.

187. Poulson, *Representing Zion*, 52.

188. Block, *Beyond the River Chebar*, 2.

189. Block, *Beyond the River Chebar*, 3.

190. Block, *Beyond the River Chebar*, 7.

to confirm that it was not God who had broken the covenant but rather the people had abandoned their God through their idolatry.[191]

Thomas Renz argues that, despite the lack of the name "Zion" in Ezekiel, there is evidence of the Zion tradition throughout the book, which falls into four categories: statements about the temple and the city of Jerusalem being destroyed by Babylon; statements about restoration and the new temple; statements about the God of Israel; other allusions to the Zion tradition.[192] Regarding the new temple, Ezekiel's vision in chapter 40 describes a highly theological task, as the prophet surveys the new sacred space God is creating for his presence. God promises that this place will be "the place of my throne and the place of the soles of my feet, where I will dwell in the midst of the people of Israel forever" (Ezek 43:7). Thus, Ezekiel sees the glory of God returning to a sanctuary, or a place that will bless those who draw near to his presence. The entire temple area has become the footstool of God, not the ark, indicating that the existence of such a place implies Yahweh's eternal presence within it.[193] Chapters 47–48 detail the relationship between the new temple and the land, describing a life-giving stream of water flowing through the temple, which recalls imagery from Eden and the Zion traditions found in passages such as Ps 46.[194] Unfading trees on either side of the river bear fruit each month, and their leaves bring healing. This imagery recalls the effects of the presence of God in Eden and is also used in Rev 22:1–5, a passage that reveals how the presence of God will bring eternal light and healing to the redeemed. Since Ezekiel's prophecy is oriented toward a future relationship between Yahweh and Israel, the poor leadership of the past, including its corrupt religious traditions, must never return. Therefore, Ezekiel sees Yahweh himself as reigning eternally over the whole of Israel, for when he assumes his rightful place in the temple, peace will come to the land.[195]

Without mentioning "Zion" by name, Ezekiel nonetheless progresses Zion, the sacred space filled with the presence of God, to a new perspective on God's eschatological purposes in Israel. The restoration of the city presented as a reallocation of the land to all twelve tribes suggests that Ezekiel 40–48 shows the renewal plan for the whole nation. Yet, the new city is not rebuilt upon the old site, but rather, it appears as a new location: at first, the

191. Block, *Beyond the River Chebar*, 7.

192. Thomas Renz, "Use of the Zion Tradition in the Book of Ezekiel," in Ollenburger, *Zion, the City*, 87.

193. Block, *Book of Ezekiel*, 571.

194. Thomas Renz, "Use of the Zion Tradition in the Book of Ezekiel," in Ollenburger, *Zion, the City*, 95.

195. Block, *Beyond the River*, 9.

new temple appears to be placed at the Temple Mount, or Mount Zion, but as Ezekiel's vision progresses, it becomes clear that this is a new location.[196] Zion, as a symbol of God's presence, was expanding through the Prophets beyond the Temple Mount or Jerusalem; Ezekiel's vision shows that God's purpose through Israel was to transform them into a light to the nations through his holy presence. Even still, the place itself is not the focus, for it is the presence of God and the blessings from it that are the centerpiece of Israel's life.[197]

Joel

Joel provides a captivating illustration of the classic Zion motif, for in its seven occurrences, it is used to describe Yahweh's sacred mountain, God's protection of the city, and the repulsion of Israel's enemies.[198] "The Lord roars from Zion" but "is a refuge to his people," indicating the nature of God's sacred space atop Mount Zion (Joel 3:16). The sons of Zion rejoice (Joel 2:23) and it is the place of salvation, where "everyone who calls on the name of the Lord shall be saved" (Joel 2:32). Zion is depicted as the place where Yahweh dwells in his holiness, avenging Israel's enemies and ushering in a glorious future (Joel 3:17, 21). Joel is primarily focused on the day of the Lord, and through his visions, the people would likely have been encouraged that God would soon vindicate Israel and crush their enemies; yet, those promises did not fully materialize in the prophet's day.[199] As opposed to Isaiah and Jeremiah, Joel connects the Zion motif primarily with Judah's safety and salvation, not its judgment. Reflecting the language of the Zion hymns in Psalms, Joel perceives Zion as the stronghold of Yahweh, the Lord's sacred mountain from which he crushes those who try to harm his holy city, and the city in which God's elect people are saved.[200]

While Zion is the place of protection and the source of judgment upon Judah's enemies, Joel's vision of eschatological salvation, the outpouring of the Spirit, and vindication for the suffering contain fulfillment in the prophet's day as well as the future.[201] This is evidenced by Peter's sermon in Jerusalem where he connects Joel's prophecy concerning the "last days"

196. Rooke, "Urban Planning," 126.

197. Thomas Renz, "Use of the Zion Tradition in the Book of Ezekiel," in Ollenburger, *Zion, the City*, 95.

198. Poulson, *Representing Zion*, 52.

199. Allen, *Joel, Obadiah, Jonah, and Micah*, 38.

200. Poulson, *Representing Zion*, 53.

201. Allen, *Joel, Obadiah, Jonah, and Micah*, 120.

with the miracles occurring on the day of Pentecost. Zion, then, symbolizes Israel as the true people of God; in the New Testament context, the true people of God become those who receive the Spirit upon hearing the truth and responding to the message of the gospel. Isaiah 2:2–4 had predicted that the gentile nations would seek Zion and submit to the God of Israel, and even though Joel is primarily concerned with Judah's protection, Joel 3:17 hints at a time when Zion will be holy and when "strangers shall never again pass through it."[202]

Zion's future destination is a time when the city has been purified and will never again be polluted by foreign conquerors but will be filled with the fullness of God's presence. As a theological symbol, Joel's use of Zion denotes the kingship of Yahweh, the enthroned king over Mount Zion, who will not allow his chosen city to be conquered and who will rise to defend the people he loves. Because of God's holy presence on Mount Zion, the city has become the eschatological location of salvation, pointing to a time when the Lord "will pour out my Spirit on all flesh" (Joel 2:28). The assurance that the Lord dwells in Zion (Joel 3:21) proves that God is jealous for his chosen place, for it is his sacred mountain from which salvation comes.[203]

Obadiah

"Mount Zion" occurs twice in the short book of Obadiah, and like Joel, Zion is portrayed as a place of salvation, which is holy and protected as a symbol of God's faithfulness to the line of Jacob.[204] The unique feature of Obadiah is its context in which the prophet condemns Edom for rising up against Israel, leading to a comparison between two mountains: Mount Zion and Mount Seir.[205] Mount Zion is the place Yahweh loves, but it had become a place of destruction; yet Obadiah is confident that Zion would once again become a holy place.[206] Reflecting on the events of 586 BC, Obadiah offers an interesting perspective on the plight of Jerusalem: Edom, the people descended from Esau, should have helped Judah but instead sided with Babylon. As a result, Obadiah prophesies that Edom will be repaid for its evil deeds, and Mount Zion will "govern the mountains of Esau" in a future restored kingdom. The statement that Mount Zion "shall be holy" resembles Joel 3:17 ("Jerusalem shall be holy") and connects the theological emphases

202. Garrett, *Hosea, Joel*, 393.

203. Hubbard, *Joel and Amos*, 85.

204. Poulson, *Representing Zion*, 54.

205. Smith, *Minor Prophets*, 49.

206. See Ps 74:7.

in each prophet's writing. Some commentators see Obadiah as a response to Lamentations and the fear that Yahweh had completely abandoned his people during the events of the Babylonian invasion. In this sense, Obadiah affirms that Yahweh is sovereign over the events on earth, and his covenant promises regarding Zion cannot be forever broken.[207]

Obadiah's language resembles many of the other prophets with a central focus on the day of the Lord and the salvation coming for Israel in that day. As the primary symbol of God's presence on earth, Zion represents both the place of God's protection and salvation, but it also serves as a symbol representing God's covenant faithfulness to Judah.[208] Obadiah also sees the nations coming into Zion in Obad 1:16–17 for judgment, not instruction, as in Isa 2:2–4; thus, Zion is the place of salvation for Israel but the place of judgment upon the nations.[209]

Micah

The word "Zion" occurs often in Micah, and among its nine occurrences, it appears four times independently: once as "Mount Zion" and four times as "daughter Zion."[210] Micah resembles Isaiah in several ways as both texts open with a court scene, Israel and Judah's punishment is a unified action by God, and the Zion symbol conveys both judgment and salvation for the people of Israel. Micah's incendiary words against the leaders of Jerusalem were likely shocking, for the city and temple were perceived as the holy place of Yahweh.[211] Micah's harsh words called on the people to mourn because "the sons of your delight," which may refer to either the towns of Judah or perhaps its armies, have been taken captive.[212] Zion's inviolability is called into question, for the arrogance of its leaders will leave them in a state of mourning.

Micah provides a unique perspective on Zion, since Micah likely originated as a prophet from the Judean countryside and then traveled to Jerusalem to represent his rural peers.[213] While speaking the word of the Lord, Micah represented the devalued and disillusioned people from rural towns in a time where the metropolitan elites had abused their influence

207. Barton, *Joel and Obadiah*, 158.
208. Smith, *Amos, Obadiah, Jonah*, 199.
209. Barton, *Joel and Obadiah*, 152.
210. Poulson, *Representing Zion*, 56.
211. Smith, *Micah–Malachi*, 35.
212. Smith, *Minor Prophets*, 294.
213. Rick R. Marrs, "Back to the Future," in Batto and Roberts, *David and Zion*, 80.

and power. Therefore, Zion appears in two ways in Micah: the present Zion, which is corrupted and weakened through the failed policies and corruption of the city's leadership, and as a future site of God's divine plans.[214]

Zion's current plight is described as Micah says, "Therefore because of you Zion shall be plowed as a field; Jerusalem shall become a heap of ruins, and the mountain of the house a wooded height" (Mic 3:12). Micah's words would not prove true for another hundred years, but even during the days of Jeremiah, some elders remembered Micah's prophecy about the city's destruction (Jer 26:1–19). These words speak to the prophet's concern for the Lord's sacred space, for through failed leadership and idolatrous practices, the purity of Zion was contaminated and destruction would ensue. This also reflects God's covenant promises and curses, for even though he had chosen Zion and loved it (Ps 132:13), his holy presence could not withstand the wickedness of Zion's inhabitants. In other words, the leaders of Zion were not reflecting the character of God, causing Israel and Judah to fail in representing his glory and dominion to the nations.[215] Zion, to Micah, represents the holy place of God and the Lord's sovereignty over the nations; therefore, judgment would come on those who polluted the Temple Mount or prevented the nations from drawing near to the Lord.[216]

Micah 4:1–3 is nearly identical to Isa 2:2–4, and in both instances, Zion is depicted as a place to which the nations will come to receive instruction from the Lord and find perfect justice in his presence. This is the goal of Zion: the nations will stream into God's presence like a river to be blessed, as God had promised Abraham (Gen 12:1–3).[217] The kingdom of God in this passage is spiritual, speaking of a kingdom that would one day be exalted over all other kingdoms of the world. Thus, perceiving Zion as "the highest of the mountains" with the nations streaming like a river portrays the blessing over the whole earth, which would come from God's presence on Zion (Mic 4:1).[218] This is Zion's future after God's sovereign plans for the city have been fully realized. As in Isaiah, Zion is on a journey in Micah: while the present city is weakened, Micah sees Zion transformed and indwelt by God's presence, which brings justice and peace to the people. This transformation will not come easily or without pain, for Mic 4:9–10 describes Zion as a pregnant woman agonizing through birth pangs. Even though Zion

214. Rick R. Marrs, "Back to the Future," in Batto and Roberts, *David and Zion*, 82.

215. Smith, *Minor Prophets*, 294.

216. Allen, *Joel, Obadiah, Jonah, and Micah*, 320.

217. Barker, *Micah, Nahum, Habakkuk, Zephaniah*, 84.

218. Smith, *Minor Prophets*, 318.

must suffer through exile, God promises, "There you shall be rescued; there the Lord will redeem you" (Mic 4:10).

Another unique perspective on Zion in Micah occurs in 4:11–13, where the nations are described as gathering around the city saying, "Let her be defiled, and let our eyes gaze upon Zion" (Mic 4:11). However, Yahweh has assembled the nations so that Zion can plunder them. Zion is described in 4:13 as "threshing" and it "shall beat in pieces many peoples"; the shift to imagery of military victory conveys the theological notion that Yahweh has definitively defeated the nations and given the spoils to his chosen city.[219] Micah's use of the Zion symbol continues the progress of Zion as an inviolable city to a transformed city, where Yahweh will execute righteous judgments on behalf of the nations, defeating Israel's enemies and welcoming those seeking instruction from the Lord.

Rick Marrs states, "Micah's creative use of the Zion tradition remains consistent. Just as Yahweh shepherded his people as a royal monarch . . . now Yahweh brings forth a ruler away from the corrupt capital."[220] Within Micah's use of Zion symbolism emerges a messianic figure, arising from "Bethlehem Ephrathah," who will "shepherd his flock in the strength of the Lord" (Mic 5:2–3). Once Zion has been transformed, the city will be ruled by a Good Shepherd who will "be their peace" and who "shall be great to the ends of the earth" (Mic 5:4–5). In other words, Zion must first go through the process of transformation before the Lord can once again dwell among the people and bring perfect peace and justice. By depicting what the Lord intends for Zion to become, Micah pushes forward the Zion symbol toward its intended destination as the place where God would eternally dwell among his people in peace.[221]

Zechariah

During the return from exile and the rebuilding of the temple in Jerusalem, Zechariah prophesied about the renewal of the covenant community and the coming of Zion's King. Zechariah 1–6 centers on the rebuilding of the temple through the power of God's Spirit (Zech 4:6), while chapters 8 and 9 focus on the Lord's love for Zion, and chapters 10 through 14 speak of how Yahweh will return to Zion.[222] Zechariah's focus is beyond the temple, which is the primary focus of his contemporary Haggai, for he places priority on

219. Rick R. Marrs, "Back to the Future," in Batto and Roberts, *David and Zion*, 89.

220. Rick R. Marrs, "Back to the Future," in Batto and Roberts, *David and Zion*, 89.

221. Rick R. Marrs, "Back to the Future," in Batto and Roberts, *David and Zion*, 93.

222. Hamilton, *God's Glory in Salvation*, 260.

the restoration of the covenant community, which impacts the infrastructure of the city, material prosperity, and global impact on the nations, all emanating from a renewed people in Zion.[223]

Zechariah 8:3 provides a clear example of the prophet's use of Zion to convey the return of Yahweh and the restoration of the city. It reads, "I have returned to Zion and will dwell in the midst of Jerusalem, and Jerusalem shall be called the faithful city, and the mountain of the Lord of hosts, the holy mountain" (Zech 8:3). This verse indicates that the full salvation of the remnant is coming because Yahweh is returning to his chosen holy mountain, resulting in an ideal future where injustice and strife have been eliminated and the most vulnerable in society will prosper.[224] Joel 3:17 contained similar language, but now Zechariah is viewing God's plans for Zion from the postexilic era. Zion can now be described as the "faithful city" because Yahweh's presence has made it so.[225]

The language of Zech 8:1–8 is reminiscent of both covenantal and relational aspects between God and his chosen people; therefore, the use of the Zion symbol points beyond a temple toward an intimate relationship.[226] Zion's restoration speaks not only to God's presence in a temple or city but rather among the people, for "they shall be my people, and I will be their God, in faithfulness and righteousness" (Zech 8:8). In a sense, the belief in a restored Zion from Isaiah and Jeremiah has come true in Zechariah because the exile is over, and the people can now rebuild a new community of faith in God.[227] The prophet sees the physical effects of Yahweh's return, yet he envisions a spiritual Jerusalem filled with citizens who have been sanctified and cleansed, thus making it a "holy mountain."[228]

Zechariah 9–11 continues the motif of Zion's protection because of Yahweh's return, for peace is proclaimed and weapons of war are destroyed. Zechariah 9:9–13 depicts the coming of Zion's king: "Rejoice greatly, O daughter of Zion! Shout aloud, O daughter of Jerusalem! Behold, your king is coming to you; righteous and having salvation is he" (Zech 9:9). In this famous passage, Zion's king is like no other, for Zion is like no other place: this king has been chosen by God to reign in a kingdom which will eventually replace all other kingdoms (Zech 9:10).[229] Psalm 72 speaks of the king ruling

223. Boda, *Book of Zechariah*, 46.
224. Boda, *Book of Zechariah*, 371.
225. Clark, *Handbook on Zechariah*, 200.
226. Duvall, *God's Relational Presence*, 160.
227. Poulson, *Representing Zion*, 59.
228. Smith, *Minor Prophets*, 568.
229. Webb, *Message of Zechariah*, 137.

"from the Euphrates to the ends of the earth," a similar construction as Zech 9:10, but the psalmist's vision of the nations being defeated and becoming subservient to this king is now seen as a vision of peace among the nations through this messianic figure. Jesus, as he fulfills these verses, sought the peaceful and universal reign of God over the nations, not through force but by belief.[230]

The New Testament identifies this king with Jesus Christ, the Son of God who was chosen to rule over all nations (Ps 2:8–9). While other kings are flawed and could only reflect God's character imperfectly, this king is the agent through whom God's salvation is made available. Thus, Zechariah interprets Zion as the place of eschatological salvation, both in a physical and spiritual sense. Physically, God's dominion began in Mount Zion, the chosen holy mountain on which God resided among the people; spiritually, Zion represents the identity of all the redeemed, for its influence will spread from "the River to the ends of the earth" (Zech 9:10).[231] These verses add depth to the coming Messiah and show that God was not merely standing behind him or supporting him but that God was present in him.[232] Because of this, the redeemed become citizens of this remade Zion because they carry the presence of God with them through faith in this coming king.

ZION AND THE MESSIANIC HOPE IN THE PROPHETS

The prophets present Zion as the symbol of God's presence and as a collective symbol describing the people of God, whether or not the people are representing God's character and reign to the nations. Zion is on a journey of transformation, beginning with Isa 1–2 as a framework to describe a broken, faithless city that will one day transform into a glorious beacon of God's presence for all people. Isaiah's vision of a restored Zion includes a vision of the suffering servant, one who represented the people before God as a sacrificial lamb, enduring severe judgment yet emerging victorious to "justify many" (Isa 53:11). Jeremiah prophesied that the Lord would create a new covenant in the hearts of men, indicating a time coming when the law would be an internal transformation instead of external obedience. Jeremiah also said, "In those days and at that time I will cause a righteous Branch to spring up for David," resulting in the nation's salvation (Jer 33:15). For Ezekiel, the failed leadership, or false shepherds, that led Israel toward apostasy and exile would be replaced through God's own intervention. God

230. Smith, *Micah-Malachi*, 257.

231. Webb, *Message of Zechariah*, 138.

232. Webb, *Message of Zechariah*, 138.

told the prophet, "I myself will search for my sheep and will seek them out . . . and will bring them into their own land" (Ezek 34:11, 13).[233] The writings of the Major Prophets weave together the theological concepts of Messiah, temple, and land to create a tapestry of God's future intentions for his people with a focus on God's own actions to accomplish it. The people were unable to maintain their covenant obligations, but because of his mercy, God himself acts on behalf of the people to restore them and bring them into a renewed land, where once again he can dwell among them in peace. Through all these prophecies, Zion does not fade from view but rather remains as the primary symbol for God's divine presence among his people. Jeremiah says, "Arise, and let us go up to Zion, to the Lord our God," indicating that God was personally drawing the people back together in Zion so they could again receive the blessings of his presence.[234] The combination of a restored Zion, renewed hearts of men, and the regathering of the remnant points to a time when God's presence would dwell intimately within the hearts of people. These images set the stage for Jesus, who came not to destroy the temple but to become the new temple within himself and to allow all men to receive the indwelling presence of God through faith.[235]

The oracles of the Minor Prophets likewise progress the imagery of Zion toward a future fulfillment with eternal ramifications. While earlier prophecies in Joel maintain the previous Zion traditions involving Yahweh's reign and defeat of Israel's enemies, the later prophets, such as Zechariah, interpret Zion as the center of God's eschatological kingdom. Within Zechariah's vision of a new covenant people arises a gentle and humble king who is "righteous and having salvation" (Zech 9:9). Jesus's triumphal entry into Jerusalem reenacts this imagery, showing that he is the fulfillment of the prophet's vision of a new messianic king who brings salvation for the people. As the prophets reflected on the Davidic covenant and its eternal implications, an image of a coming Messiah emerges: Isaiah saw a branch arising from Jesse's stump (Isa 11:1–2); Micah saw a new leader arising from the humble town of Bethlehem (Mic 5:2), and Zechariah foresaw the humble king entering Zion victoriously (Zech 9:9–10). All these images paint a picture of God himself providing salvation through a new king who will open a new chapter in history, where God again will dwell among his people in righteousness and peace.[236]

233. Chae, *Jesus*, 91.

234. Duvall, *God's Relational Presence*, 133.

235. Perrin, *Jesus the Temple*, 8.

236. D. G. Firth, "Messiah," in Boda and McConville, *Dictionary of Old Testament: Prophets*, 1174.

Zion, as a theological symbol, develops and expands through the Prophets, blooming into a beautiful picture representing God's intent to eternally dwell among his people. The presence of God remains the focus, but by the end of the Old Testament, Zion is no longer only a physical Temple Mount but rather symbolizes a restored people of God's choosing. It is within this setting that Jesus Christ emerges: "For while we were still weak, at the right time Christ died for the ungodly" (Rom 5:6). The imagery of a restored Zion and renewed people sets the table for the entrance of the Messiah, who, at the right time, would himself create the way for people to dwell again in the presence of God.

4

Zion Transformed in Jesus Christ

The development of Zion symbolism in the Old Testament reveals a progressing theological idea regarding the presence of God. God's desire to dwell among people was corrupted by sin, yet God himself created a plan to draw rebellious people back toward his holy presence, where they would find eternal peace and rest. Within the Psalms and Prophets emerges a messianic expectation that God's covenant promises to David would be fulfilled in a future king who would establish an eternal kingdom filled with redeemed people. The Hebrew *Māšîaḥ* occurs several times in the Old Testament, often in reference to human kings or priests and their "anointing" received by God.[1] However, the later, fuller revelation developed in the New Testament reveals a deeper, more profound meaning for this figure, which is fulfilled in Jesus Christ.[2] The Gospels interpret the Old Testament messianic passages through the lens of Jesus, showing that the undercurrent of the Old Testament messianic hope was flowing toward its fulfillment in Jesus. Within that messianic expectation, the Zion symbol is an important aspect, since it represents the presence of God among his people. Even though the term "Zion" is rare in the Gospels, the symbol and its related theological expressions are an important aspect to Jesus's ministry and teaching, particularly regarding the role of the church as a new temple.

This chapter will demonstrate that the hopes for a renewed Zion in which the presence of God dwelled among the people is fulfilled in Jesus Christ as he transforms the imagery from an earthly kingdom to a spiritual

1. Porter, *Messiah*, 14.
2. Porter, *Messiah*, 34.

kingdom, in which the Spirit of God indwells the hearts of those who believe. The Second Temple period in which Jesus ministered contained a wealth of literature regarding the coming Messiah, and within that expectation, alongside the Roman occupation, emerged Jesus of Nazareth, an itinerant preacher with a radical message. Sectarian groups, such as the one at Qumran, developed the idea that the Messiah was coming soon and that God would redeem those who refused to participate in the corrupt practices of the current leadership and remained faithful to him. Through a brief examination of key literature produced near the time of Jesus, a reinterpretation of Zion's restoration emerges. Ultimately, Jesus would fulfill the promises of a restored Zion through the inauguration of God's eschatological kingdom through his death and resurrection. Because of Christ, all who enter "Zion" through faith in Jesus are given access to the presence of God forever. Jesus, then, is the goal of Zion and its eschatological fulfillment.

The Gospel writers do not ignore the temple and its related imagery but rather, they expose the original intent of the temple through the life and ministry of Jesus: God has always desired to dwell among his people. Jesus's primary message, "The time is fulfilled, and the kingdom of God is at hand," reveals that Jesus's focus was preaching a gospel of repentance so that people could join in him in this new kingdom made up of those who believe (Mark 1:15).[3] Furthermore, by the end of his earthly ministry, Jesus's desire is that his disciples would "abide in me, and I in you" (John 15:4), and that his followers "may all be one, just as you, Father, are in me, and I in you, that they also may be in us" (John 17:20). This language is relational, suggesting that oneness with the Father, or remaining in his presence, was the goal of Jesus's ministry and the eternal effect of the salvation he brought. Therefore, through Jesus's life, ministry, and sacrificial death, the Zion symbol is transformed as the presence of God in the temple is transferred into the individual heart, creating a new "temple" inside each believer and unifying them all through the Holy Spirit. Zion is not abandoned but is fulfilled through Jesus's sacrificial death and resurrection, creating a new "temple" inside the heart of individuals and uniting them through the Spirit's presence.

SETTING THE STAGE: THE MESSIANIC EXPECTATIONS OF THE SECOND TEMPLE ERA

The historical period in which Jesus ministered was inundated with teaching, literature, and ideas about the identity, purpose, and mission of the Messiah. The term "messianism" is a modern word to express the various

3. Stein, *Jesus the Messiah*, 82.

Jewish expectations regarding the ones who would rise to action in accordance with God's eschatological plans.[4] While there were many ideas of the kind of leader this person would be, a majority of the writing during the Second Temple period speaks of a new leader who would reestablish Israel as an independent kingdom and rule over the people with justice and righteousness. For some, this messianic figure would overthrow Rome or the corrupt Hasmonean leadership in Jerusalem, but for others, he would primarily be a religious or spiritual leader.

Important Jewish leaders, such as Judas Maccabeus and his brother Jonathan, had left a significant impression on the Jewish people regarding messianic figures, the kind of leadership needed to mitigate oppression by other nations, and a renewal of religious fervor.[5] Even in the decades before and after Jesus's ministry, several messiah-like individuals had risen and commanded a following among the Jews. Josephus chronicles the stories of figures claiming to be prophets, such as Theudas, a man called "the Samaritan," and another called "the Egyptian Jew."[6] In each instance, these "prophets" gathered a crowd to a specific location with lofty promises regarding spiritual blessing or the revealing of an ancient artifact, yet they were thwarted by Roman officials and quickly crushed. However, such stories point to growing angst among the people for a new prophet to arise and bring salvation. Furthermore, the dissatisfaction with the temple and the priesthood undergirded the longing for rescue. The promise of a restored Zion had not been forgotten, but how it would happen or when it would come was still unsure among the Jews.

While the concept of messianic figures developed foremost from scriptural traditions, it cannot be separated from the changing tides of the contemporary issues facing the Jews.[7] One of the most significant factors relating to Jesus's day and the decades prior was the entrenchment of top-level Jewish leaders within the temple system who were corrupt or essentially behaved as gentiles.[8] Remaining under gentile rule was a tragedy, but as the temple system, the primary symbol of the Jews' unique identity, became subservient to Greek or Roman rule, the Jews began to interpret such events as a sign of impending tribulation. Writers and various sects during the Second Temple period believed that a time of testing, which included foreign rule and great apostasy among the people, would usher in a time when the

4. Dodson, *Exploring Biblical Backgrounds*, 189.
5. Schürer, *History of the Jewish People*, 1:235.
6. Whiston, *Works of Flavius Josephus*, 492, 563.
7. Perrin, *Jesus the Temple*, 18.
8. Perrin, *Jesus the Temple*, 19.

Lord's faithful remnant would await the appearance of God's Messiah, who would bring judgment and salvation.[9] It is within this sentiment that several Jewish groups developed literature, and it is also likely that counter-temple movements, such as the one led by John the Baptist, arose from these beliefs.

Alongside a growing expectation of a messianic ruler was a vision for a future temple, which would once again be filled with the glory of God. Tobit, dated around the second or third century BC, expected a coming restoration involving a temple gathering that included gentiles.[10] First Enoch attests to an old temple torn down and replaced by a new one, to which all peoples of earth are drawn, and the Temple Scroll from Qumran anticipated a new eschatological temple, filled with God's presence and glory.[11] These expectations from Jewish literature reveal, from different theological perspectives, that a new temple as Isaiah and Ezekiel envisioned would come in the eschaton. The Gospels were written within this historical context and reflect a new Zion, or a new temple through Christ, who is both the awaited Messiah and is himself the inauguration of a new temple residing in the hearts of his followers.

The Messiah in Psalms of Solomon

Psalms of Solomon, written in the late first century BC, reflects the beliefs of a group of Jews who despised Hasmonean and Roman rule in Israel and serves as an example of the messianism arising in the decades before Jesus.[12] The seventeenth psalm speaks of a "Lord Messiah" (Χριστὸς κύριος) who will "gather together a holy people, whom he shall lead in righteousness" and "purge Jerusalem, making it holy as of old."[13] Likely reflecting on Pompey's incursion into the temple and the holy of holies, the psalmist appears to interpret this tragic event through the prophetic lens of the Old Testament.[14] In other words, Israel's covenantal unfaithfulness had resulted in God sending the gentiles as punishment. If the temple was profaned in this way, the community responsible for these psalms interpreted the events as a signal for the day of the Lord. Psalms of Solomon 11:1 exclaims, "Sound in

9. Perrin, *Jesus the Temple*, 19.

10. Kirk, "Time for Figs," 515.

11. 1 En. 90:28–29.

12. All quotations of the Pseudepigrapha are taken from *Pseudepigrapha of the Old Testament*, edited by Robert H. Charles (Clarendon, 1913).

13. Pss. Sol. 17:26, 33. The phrase Χριστὸς κύριος also appears in Lam 4:20 (LXX) and in Luke 2:11 as "Christ the Lord."

14. Perrin, *Jesus the Temple*, 23.

Zion the signal trumpet of the sanctuary, announce in Jerusalem the voice of him that brings good news."[15] The imagery in this passage, similar to Isa 40, envisions a cleansing of the temple of its wicked leaders and a future remnant that will live in peace in Jerusalem. The sectarians responsible for these psalms understood their prayers as a catalyst for the time of the Messiah, and their waiting for such a time provides a theological backdrop for figures such as John the Baptist and Jesus, especially regarding their words against the temple establishment.[16]

The messianic hope in Psalms of Solomon is connected to David's dynasty and appears to align with much of the imagery Isaiah uses to describe Israel as a servant in the process of being sanctified by a new king.[17] This psalm also recalls the imagery of the Davidic Messiah from Ps 2, speaking of his iron rod with which he will shatter godless nations and cleanse Jerusalem. By stitching together the motifs from passages such as Ps 2, Isa 11, and Isa 53, the Psalms of Solomon reflects a deep yearning from within certain groups of Jews for God to act through the sending of the long-awaited Messiah. Through this figure, the people would return to righteousness and holiness, being finally delivered from their enemies so they could heed the word of the Lord and be sanctified.

The phrase "son of David" appears in Pss. Sol. 17:21, and it also occurs in Matthew's Gospel nine times to designate Jesus as the Messiah.[18] In both sources, the writers portray the royal Messiah as a contrast to the failures of the Hasmonean or Herodian leadership over Israel. By emphasizing the coming Messiah's royal lineage and right to rule over Israel, the psalmist is pointing to one who will rule with godly authority, not with the corrupt and godless leadership seen in the present rulers. Psalms of Solomon 1 condemns the priests, even the high priest, of greed and dishonest gains, saying, "But they became insolent in their prosperity . . . their transgressions went beyond those of the heathen before them."[19] Such statements indicate that Zion, the place of God's presence, had become corrupted by failed leaders, and since the writing likely came from an educated group and was written for a community in Jerusalem, such charges against the high priest likely were substantive.[20] Similar to Micah's condemnation of Jerusalem's leadership in his day, Psalms of Solomon reveals a community that longed for a

15. Pss. Sol. 11:1.

16. Perrin, *Jesus the Temple*, 28.

17. Johnson, "Rendering David a Servant," 244.

18. Willitts, "Matthew and Psalms," 33.

19. Perrin, *Jesus the Temple*, 25. Pss. Sol. 1:6, 8.

20. Perrin, *Jesus the Temple*, 26.

Messiah to purify Zion. Hope in the current priesthood was lost, and only through God's eschatological plans would Israel be redeemed. Therefore, Psalms of Solomon serves as a unique example of the messianism developing in the century before Jesus, setting the stage for the Coming One who would not only purify the temple but would himself become the purifying presence of God among those willing to repent and believe.

The Messiah in 1 Enoch

Within the larger composition of 1 Enoch is a section usually entitled Similitudes, which is a pseudepigraphic "vision" given to Enoch, including descriptions of a Messiah who will come during a time of tribulation.[21] First Enoch 48:10 describes the Messiah's judgment on those who reject him, saying, "For they have denied the Lord of Spirits and His Anointed." Without much explanation, this text appears to assume a preexistent "Son of Man" or "Lord of the Spirits" who will deliver those who are righteous upon his arrival. God's ideal ruler stands in stark contrast to the wealthy elites who oppress the people and dominate the land.[22] However, different from Psalms of Solomon, Similitudes does not link this figure with the Davidic dynasty nor are there explicit references to his role in fulfilling covenant promises. First Enoch expresses a longing for a righteous "Son of Man," likely influenced by Daniel, who will rise and vindicate the righteous, thus ushering in a time of restoration.[23] Furthermore, 1 En. 90:29 foresees a "new house," representing a new Jerusalem, descending from above and leading to a time when a messianic figure transforms the members of God's kingdom.[24] This figure becomes a lamb and represents the nation's leader, who has brought the people into everlasting life, resembling what Adam originally experienced in Eden. Robert Charles notes that this figure "is not angelic, but human, yet superior to the righteous symbolized by sheep. As human he corresponds to the Messiah of the prophets."[25]

Relating to Zion symbolism, 1 Enoch exists alongside other Second Temple literature in that it is located within a complex landscape of beliefs and sentiments regarding the temple. While the Second Temple stood near Mount Zion, it did not have the glory of Solomon's temple, for it was now primarily a house of prayer or a meeting place. Furthermore, the discontent

21. Porter, *Messiah*, 98. Similitudes comprises chapters 37–71 of 1 Enoch.

22. Porter, *Messiah*, 100.

23. 1 En. 48:2.

24. Charles, *Commentary on the Pseudepigrapha*, 2:260.

25. Charles, *Commentary on the Pseudepigrapha*, 2:260.

with the current priesthood led to much criticism regarding how the temple duties were carried out and the people's relationship with the temple itself.[26] First Enoch 14 envisions a heavenly temple with a lofty throne, with "streams of flaming fire," and "the Great Glory" whose "raiment shone more brightly than the sun."[27] This imagery reflects the theological concept of the heavenly temple filled with God's glory as depicted in passages such as Isa 6 and Ezek 1. This also points to the Second Temple belief that the present temple was not filled with the same glory as the original: the earthly temple was empty, but the heavenly one was filled with glory.[28] This longing for the presence of God to be made manifest among the people would only come when God's Messiah arrived, redeeming the faithful and judging the wicked. First Enoch provides an example from a Jewish perspective near the time of Jesus that highlights the desire for God's Messiah to purify Israel and release the people from oppression. For Zion to once again be the intersection between heaven and earth, the place where the divine presence met with humankind, the "Son of Man," or God's righteous future king, would need to arrive and inaugurate God's eschatological kingdom on earth. In other words, the glory that once filled the original temple on Zion would not come until the Messiah established his new kingdom, a kingdom filled with people who were faithful to God alone and who would enjoy his presence forever.

The Qumran Community

The Qumran community, responsible for the Dead Sea Scrolls, provides another glimpse at Jewish sectarian groups who wrote on a coming Messiah, both through reflection in Scripture and because of contemporary sociopolitical issues regarding the governance of Israel and the temple. The diversity of messianic expectations can be seen in the Qumran documents as well, for Rule of the Community (1QS) speaks to the "prophet" and "messiahs of Aaron and Israel" and men being set apart as "a holy house for Aaron."[29] The messianic focus was on a future leader who would rule the faithful of Israel with righteousness and justice. Whether in the form of a prophet or priest, the outcome was the coming of God's kingdom and the expulsion of Israel's enemies from the land.[30]

26. Bokhorst, "Enoch's Vision," 246.

27. 1 En. 14:19–20.

28. Bokhorst, "Enoch's Vision," 260.

29. Dodson, *Exploring Biblical Backgrounds*, 192.

30. Brown, "Messianism of Qumran," 57.

The notion that a coming king could be regarded as "son of God" can be traced to the pre-Christian Judaism as well, for Rule of the Congregation (1QSa) speaks to a time when God "begets" the Messiah.[31] However, many of the messianic texts from Qumran identify the figure in primarily military terms, as one who will crush Israel's enemies as the "branch" of Isa 11 and as the royal warrior sent from God to cleanse the land.[32] As the political situation of Israel intensified, and as the priesthood failed to remain faithful to the Torah, groups such as the one at Qumran saw themselves as the faithful remnant, awaiting the time when God would redeem his people through the victory of the Messiah.

The Damascus Document contains a unique insight on how the Qumran community perceived the high priest and the temple, for the community essentially created a new "temple" that did not require a building. All that was needed for their "temple" was a faithful people.[33] This document details the creation of a new temple order, including priests who would "preserve faith" by "atoning for sin by working justice and suffering affliction."[34] The faithful leaders at Qumran are described as "an eternal planting" and "a temple for Israel," alluding to both the eschatological hope of a renewed Eden and to the sacred space where the divine and the earthly meet.[35] In terms of the Zion symbol's transformation, the Damascus Document reveals how a sect had not only departed from the temple in Jerusalem as the primary source of their spiritual identity but had then created their own community in which faithfulness to the Torah and one another were now prime virtues. The community itself would be the fulfillment of Isa 28:16 and become the "tested cornerstone" with unshakable foundations. The new order of priests and the laity would then become the spiritual cornerstone and the walls of the temple. The creational and redemptive symbolism within the Qumran community's beliefs echo imagery from Isaiah: the "cornerstone" of Isa 28:16 now applied to the people. In other words, the community was not merely doing the works of the temple, but they became a new temple.[36]

Zion's restoration was a major theme in Isaiah, but the Qumran community began to interpret it through a different lens. Nicholas Perrin states, "They saw themselves not merely as part of an *ad hoc* measure until the personnel at Zion could straighten themselves out; rather, the Qumran

31. Joseph, *Jesus, the Essenes*, 72.
32. Joseph, *Jesus, the Essenes*, 75.
33. Perrin, *Jesus the Temple*, 31.
34. Perrin, *Jesus the Temple*, 32.
35. Perrin, *Jesus the Temple*, 33.
36. Perrin, *Jesus the Temple*, 34.

community envisaged itself as the threshold to a larger and infinitely more glorious temple."[37] The Second Temple was missing key elements, such as the ark, the tablets, the Urim and Thummim, and most of all, the Shekinah presence of God; thus, the mindset of those faithful to Yahweh began to shift away from the holy of holies toward inner transformation.[38] Zion was transforming into a symbol of God's presence within his people instead of among his people in a particular place.

John the Baptist

As the embodiment of the "voice of one crying out in the wilderness" from Isa 40:3, John the Baptist represents an important movement since he baptizes Jesus and, from there, appears to step aside as Jesus begins to minister in Galilee (John 1:23). All four of the Gospels speak of John's ministry and provide glimpses of his teaching, thus his statements that deny he himself was the Messiah as well as his affirmation of Jesus set the stage for Jesus's ministry. John likely did not belong to an organized sect such as the one at Qumran or the Essenes, yet he does belong to the long line of dissident voices that pointed to the end of the old order and the near arrival of a new temple.[39] Luke's account of John the Baptist provides more extensive detail into John's teaching, for Luke writes, "As the people were in expectation, and all were questioning in their hearts concerning John, whether he might be the Christ" (Luke 3:15). Crowds were approaching John to be baptized, including tax collectors and soldiers, wondering if he might be the one called Christ, yet John replied, "He who is mightier than I is coming . . . He will baptize you with the Holy Spirit and fire" (Luke 3:16). These verses indicate that the people were looking for a messianic figure, and John's bold preaching and radical ethics stirred the crowds toward a hopeful expectation in a deliverer.[40]

John the Baptist also represents the beginning of the time of fulfillment when the promises of Isa 40 were becoming reality and when the transformation of individual hearts would be God's primary means of salvation. In this sense, the Baptist is the final prophet, the last voice in the age of promise, who introduces Jesus as the fulfillment of God's promises to Israel and as the singular figure to bring the eschaton into reality.[41] By the time

37. Perrin, *Jesus the Temple*, 34.

38. Edersheim, *Temple*, 62.

39. Perrin, *Jesus the Temple*, 37.

40. Marshall, *Gospel of Luke*, 145.

41. Bock, *Luke 1:1—9:50*, 279.

of Zechariah, the Zion motif was centered on the return of God's presence through a future king, or the theological idea that God's divine presence, along with a new kingdom, would come through this new figure whose roles include prophet, priest, and king. Thus, John the Baptist serves as a bridge between the Old and New Testaments, between the age of promise and the age of fulfillment. His teaching pointed people toward repentance and faith, not ritualistic obedience. John taught against greed and against the corrupt practices that had defined many of the religious elite, pointing to the passing away of the current temple system in favor of a new temple based upon "fruits keeping with repentance" (Luke 3:8). In Matthew, John targets the religious elites, calling the Pharisees and Sadducees a "brood of vipers," indicating once again the discontent toward the religious elites and a break from the established temple religion in Jerusalem (Matt 3:7).[42] John also said, "Even now the axe is laid to the root of the trees," depicting the old religious order as ready to be chopped down in favor of a new, spiritual kingdom based upon repentance. The way in which John the Baptist speaks of the established religious leaders, especially in Matthew and Luke, reveals a continuity with the prophets, such as Micah, who spoke of the corruption of Israel's leadership and judgment coming upon Zion.[43]

Jesus began his ministry among the Jewish people in a time of unrest and uncertainty regarding the future. The temple was still standing in Jerusalem, but despite its grandeur, many groups within Judaism were dissatisfied with the corrupt behavior of priests as well as the Roman influence upon them. Prophetic figures like John the Baptist typify this time period, yet John is unique in that he willingly stepped aside and pointed others to Jesus as the true Messiah.[44] "He who is mightier than I" was soon coming, one who would accomplish what no previous prophet could: this Messiah would "baptize you with the Holy Spirit," indicating that the presence of God was descending not only upon Jesus but upon all those who are united to him through faith (Luke 3:16).

JESUS, THE FULFILLMENT OF THE TEMPLE

The Jerusalem Temple is a key location for Jesus's ministry in the Gospels; however, Jesus's words and actions regarding the temple and its leadership reveal that, while he had profound respect for his Father's house, he also

42. Morris, *Gospel According to Matthew*, 58.

43. See Mic 3:5–12.

44. Marshall, *Gospel of Luke*, 146.

knew the temple would soon be destroyed.[45] The Gospels present Jesus as having authority over the temple, especially as he cleared out the money-changers and spoke of himself as a new temple. For the Jews, the temple was the primary symbol of God's presence, the place of prayer, offerings, and teaching.[46] It represented the core of a Jew's identity and was the gathering place for Jews near to and far from Jerusalem. Even though there was a growing dissatisfaction with the priesthood and the way in which they fulfilled their duties, the temple nonetheless was revered as the center of Israelite life.[47]

The Gospels portray Jesus as the fulfillment of the temple, for he himself brought the presence of God near through his sacrificial death and atonement for the sins of mankind. Furthermore, Jesus's teaching represents the ideal of what the temple represented: as people drew near to the presence of God and heard from the Law, the response should have been repentance and obedience. Yet often the people fell into heartless repetition as Isa 1:2–31 indicates. Therefore, Jesus represents the fulfillment of the promises regarding Zion because he represents the divine connection between heaven and earth, the "place" where redemption is offered freely to individuals who draw near in faith. Although each Gospel story has a unique perspective on Jesus, each book portrays Christ as the fulfillment of the temple and the beginning of God's eschatological kingdom, which would no longer require adherence to temple ritual but instead be built upon faith in the Son of God, who imparts the presence of God to individuals, making them a new temple.

The longing for Zion's restoration from Isa 65:17–25 is not left behind in the Gospels; rather, this hope is transformed as Jesus himself becomes the fulfillment of those hopes, transforming the imagery of the city of God into a redeemed people of God. Matthew presents Jesus as fulfilling eschatological expectations regarding the kingdom of God, and within those expectations is the belief in an eschatological temple with a renewed priesthood.[48] Mark emphasizes Jesus as the "Son of God," modeling the suffering servant of Isaiah and the one to accomplish God's redemptive mission. Mark's interest in the religious experts, who ironically seem to have the least understanding and are most resistant to faith in Jesus, also supports his belief in the

45. Joseph, *Jesus and the Temple*, 69.

46. Joseph, *Jesus and the Temple*, 70.

47. Edersheim, *Temple*, 61.

48. Barber, "Jesus as Davidic Temple Builder," 936.

radically new kingdom of God that will include gentiles and those previously considered outsiders.[49]

In Luke and Acts, Jesus is portrayed as the fulfillment of prophecy, bringing blessings upon those who respond to the message of Jesus as they enter the kingdom of God. This kingdom, however, is one of self-denial and wholehearted discipleship against the temptations of the world.[50] Luke also emphasizes the new community of faith, which has no boundaries and extends to all who believe the message of Jesus; thus, as the early Christians met in the temple to teach and pray in Acts, they had become a new temple through the Holy Spirit and were transformed into a family focused on love and service to those in need.[51] Therefore, though at times subtle, the synoptic Gospels portray Jesus as the fulfillment of prophecy and the one who would bring the kingdom of God to earth, a kingdom not based upon ethnicity or religious duty but upon faith in the Son of God. In Isa 2:2–4, the prophet envisioned a new Zion, a place into which the nations would flow, seeking justice and peace from the presence of God. The Gospels present such a place as the coming kingdom of God, entered only by faith in the Son of God.

The Fulfillment of Messianic Prophecy in Matthew

Matthew's understanding of Jesus as the fulfillment of the eschatological hopes of Israel begins in the opening verse by calling Jesus "the son of David, the son of Abraham" (Matt 1:1). The very first verse of the New Testament recalls God's promise to provide a "seed" to Abraham, who would bring forth a nation.[52] By also calling Jesus "the Son of David," Matthew associates Jesus's ministry with the covenant promises delivered to Nathan in 2 Sam 7:12–14, that a son of David would have his kingdom established by God, that he "shall build a house for my name," and "I will be to him a father, and he shall be to me a son" (2 Sam 7:13–14). Therefore, Matthew signals in his first words that Jesus would be both the seed of Abraham and the seed of David, completing the promises given to Israel's patriarch and king.[53] Matthew portrays Jesus as a new Israel as Jesus's story recaptures the exodus from Egypt (Matt 2:19–20), the crossing of the sea (Matt 3:13–17), temptation in the wilderness (Matt 4:1–11), and the arrival of the people at

49. Edwards, *Gospel According to Mark*, 19.

50. Marshall, *Gospel of Luke*, 35.

51. Bock, *Luke 1:1—9:50*, 37.

52. Lister, *Presence of God*, 132.

53. Lister, *Presence of God*, 132.

Sinai to receive the law in Jesus's sermon on the mount (Matt 5:1–2). Jesus does what Adam could not do and what God's chosen nation failed to accomplish, thus restoring God's eschatological plans.[54]

Matthew's unique focus on Jesus as "Immanuel" further conveys his picture of the kingdom of God as present among Israel because Christ has accomplished God's eschatological objectives (Matt 1:23). The beauty of Eden, the fearful sights and sounds of Sinai, the potent reminders in the tabernacle, and the manifest glory of God in Solomon's temple all spoke to one thing: the presence of God.[55] The primary component to the Zion symbol was that the presence of God rested on earth in a place: the permanence of Zion portrayed often in Psalms was not entirely eradicated by exile nor was it reinstated by the construction of the Second Temple; rather, the Gospels point to the Son of God himself as the "place" where heaven touches earth and where people find peace, healing, and the teaching promised in Isa 2:4. Prior to the sermon on the mount, Matthew records, "And he went throughout all Galilee, teaching in their synagogues and proclaiming the gospel of the kingdom and healing every disease and every affliction among the people" (Matt 4:23). Great crowds were following Jesus, longing to be near him or in his presence because, as they drew near to him, they were healed and were taught about the true nature of the kingdom of God.

When feeding the five thousand, the large crowd was willing to follow Jesus into a desolate place, apparently without access to food, in order to be near him (Matt 14:13–21). Again, Matthew is communicating that Jesus was fulfilling the eschatological promises concerning the kingdom of God: what prophets such as Isaiah saw through a blurry lens, the people drawing near to Jesus witnessed with their own eyes.[56] While the synoptic Gospels bear much resemblance, Matthew's keen interest on Jesus as the fulfillment of the promise of Yahweh's presence is developed through his repeated use of Old Testament typology and through his presentation of Jesus as the Messiah, whose kingdom is the new Israel.[57]

In Matt 16:18, in response to Peter's confession of Jesus as Messiah, Jesus promises to "build my church" upon "this rock," utilizing the imagery of temple construction to describe the way in which the church would be built.[58] Zechariah 4:7–9 spoke of the building of a temple during the time of Zerubbabel, but since the action of building the temple is linked with the

54. Lister, *Presence of God*, 133.

55. Duvall, *God's Relational Presence*, 170.

56. Stein, *Jesus the Messiah*, 84.

57. Duvall, *God's Relational Presence*, 179.

58. Barber, "Jesus as Davidic Temple Builder," 940.

prophet's teaching on the eschatological rebuilding of the temple, it is likely that such imagery was interpreted messianically.[59] Jesus is the Son of David who would build the eschatological temple; thus, Matthew is communicating in this passage that the church, through their confession of Christ as Messiah, is that temple.[60]

Zion in Isaiah was an image of both God's present and future actions toward his people, resulting in a restored kingdom and a redeemed people. Therefore, Matt 16:18 picks up that language regarding the church, or the new temple community, who represents the presence of God on earth through their confession of Christ. Furthermore, Jesus promises that "the gates of hell shall not prevail against it," meaning that the kingdom of God in the church would never die.[61] Just as the Zion tradition had developed the theological belief of God's sacred space from which the enemy was repulsed, the church would never be overthrown. Through this imagery, Jesus assured his followers that their confession of faith would be the cornerstone of the new temple, the church, built by faith that could not be shaken.

Matthew also connects Jesus with the temple in Matt 21:42 as Jesus cites Ps 118:22–23 during the parable of the tenants. In this context, it is plausible Jesus is speaking from within the temple, thus Matthew's identification of Jesus with the "cornerstone" of Ps 118 develops the theological concept that Jesus is a new temple.[62] Beyond this, however, Jesus had already stated, "I tell you, something greater than the temple is here," indicating that his role was greater than the temple or the Sabbath (Matt 12:6). In this sense, Matthew asserts that Jesus is of greater importance than the regulations held dear by the priests regarding the temple or Sabbath.[63]

Matthew focuses on Christ as the fulfillment of prophecy, and through this he connects the Zion theology of the Old Testament to the person of Christ. Not only does Christ fulfill all that Zion and its related prophecies represent but he also unpacks its intended meaning.[64] While many Old Testament prophecies concerning Zion and the temple included a physical sanctuary, several others portrayed Zion in ways unassociated with a structure. The temple would extend over all Jerusalem (Isa 4:5–6), over the whole land (Ezek 37:26–28), and even over the whole earth (Dan 2:44–45).[65] By

59. Barber, "Jesus as Davidic Temple Builder," 941.
60. Barber, "Jesus as Davidic Temple Builder," 941.
61. Morris, *Gospel According to Matthew*, 425.
62. Barber, "Jesus as Davidic Temple Builder," 943.
63. Nolland, *Gospel of Matthew*, 484.
64. Beale, *New Testament Biblical Theology*, 642.
65. Beale, *New Testament Biblical Theology*, 642.

associating Jesus with the cornerstone of Ps 118, by emphasizing Peter's confession of faith as the foundation of the church and by portraying Jesus as a greater temple, Matthew recaptures the primary drive of the Zion symbol: the presence of God that restores and redeems the righteous and expels darkness. The essence of the new temple in Christ is still the presence of God and his glory filling the earth, yet now the "temple" has become the worldwide community of faith in Christ through the Spirit.[66]

Jesus and the Temple in Mark

Where Matthew focused on Jesus as the fulfillment of prophecy and the one who would usher in a new kingdom of God and a new temple community, Mark portrays Jesus primarily as a man of action.[67] The kingdom Jesus preaches and inaugurates is not definable by the existing social norms; rather, it is based upon Jesus himself. This new kingdom contains outsiders, gentiles, and others thought to be unclean and unworthy of the Messiah's domain.[68] Mark's Gospel can be divided into two with the northern, Galilee ministry first and the events of Jerusalem last; within this, as Jesus's journey enters Jerusalem, Mark signifies Jesus's new kingdom through the rejection of the temple and a series of traps and tests Jesus encounters in chapters 11 through 13. Mark, sensitive to a gentile audience, portrays Jesus as the one who predicted the fall of the temple and its institutions and the arrival of the new kingdom of God. At the same, Mark also portrays Jesus as the true Son of God whose kingdom has broken out of the old temple into the new.[69] Zion, as a symbol of God's restorative acts toward Israel, was fulfilled as Christ replaced the old temple with a new kingdom based upon faith in the Son of God.

One of the most significant passages regarding Zion theology and the role of Jesus in transforming its meaning is Mark 11:1–19.[70] While there are numerous exegetical considerations surrounding the pericopes of both the cursing of the fig tree and the cleansing of the temple, taken together, the stories portray Jesus in a prophetic capacity, signaling the end of the old temple system and the beginning of the new. Jesus's entry in Jerusalem in Mark 11:1–10 connects to the Zion theology of Zechariah, where the

66. Beale, *New Testament Biblical Theology*, 643.

67. Edwards, *Gospel According to Mark*, 13.

68. Edwards, *Gospel According to Mark*, 18.

69. Beale, *New Testament Biblical Theology*, 647.

70. The cursing of the fig tree also appears in Matt 21:18–19; the cleansing of the temple is also found in Matt 21:12–13, Luke 19:45–47, and John 2:14–16.

prophet said, "Rejoice greatly, O daughter of Zion! Shout aloud, O daughter of Jerusalem" (Zech 9:9). Through metonymy, passages such as this equate Zion with Jerusalem, the temple city; thus, the triumphal entry portrays Jesus as fulfilling his role as a messianic king-priest.[71] However, Mark 11:11 shows that Jesus's first action in Jerusalem after the triumphal entry was to enter the temple, where he "looked around at everything" (Mark 11:11). The allusions to Zech 9:9–15 draw forth the theological focus on the prophets' "day of the Lord," but also recall Jesus's first words in Mark that "the time is fulfilled" (Mark 1:15).[72] Therefore, Mark's presentation of Jesus's arrival into Jerusalem and the temple, in conjunction with the cursing of the fig tree and the cleansing of the temple, point his audience to Jesus as the new temple.[73] Mark's presentation of Jesus's entry into Jerusalem is striking because of what does not happen, namely that, after Jesus arrives, he walks around the temple and then leaves for Bethany with his disciples.[74] Mark is indicating to his audience that the temple is not the home of the Son of God. Edwards notes, "Jesus is indeed the Messiah, but he is veiled and unrecognized. Even when he stands at the center of Israel's faith, he stands alone."[75] Despite the clamor of Jesus's entry into the city, he received no notice in the temple. This detail is unique to Mark, showing that the old Zion was fading, not to be deleted but to be remade through the Son of God.

The story of the cursed fig tree in Mark 11:12–14 is an example of intercalation, or the sandwiching of one story inside another.[76] This allows the stories of the fig tree and temple cleansing to be mutually interpreting, signaling that Mark's placement of the fig tree story predicts the destruction of the present temple.[77] In this sense, the priesthood has withered and Jesus represents the new temple that would replace the old ways. However, the allusion to Jer 7:11 in Mark 11:17 recalls an important motif regarding Zion: Zion's leadership had failed, and as God was looking for good fruit, he found none. Therefore, for Zion to be restored, God removed the leadership of Jeremiah's day through the Babylonian exile. To this, George Guthrie notes, "Might, then, we read Jesus' cursing of the fig tree in part as a dramatic enactment of this form of judgment?"[78] Furthermore, the quote from

71. Alvarez, "Temple Controversy in Mark," 133.

72. Alvarez, "Temple Controversy in Mark, 135.

73. Alvarez, "Temple Controversy in Mark, 148.

74. Edwards, *Gospel According to Mark*, 338.

75. Edwards, *Gospel According to Mark*, 338.

76. Guthrie, "Tree and the Temple," 27.

77. Guthrie, "Tree and the Temple," 27.

78. Guthrie, "Tree and the Temple," 32.

Isa 56:7 in verse 17 recalls another aspect of Zion theology important to Isaiah: the restored Zion would become a place where all the nations would seek Yahweh and be blessed by his presence. In Isa 56:7, Yahweh promised to "bring them to my holy mountain," indicating a time where a restored temple, after the unrighteous leaders were removed, would welcome in any who came to "love the name of the Lord" and "become his servants" (Isa 56:6–7). As Jesus explains the meaning of the fig tree in Mark 11:23, the context suggests that "this mountain" that can be thrown into the sea is the Temple Mount; thus, Jesus is speaking of the temple's removal because it had failed to produce the life it advertised.[79] Jesus himself would have to become the cornerstone of a new temple in order to provide life in abundance.

Mark portrays Jesus as the fulfillment of Zion symbolism in Mark 11 by portraying him as the one through whom Zion's failed leadership would be judged so that the temple could once again serve its purpose of drawing all people toward the presence of God. Jesus functions as a prophet as he curses the fig tree and cleanses the temple of its greedy practices because the people were not using the temple as it was intended. Jesus is not merely frustrated at the economic practices happening at the temple, but rather he showed that the purpose of the temple was the glory of God, and Israel's mission as a light to the nations had been dimmed.[80] Christ's radical action in the temple serves as a parable of judgment against the temple because it represented Israel's rejection of God's word and, ultimately, of Christ himself.[81]

Beyond fulfilling the hopes of a restored Zion from the Prophets, Jesus becomes the temple foreseen centuries earlier. By citing Isa 56:7 in Mark 11:17, Jesus is saying that the temple must be replaced because it was not fulfilling its eschatological goal of being a place that drew the nations to God's presence.[82] Sacred space is transformed in Mark 11–13 without emphasizing the temple in Jerusalem because Mark emphasizes the conflict between the teachings of Jesus and the temple in such a way that the two can no longer coexist as part of God's redemptive plans.[83] Isaiah spoke frequently of Zion as a sacred space, as God's holy mountain from which the Holy One of Israel reigned over the earth, and from which one day the Lord would restore his people. Mark presents Jesus himself as that sacred space, replacing the present system and inaugurating a new kingdom. At the

79. Beale, *God Dwells Among Us*, 81.

80. Carey, "Teachings and Tirades," 105.

81. Beale, *Temple and the Church's Mission*, 196.

82. Beale, *Temple and the Church's Mission*, 196.

83. Wenell, "Contested Temple Space," 323.

crucifixion in Mark's account, the temple curtain is torn in two from top to bottom immediately as Jesus takes his final breath, signaling the end of the temple's centrality to Israel's faith and the beginning of a new temple based upon the person of Jesus Christ.[84]

Where the physical place of Zion had been a primary concern in the Prophets, Mark reformulates the concept of sacred space in terms of the new kingdom the Son of God was building. Thus, Mark captures the ultimate hope of Isaiah's vision of a restored Zion and Ezekiel's vision of a new temple, which would be an everlasting, worldwide kingdom.[85] Mark understands the kingdom of God to be an active reign of God in the hearts of individuals, not a physical territory. The term "Zion" may be absent from Mark's theology, but the ultimate hope of the restored Zion expressed in the Prophets is fully realized through Christ's new kingdom, which creates a worldwide reign of God through faith in the Son of God.

The Church Becomes the New Zion in Luke–Acts

One striking feature of the New Testament concerning Zion is that the divine election of Jerusalem is nowhere to be found, at least explicitly.[86] Whereas passages such as Pss 46 and 132 expressed Zion's election by God as the source of confidence in God's covenant promises, the New Testament does not appear to be as concerned with the physical city of Jerusalem. However, the New Testament, perhaps Luke–Acts most clearly, does utilize Jerusalem as a motif to express its central purpose in the life and death of Jesus. Zion was the center of God's activity from the time of David through the time of Christ, and in Luke–Acts, it becomes clear that the temple in Jerusalem would become the launching pad for the new temple, the church.

Scholars have noted that the location of sacred space and the divine presence is transferred from the temple to Jesus and then to his followers, but this becomes essential as the mission of the church in Acts.[87] Klaus Baltzer sees a clear transfer of the presence of God to Christ and then to the members of the church through the Spirit. He said, "For the Christians the problem of the Temple was not solved by the destruction of the Temple . . . Luke solved the problem by means of his Christology. For him, Christ is the presence of God."[88] Acts further demonstrates this as the church meets

84. Wenell, "Contested Temple Space," 325.

85. Wenell, "Contested Temple Space," 337.

86. Schreiner, "Election and Divine Choice," 147.

87. Moore, "He Saw Heaven Opened," 38.

88. Baltzer, "Meaning of the Temple," 277.

openly in the temple courts but is then cast out in the stories of the apostles. Joel Green sees the temple's function transferred to Christians through their prayer and through the inclusive nature of Christ's kingdom in the sense that the presence of God is now realized in the individual's witness.[89] Similarly, another view highlights Luke's focus on the household as the new symbolic center for the followers of Jesus. What was once centered on the cultic function of the temple is now recreated through the prayer, worship, and testimony of the believers within everyday homes.[90] Either way, Luke's primary emphasis is that the temple's original purpose, the glory of God, is now alive and present within the community of Christ's followers, the Way. Ethnicity, socioeconomic status, and other previous limitations no longer matter because the outpouring of the Spirit through the gospel's witness has created a new temple community.

Luke's theological emphasis on this new temple can be seen in several key moments in both his Gospel and in Acts. While Luke follows Mark in the story of Jesus's triumphal entry into Jerusalem, he also adds his own unique view based upon his theological perspective as noted above. First, in Luke 19:46, he quotes Isa 56:7 without the phrase "for all nations" as Mark did, perhaps indicating that the temple had not become as such and was instead a home for Jewish avarice and arrogance.[91] Luke speaks of prayer as the revelatory actions of God in human affairs, so instead of a place that invited all nations to seek God, the temple's original function as the dwelling place of God was a "den of robbers" (Luke 19:46).[92] Secondly, unlike Mark, Luke precedes the pericope of Jesus clearing the temple with Jesus weeping over Jerusalem in Luke 19:41–44. Jeremiah had a similar lament, saying, "Behold, the cry of the daughter of my people from the length and breadth of the land: Is the Lord not in Zion? Is her King not in her?" (Jer 8:19). In Jeremiah's day, many of Jerusalem's leaders believed they had peace, but in reality, they had none. Similarly, Jesus laments that the city could have known peace with God, yet it did not because it rejected him.[93] An essential component to the Zion symbol in Jeremiah was that the presence of God had abandoned the city because the people had abandoned God. Likewise, Jesus, in a prophetic capacity, mourns over the condition of God's chosen city, knowing that he himself represented the peace the city needed but rejected. This furthers Luke's emphasis on Christ as the new temple, for no

89. Moore, "He Saw Heaven Opened," 39.

90. Moore, "He Saw Heaven Opened," 39.

91. Marshall, *Gospel of Luke*, 721.

92. Green, *Gospel of Luke*, 693.

93. Bock, *Luke 1:1—9:50*, 1561.

longer would peace be found in the temple or its city; rather, it could only be found in Jesus himself. In this sense, Jesus reenacts Jeremiah's lament over Jerusalem, but now the threat of physical exile is not in focus, for Jesus weeps over the spiritual emptiness within God's chosen dwelling place. In other words, Jesus fulfills the Zion symbolism that had conveyed a glorious restoration following judgment, and Jeremiah's new covenant would finally become reality through Christ's death and resurrection.[94]

Luke's emphasis on the temple as the launching pad for the new Christian movement can also be traced through his more positive presentation of the temple and his avoidance of describing the temple in direct opposition to Jesus.[95] Luke prefers to picture Israel's leaders in opposition to Jesus rather than the temple as a whole, as Mark does, for in passages such as Luke 19:47–48 and 21:37–38, Jesus teaches in the temple as crowds gather to hear him.[96] Luke had already cast a favorable light on figures in the temple, such as Zechariah, Simeon, and Anna in Luke 1–2; therefore, this follows his perspective that Jesus, and those who follow him, were becoming a new temple regardless of their affiliation or role within the temple institution.

In Luke 21:1–9, Luke presents another important perspective on the temple, its role in the present, and its destruction in the future. Ironically, Jesus praises a poor widow who places two small copper coins into the treasury box at the temple, affirming such an action as a sign of faith. Yet, as he listens to others speaking of the ornate nature of Herod's temple, Jesus foretells of its destruction, saying "the days will come when there will not be left here one stone upon another that will not be thrown down" (Luke 21:6). This scene is significant for the transformation of Zion symbolism, for it depicts Jesus as the turning point between the old system and the new. Micah prophesied harsh words against Jerusalem's leadership in Mic 3:1–12, claiming that the leaders "build Zion with blood" and that "because of you Zion shall be plowed as a field" (Mic 3:10, 12). Yet, in Mic 4, the prophet envisions a restored mountain becoming the place of righteousness and justice for those in need. Luke follows this thinking, showing that the temple itself was not standing in judgment but rather the rich leaders who had corrupted it would be judged.[97] The poor widow is praised by Jesus because she represents the kind of person for whom Jesus's gospel is intended, for she sacrificed much: literally "all her life," from the Greek *bios*.[98] The

94. Beale, *Temple and the Church's Mission*, 206.

95. Weinert, "Meaning of the Temple," 86.

96. Weinert, "Meaning of the Temple," 86.

97. Bock, *Luke 1:1—9:50*, 1645.

98. Bock, *Luke 1:1—9:50*, 1646.

widow typifies the new temple, filled with people whose faith leads them to sacrificial living and a rejection of worldly pleasures in pursuit of the kingdom of heaven.

If Jesus is the new temple, then like the previous versions in Eden, the wilderness, and on Mount Zion, the eschatological imperative is to expand the temple over the earth.[99] This falls in line with Luke's more favorable approach to the temple as a symbol of God's presence and of authentic Jewish life, for from there, the church begins its mission of expanding the gospel's influence on the earth. In the earlier chapters of Acts, the apostles are seen teaching and praying in the temple, based upon Jesus's own command that they were "not to depart from Jerusalem" until they were "baptized with the Holy Spirit" (Acts 1:4–5). In a sense, Jesus's presence among the disciples in Acts is reminiscent of God's activity among Israel in the Old Testament. To this, Douglas Buckwalter says Luke "depicts in Acts the exalted Jesus as present within the church in the same way that the OT describes transcendent Yahweh as immanently involved with Israel."[100] Luke builds upon this background in Acts through the works of the Holy Spirit as God's presence in the first church brings salvation to an expanding group of believers in Jerusalem and beyond.

Isaiah 66:18–23 depicts the eschatological kingdom of God as a place where the nations will come and see the glory of God, resulting in a regathering of God's people and even gentiles becoming like priests in his presence. On the day of Pentecost in Acts 2:7–12, Luke describes a large crowd filled with people from many nations gathered to hear Peter preach the good news of Jesus. The prophets' vision of a restored Zion was emerging as the nations gathered in Jerusalem to hear "the mighty works of God" as displayed in Jesus Christ (Acts 2:11). Peter cites Joel 2 in Acts 2:17–21, connecting the prophet's day of the Lord with the outpouring of the Holy Spirit. Thus, the presence of God in their midst had transferred from the Temple Mount to the hearts of individual believers.[101] The presence of God would now be dispersed by individuals from all nations who heard the gospel, repented, were baptized, and then returned home to the various nations listed in Acts 2:9–11. This evidences the progressive nature not only of God's redemptive acts toward humanity but also the way in which his presence dwells among people. Zion, as a theological symbol of God's presence,

99. Beale, *New Testament Biblical Theology*, 644.

100. Douglas Buckwalter, "Divine Saviour," in Howard and Peterson, *Witness to the Gospel*, 133.

101. Duvall, *God's Relational Presence*, 207.

was not being erased by the emerging church; rather, the church became the fulfillment of it as the physical temple was passing away.

Another important aspect of Zion symbolism in Acts is portrayed in Stephen's sermon. Zion represents the intersection of heaven and earth, or the sacred space from where the presence of God emanates to accomplish his will. Stephen's indictment of the religious leaders in Acts 7 is not as much against the temple as the people's attitude toward it and the God whose presence it represents.[102] Stephen, then, represents the beliefs of the early Christians, especially regarding their understanding of Scripture as pointing to Christ and the tendency of Israel's leaders to disobey God's word.[103] Toward the end of his speech, Stephen speaks of God's dwelling in heaven, quoting Isa 66:1–2, which reads, "Heaven is my throne, and the earth is my footstool. What kind of house will you build for me, says the Lord, or what is the place of my rest?" (Acts 7:49). Stephen's construal of heaven as the permanent sanctuary of God sets up the ending of the story, for as Stephen is nearing death, he gazes into heaven and sees God's glory, and Jesus standing, not sitting, at God's right hand.[104] Ultimately, Zion is fulfilled in heaven where the glory of God rests eternally. The earthly tabernacle and temple provided a house in which God chose to reveal his glory, but because of Jesus, Stephen sees his savior standing as a priest, serving in the heavenly temple on behalf of those who believe in him.[105] After this point in Acts, the church is pushed out of Jerusalem and the gospel begins to expand outward toward the nations. Thus, Stephen's story represents another turning point in the church's identity as a glimpse of heaven on earth; as they move forward by the Holy Spirit, the glory of God goes with them through the Spirit's power. As result of Stephen's speech, the focal location of God's activity shifts away from Jerusalem toward the nations.[106] Zion's goal in Isa 2:2–4 included the teaching of the nations in the presence of God, so as the church was expelled from Jerusalem, they took with them the good news of Jesus and the presence of God through the Spirit's indwelling. As in the Gospels, Acts provides a picture of a new Zion unbound by physical walls, which stretches across the earth to fill it with the glory of God. For creation to once again become a sanctuary for his glory, God commissioned the first Christians to become a new temple, carrying his presence to the ends of the earth.

102. Moore, "He Saw Heaven Opened," 44.

103. Padilla, *Acts of the Apostles*, 165.

104. Moore, "He Saw Heaven Opened," 44.

105. Moore, "He Saw Heaven Opened," 45.

106. Padilla, *Acts of the Apostles*, 168.

The Temple of Jesus's Body in John

Early in John's Gospel, the beloved disciple presents Jesus uniquely as the preexistent Son of God, who "became flesh and dwelt among us . . . full of grace and truth" (John 1:14). In his introduction, John communicates that Jesus is what the temple was pointing to, or that in himself, he was the fullness of the presence of God among the people.[107] John 1:14 expresses John's theology in a way that intentionally connects with the Old Testament portrayal of the word of God as God's self-expression. Thus, as Jesus "dwelt" among his creation, the presence of God was being revealed.[108] The goal of Zion was that the glory of God would stretch across the earth, filling it as a cosmic sanctuary once God purified his people and righteously judged those who refused to acknowledge him. This "realized eschatology" emphasizes Jesus's role as the fulfillment of the Old Testament messianic prophecies as well as the incarnate Word of God, now dwelling upon earth to complete God's redemptive plans for humanity.[109] Moses had experienced the glory of God in Exod 33 and the Lord had promised him, "My presence will go with you," yet even Moses was prevented from seeing the fullness of God's glory. Jesus, the incarnate Word, represented God in the fullness of grace and truth so that people could experience the presence of God as Moses had.[110] The incarnational presence of God in Jesus Christ is the primary way John portrays the fulfillment of the Old Testament Zion motif: Jesus represents new creation, a new temple, and a new and final priest, for only the Word of God could fulfill God's purposes.[111]

John 2: New Creation and New Temple

The fact that John begins the narrative of Jesus's ministry in John 2 with the wedding in Cana and the cleansing of the temple reveals his theological emphasis on the person of Jesus. The water at Cana was contained in jars for purification rites, and the Jerusalem temple was the central sanctuary for all of Israel: these stories foreshadow Christ's death, pointing the audience to Jesus as the centerpiece of a new temple.[112] In Cana, Jesus revealed his divinity through the miracle of transforming water into wine, and as the

107. Köstenberger, *John*, 41.
108. Duvall, *God's Relational Presence*, 282.
109. Keener, *Gospel of John*, 382.
110. Keener, *Gospel of John*, 449.
111. Duvall, *God's Relational Presence*, 286.
112. Koester, *Symbolism in the Fourth Gospel*, 82.

story spread, both Jews and Greeks would have understood this to be a sign that a deity was among them.[113] The restoration of the Davidic kingdom was associated with the presence of abundant wine (Amos 9:13), and the blessing on Judah in Gen 49 spoke of a future ruler who "washed his garments in wine" (Gen 49:11). The sheer volume of wine at the wedding miracle, possibly over 120 gallons, expresses the fulfillment of such prophecies and provides a hint to the theological depth of the miracle.[114] This explains how after Mary's simple request to remedy the lack of wine, Jesus responds that "my hour has not yet come," indicating that Jesus is interpreting this event through his messianic purpose.[115] Even the filling of the water jars to the brim indicates that the time for ceremonial purification is fulfilled: Jesus's new temple community, symbolized here by wine, would be permanently purified by his sacrificial blood.[116] These messianic symbols are reflected in Jesus's actions in Cana, and as a result, John wrote that Jesus "manifested his glory. And his disciples believed in him" (John 2:11). Scholars have further noted that John's chronology in chapters 1 and 2 point to a sense of realized eschatology.[117] John's counting of days suggests that "on the third day" in John 2:1 follows the previous section, meaning that the wedding miracle happened on a Sabbath, the seventh day. Jesus also heals the man at Bethesda (John 5:9–10) and restores the sight of the blind man (9:13–14) on the Sabbath; therefore, these signs produce a message that, with Jesus, there is new life.[118]

John intentionally connects the miracle at Cana with the cleansing of the temple in John 2:13–22, for John presents the story, found in the Synoptics close to passion week, as a prophetic event that would shape John's theological purposes throughout his gospel.[119] Furthermore, Jesus's conversation with the Jews is unique from the Synoptic account, for Jesus appears to allude to Zech 14:20 instead of Isa 56, as in Mark's account.[120] Jesus's words, "Destroy this temple and in three days I will raise it up," may point to

113. Koester, *Symbolism in the Fourth Gospel*, 86.

114. Kerr, *Temple of Jesus' Body*, 69.

115. Carson, *Gospel According to John*, 172.

116. Carson, *Gospel According to John*, 174.

117. Kerr, *Temple of Jesus' Body*, 70.

118. Kerr, *Temple of Jesus' Body*, 70.

119. Carson notes that the most likely view of the temple cleansing so early in John 2 is that John moved this story toward the beginning of his narrative for programmatic reasons. A small number of scholars believe John's timing is correct while the Synoptics moved the story later; some also hold to two temple cleansings. Carson, *Gospel According to John*, 177.

120. Koester, *Symbolism in the Fourth Gospel*, 87.

the Jewish eschatological belief in a glorious new temple built in a new age of salvation, but John is quick to narrate that Jesus "was speaking about the temple of his body" (John 2:19, 21). It is possible that Jesus is unconcerned with the physical temple in this scene, but more likely, this has a double meaning: on one level, he was speaking to the destruction of the temple that would be raised up in a new form as the church, and on another, he was describing what would happen to him as he would die and be raised to life again.[121] In this sense, the cleansing of the temple parabolically captures the essence of Jesus's ministry: he came to establish a new kingdom built upon the temple of his own body.[122] In other words, Jesus is the presence of God that the temple represented; thus, through his death and resurrection, there would be no need for the Jerusalem temple. Zechariah 6:12–13 spoke of the messianic "branch" who would build a temple and rule in glory, and the Davidic covenant in 2 Sam 7:12–13 also pointed to the final building of the temple as a messianic task.[123] Therefore, John's presentation of Jesus cleansing the temple rests in his introduction of Jesus as "the Word," which "became flesh, and dwelt among us" (John 1:14). Jesus is a better temple, a complete temple without flaw and the final sacrificial offering to fulfill the hopes of a purified Zion, free from the threat of enemies and free to enjoy the presence of God.

If Jesus is the new temple, then the life of that temple is only found in him. The Old Testament depicted this life in the river that flowed from God's presence in the Eden sanctuary and the tree of life therein, and Ezekiel saw an eschatological temple with trees of life that bring healing.[124] Zion was the intersection between heaven and earth, a symbol of God's covenant promises to David and his divine choice of Israel among all the nations. The temple was the physical symbol of all this, and it represented God's presence among the people. However, the temple in Jesus's day, while still significant for its symbolic meaning and religious function, did not contain the same glory experienced in Solomon's time. John presents Jesus as the true temple because through him was the way to true worship of God. George Beasley-Murray states, "This again is to be understood in terms of eschatological fulfillment rather than condemnation of the old order of worship; for the death that puts an end to all sacrifices is one with the exaltation of Christ to Lordship and leads to the age of the Spirit."[125] In John 2:21, "body," from

121. Beale, *Temple and the Church's Mission*, 211.

122. Perrin, *Jesus the Temple*, 91.

123. Beale, *Temple and the Church's Mission*, 212.

124. Beale and Kim, *God Dwells Among Us*, 85.

125. Beasley-Murray, *John*, 40.

soma, is only used three other times by John, all in the context of the crucifixion and resurrection.[126] It is plausible, then, that in foreshadowing Jesus's death in chapter 2, John is communicating that Jesus is the new temple, for through his death and resurrection, all who believe become united with Christ as his body. This is why John includes in 2:22 that "when therefore he was raised from the dead, his disciples remembered that he had said this" (John 2:22). Because of this post-resurrection perspective, John indicates that Jesus is the new creation in the miracle at Cana, and he is the new temple in the cleansing of the temple grounds.

John 4: Jesus, the New Place of Worship

Another way in which John conveys the transformation of Zion symbolism in Christ is through the story of the woman at the well in John 4. In John 2:17, Jesus had revealed that he would become the ultimate Passover lamb, fulfilling and replacing the need for any future sacrifice. Jesus replaces both the temple and the rituals associated with it, becoming a new temple through which his followers would experience life and joy in the presence of God.[127] Therefore, Jesus's discourse with the Samaritan woman further proves that Jesus is himself the replacement of the temple structure because he has become the "place" of worship for all people. In John 4:20, the Samaritan woman argues that her ancestors chose Mt. Gerizim ("this mountain") for the worship of God, yet "you [plural] say that in Jerusalem is the place."[128] While her argument may be a deflection from Jesus's personal knowledge regarding her husbands, she nonetheless opens the door for Jesus to announce "the hour is coming . . . when the true worshipers will worship the Father in spirit and truth, for the Father is seeking such people to worship him" (John 4:23). Jesus chooses neither site as the proper place of worship, but rather states his arrival ("the hour is coming, and is now here") is bringing forth a time when true worship will be through the Spirit (John 4:23).[129]

Such a statement from Jesus aligns with the previously established claims in John's Gospel that Jesus would become in himself the new temple, the new "place" people experienced the presence of God and worshiped him in spirit and truth. The Word, standing before the Samaritan woman, is the incarnate presence of God, God's own self-expression that leads people to

126. Kerr, *Temple of Jesus' Body*, 93.

127. Kerr, *Temple of Jesus' Body*, 167.

128. Köstenberger, *John*, 155.

129. Beasley-Murray, *John*, 62.

true worship.[130] D. A. Carson says, "In that Word, now become flesh, he may be known as truly as it is possible for human beings to know him."[131] The essence of Zion symbolism in Isa 2 was that "out of Zion shall go forth the law, and the word of the Lord from Jerusalem" (Isa 2:3). In addition, Isa 4:2–5 foresaw a day when the Lord's branch would purify the remnant of Jerusalem and fill the city with the glory of God. These images are recaptured through Jesus as he became the true place of worship, for as those who believed in him were purified to express true worship, they received the Word and were transformed by him. The Samaritan's argument over the center for worship was now irrelevant, because the one who would free people to worship in spirit and truth had come.

John 14: The Father's House

In Jesus's farewell discourse with his disciples, he speaks of his "Father's house" that contains "many rooms" (John 14:2). While the reference to the "Father's house" is often interpreted as a reference to heaven, it could also be speaking to the temple of Jesus's body, which is a recurring theme in John.[132] Through John, temple language had changed from the "holy place" (*hieron*) in 2:14, to "Father's house" (*oikos*) in 2:16, to "temple of his body" (*naos*) in 2:21, moving away from the earthly structure toward Christ himself.[133] This movement in John continues as it extends beyond one person to a group in a household, living like a family in the ancient world as extensions, or rooms, were added onto a father's house.[134] Furthermore, the mention of "rooms," from *mone*, can best be understood as the dwelling of the Father and Son within the believer, not only as a spatial term.[135] In this sense, the purpose of Jesus's words to his disciples was to bring them comfort due to his impending departure by reminding them that his presence was the gift they needed most. The Spirit would come as a result of Jesus leaving earth, resulting in the permanent indwelling of the presence of God within his disciples. In other words, the community of believers becomes the household of God through the indwelling Spirit.[136] To this, Robert Gundry notes, "The Father's

130. Carson, *John*, 225.
131. Carson, *John*, 225.
132. Keener, *Gospel of John*, 916.
133. Behr, *John the Theologian*, 173.
134. Behr, *John the Theologian*, 173.
135. Behr, *John the Theologian*, 173.
136. Behr, *John the Theologian*, 174.

house is no longer heaven, but God's household or family."[137] As the people became a new temple, they took on the functions of it and served one another as God's priesthood.[138] Zion, as a term often referring to the renewed people of God, is fulfilled in Christ who, through the Spirit, regenerates believers and unites them under one household. The permanence of Zion is also reflected in John 14, for Jesus promises to return to his own, "that where I am you may also be" (John 14:3). Jesus reaffirms this in 14:18, saying, "I will not leave you as orphans," once again speaking to the familial nature of God's household and Jesus's unity with both the Father and his disciples. If the goal of Zion is to fill the earth with the glory of God, it follows in John 14 that this would be accomplished through the indwelling presence of God in this new temple as they spread across the earth. As people came into the Jerusalem temple to seek forgiveness and atonement, now Jesus and, by the Spirit, his followers would become the source for the whole world to hear the good news of forgiveness through the Son.[139]

In context of Jesus's departure, the Father's house, with its many rooms, would be filled because of Jesus's sacrificial death and resurrection; thus, Jesus reassures his disciples that if he departs, he will return. The structure of the Jerusalem temple is no longer the center of God's purposes, for Jesus has become what the temple could never be. In Solomon's day, the people stood in awe of the glory of God revealed at the temple (1 Kgs 8), but now the disciples were meeting face to face with God's final Word. If the temple of Jesus's body is in view in this passage, then this expresses the transformation of the temple from the static location in Jerusalem into the person of Jesus Christ. This is further evidenced by Jesus's statement that "you know the way to where I am going" (John 14:4). Jesus himself was the way (John 14:6), indicating that no longer would the Father's house be represented by a building but rather Christ himself.[140]

G. K. Beale stated, "The substantial essence of the new temple is still the glory of God; however, that glory is no longer confined within a material building but instead is revealed openly to the world in Christ."[141] For followers of Jesus, knowing him equates to knowing the Father; thus, dwelling in Christ equates to dwelling with the Father in both a present and eternal sense. In Rev 21:22, John sees "no temple in the city, for its temple is the Lord God the Almighty and the Lamb." In John 14, Jesus reveals that the

137. Gundry, "In My Father's House," 70.

138. Behr, *John the Theologian*, 175.

139. Beale, *Temple and the Church's Mission*, 217.

140. Barker, *King of the Jews*, 351.

141. Beale, *New Testament Biblical Theology*, 642.

place prepared for his followers is less about heavenly rewards and more about unity with God in his presence. The way to God, the truth about who God is, and the abundant life God provides, all exist through the Son and because of his role as the final sacrifice and high priest before God.

JESUS, THE NEW ZION

In the Prophets, the Zion symbol was moving toward its eschatological fulfillment, for God had promised he would redeem a people for himself (Jer 31:31–34), return to Zion in glory (Isa 40:3–5), and draw the nations to his presence and make people priests to declare his glory (Isa 66:18–23). Alongside the hope of a restored Zion was the imagery of the Lord's branch, from the stump of Jesse, who would be filled with the Spirit of the Lord and bring peace to the nations (Isa 11:1–10). The Gospels and Acts confidently and without reservation present Jesus Christ as the fulfilment of these prophecies. Jesus is not only the Savior of the world but he is the fullness of God's presence among his people as Immanuel (Matt 1:23). Jesus, then, is the fulfillment of the Zion symbol in his capacity as the Word of God who indwells individual believers with the presence of God through the Spirit. The purification of Zion, the holy mountain from which righteous teaching extends, and the place to which the nations would flow, are depicted in the Gospels and Acts as being completed in the person of Jesus. Moses, the Jewish faith, and the temple in Jerusalem could not accomplish what Jesus did, so the Gospels proclaim Jesus as the only true source of forgiveness and abundant life.[142] Christ is the temple to which all previous versions pointed and anticipated because he is the incarnate presence of God on earth.[143]

Essential to Acts is the picture of Christ as the cornerstone of the new temple in the emerging church. The statement, "This Jesus is the stone that was rejected by you, the builders," is perhaps the most direct identification of Jesus with the beginning of a new temple (Acts 4:11).[144] The allusion to Ps 118:22 (also found in Mark 12:10 and Matt 21:42) refers to the chief stone of the temple.[145] Therefore, Christ is identified as the cornerstone of the true temple. Acts 3:25–26 identified Jesus with the blessing of the nations in Gen 22:18, so with the imagery of the covenant with Abraham alongside the building of a temple, Christ is portrayed as the fulfillment of that recurring

142. Porter, *Messiah*, 188.

143. Beale, *New Testament Biblical Theology*, 632.

144. Beale, *Temple and the Church's Mission*, 237.

145. Beale, *Temple and the Church's Mission*, 237.

promise.[146] In the first-century context, it is virtually impossible to separate obedience to the Law, adherence to the temple cult, and faithfulness to God: all these are essential aspects of what it meant to be Jewish in the time of Jesus. In the Protestant tradition, it is an easier task to break away from the temple as the center of faith because Jesus himself has become that "place."[147] In other words, Jesus's purpose was always to fulfill what Zion hoped for: the glory of God filling the earth. Through Jesus, the imagery associated with Zion expands beyond Jerusalem to a spiritual kingdom, and as the Holy Spirit pushed the church outward from the city, the message of Jesus went with it. Jesus is the new Zion, because in him the poor and oppressed find justice, the repentant find forgiveness, and the lost sheep of Israel are reunited with their Shepherd.

Finally, Jesus is the new Zion because his suffering, death, and resurrection are described as the destruction of the Jerusalem temple in John 2:19.[148] In the Prophets, it becomes clear that Zion must suffer through judgment before it can be purified and redeemed for God's glory. Isaiah's suffering servant in Isa 52–53 represented Israel as a whole but also pointed to one who "poured out his soul to death and was numbered with the transgressors; yet he bore the sin of many, and makes intercession for the transgressors" (Isa 53:12). In his capacity as both the suffering servant and the high priest before God, Jesus suffered and was crushed for the sins of his people; yet after his death, he was resurrected as vindication of his righteousness. Jeremiah described Daughter Zion as desolate, unrepentant, and exposed before her enemies; yet, after her time of punishment, God promised to remake his people and fulfill what he started in Eden. The Lord promises, "I will put my law within them, and I will write it on their hearts. And I will be their God, and they shall be my people" (Jer 31:33). This, too, is reenacted and completed in Christ's death and resurrection, for as he returned to heaven, the Spirit indwelt the believers and created a new people, or a new temple community, gathered by God for his glory upon the earth.[149] Jesus is the fulfillment of Zion symbolism and is himself the new Zion, for no longer do people need to approach a temple to access the presence of God because he now indwells the hearts of individuals.

146. Beale, *Temple and the Church's Mission*, 237.

147. Perrin, *Jesus the Temple*, 184.

148. Son, *Zion Symbolism in Hebrews*, 66.

149. Porter, *Messiah*, 244.

5

Transformed Zion Symbolism in the New Testament Letters

Zion, the symbol of God's presence on earth, continues to find new meaning through the church of Jesus Christ as individual believers live with the indwelling presence of the Spirit and become unified as a new temple community called the body of Christ. Christ, then, is the beginning of the fulfillment of all the prophecies regarding an eschatological temple.[1] Paul wrote, "All the promises of God find their Yes in him," indicating that Jesus is the beginning and the fulfillment of God's eschatological plans (2 Cor 1:20). In this sense, the promises regarding Zion and the hope built into the Prophets concerning both the day of the Lord and a future restored kingdom point to Jesus and are complete in him. If this is true, it is also true that the members of the church, Christ's body, as agents of reconciliation upon earth (2 Cor 5:19) represent him in their capacity as "a spiritual house, to be a holy priesthood, to offer spiritual sacrifices acceptable to God through Jesus Christ" (1 Pet 2:5). Followers of Jesus are "living stones," built upon "him, the living stone" as God's new temple, which is not based upon a hill called Zion (1 Pet 2:4). The imagery associated with the future Zion is transferred to the church, maintaining the theological significance of the presence and glory of God, which emanate from the place he inhabits.

Paul primarily expresses the Zion symbol and its related theology through an explanation of the church as a new temple community, both at an individual and corporate level. Key passages in Paul's writing include Rom 11:25–36, 1 Cor 3:16–17, and Gal 4:21–31. Paul develops this theology

1. Beale, *New Testament Biblical Theology*, 633.

of the church as a new temple through his exegesis of the Old Testament and through the lens of Christ as the fulfillment of the messianic hope for Israel. Paul's emphasis on the church as the unified body of Christ and the role of the individual believer as a temple of the Spirit reflects his understanding of the priesthood of believers as representatives of God's presence on earth. For Paul, the Spirit is the renewed presence of God among his people, building the church into a spiritual house with Christ as the cornerstone.[2] The symbolism of Zion as the center of God's eschatological plans has been transformed as Christ, through the work of the Spirit, has indwelt believers and made them into a new temple stretching across the earth.

Hebrews 12:18–24 provides one of the clearest examples of how Zion symbolism has transformed in the New Testament, now representing the eschatological kingdom of God in an already-not-yet fashion. The author's present perfect verb in "you have come to Mount Zion" reflects the realized eschatology in the death and resurrection of Christ, encouraging the reticent believers to hold fast to their faith because it is both now and not yet (Heb 12:22).[3] Through Christ, the heavenly Zion has become reality in the present but also a confident hope for the future.

Revelation mentions Zion as the location where Jesus will stand victoriously with his redeemed saints (Rev 14:1), which creates an image of Zion as the final place of victory for the Lamb over evil. Coupled with that imagery is John's vision of the new Jerusalem, coming down from heaven and resting in God's eternal presence. Both images convey the church's relationship to God and its status as the eternal people of God. In the end, Zion finds its home upon the new earth, where no temple is needed because the presence of God is now the center of existence, and God's people eternally dwell with him in complete peace and joy.[4] This chapter will demonstrate that key passages in the New Testament epistles and Revelation show how the Zion symbolism prevalent in the Old Testament has been transferred to the church through Christ and finds its ultimate fulfillment in the heavenly city of God where his people dwell with him forever.

2. Fee, *Paul, the Spirit*, 11.

3. Son, *Zion Symbolism in Hebrews*, 173.

4. Schreiner, *Joy of Hearing*, 156.

THE CHURCH AS THE NEW TEMPLE IN PAUL'S THEOLOGY

The term "Zion" occurs twice in Paul's letters: in Rom 9:33 and 11:26 within quotations of Isa 28:16 and Isa 59:20–21, respectively.[5] In the context of Rom 9–11 with Paul's teaching about the spiritual hardening of Israel, the salvation that has come to the gentiles, and the eschatological redemption of Israel, these two references to Zion recall the major Zion themes associated with Israel's judgment and restoration brought about by God himself. In another key passage, Gal 4:21–26, Paul allegorizes Sarah and Hagar, citing two versions of Jerusalem: the present, and "the Jerusalem above," described as "free" and "our mother" (Gal 4:25). This passage indicates Paul's understanding of a future city of God, a heavenly city that corresponds to those who have faith in Christ, as opposed to the present city that corresponds to the law and those who are not "children of promise" (Gal 4:28). A third important Pauline text is 1 Cor 3:16–17, which speaks to the concept of the church, at a corporate level, becoming "God's temple" that is "holy" (1 Cor 3:17). In each of these instances, Paul's theology draws from Zion symbolism, especially regarding its transformation in Christ and how the church has become the new temple community that represents the presence of God upon the earth.

Zion in Romans 9–11

In Rom 9:30–33, Paul writes about saving faith and the reality that Gentiles were obtaining righteousness through faith, although many Jews were stumbling over Christ in their efforts to obtain righteousness by following the law. He connects both the "tested stone" of Isa 28:16 and the "stone of stumbling" from Isa 8:14 to Christ. Christ is this rock, the foundation stone laid in Zion that causes some to build a life of faith while others stumble over it.[6] First Peter 2:4–8 uses the two Isaiah passages in a similar way, leading some scholars to suggest that utilizing the motif of Christ as the Old Testament "stone" had become a common practice in the early church.[7] What was true in Isaiah's day continued to be true in Paul's day: Israel was given a sure foundation, yet for many, it had become a hindrance to faith. In other

5. The reference to the "stone of stumbling" in Rom 9:33 may also be in reference to Isa 8:14, which says, "He will be a sanctuary; but for the two houses of Israel, He will be a stone to stumble over and rock to trip over."

6. Morris, *Epistle to the Romans*, 376.

7. Morris, *Epistle to the Romans*, 376.

words, Zion was a symbol that should have led the Israelites toward faith in God alone, for he was their source of life, protection, and wisdom; yet, in their idolatry and pride, Israel failed to pursue God by faith.[8]

Romans 9:33 is an example of Paul's exegesis of key Old Testament passages relating to Zion symbolism: in his quotation of Isaiah, he interprets the stone to be Christ himself. Isaiah 28:16 reads, "Whoever believes will not be in haste," yet Paul wrote, "whoever believes in him will not be put to shame" (Rom 9:33).[9] Paul's theological emphasis is consistent with the purpose of the Isaiah passages: those who place their faith in God alone will find refuge, but those who seek security in other places will be judged. Paul understands this as part of God's sovereignty, leading some Jews to believe and others to be hardened.[10] God's cornerstone, a precious stone and a stumbling stone, is Christ himself. Zion's symbolic function in Rom 9:33 is to connect the lack of faith in Isaiah's day with the lack of faith by many Jews in Paul's day: both are a result of God's sovereignty, but they also point to Christ as the true Zion, the rock on which God's household of faith would be built. This faith that spared believers in Isaiah's day from judgment would likewise provide believers in Christ with an eschatological hope centered on what Christ had done.[11] Zion in Rom 9:33 represents the "place" of eschatological salvation from judgment, but that place is no longer a city or a physical temple but Jesus Christ.

In Rom 11, Paul continues this line of reasoning, appealing to the Old Testament to show that God had not forsaken his people but, because of their disobedience, a "partial hardening" had come upon them (Rom 11:25). Paul then quotes Isa 59:20–21 as proof that "all Israel will be saved" after "the fullness of the Gentiles has come in" (Rom 11:25). One aspect of Zion symbolism in the Prophets, especially in Jeremiah, is that Zion (the people) had become more like its enemies than the people of God; thus "Daughter Zion," the vulnerable and weak people, were exposed to exile and judgment by God. Ironically, Zion was judged as if it had become like the foreign nations.[12] Jeremiah exclaimed, "Has a nation changed its gods, even though they are no gods? But my people have changed their glory for that which does not profit" (Jer 2:11). In Rom 9–11, Paul speaks of Israel's salvation in similar terms, pointing to Christ as the stumbling stone but also

8. Keener, *Romans*, 123.

9. Paul's quotations of Isa 28:16 and 8:14 follow the LXX, but he quotes neither verse exactly. Schreiner, *Romans*, 540.

10. Schreiner, *Romans*, 541.

11. Keener, *Romans*, 123.

12. Beale, *We Become What We Worship*, 208.

showing that the reality of Israel's condition was God's sovereign plan. Paul calls this a "mystery," meaning that he was speaking of something previously hidden that has now been revealed by God so all could understand.[13] Therefore, the "mystery" is that now Christ has been revealed, and the prophesied "deliverer from Zion" has come, opening the door for Israel and the gentiles to receive salvation. The promises of a restored Zion and a redeemed Israelite nation gathering as the Lord returns were not forsaken or forgotten; rather, they have become fully realized in Christ. The hope that all the nations would stream to Zion is fulfilled in Christ, because only in him will both Israel and the nations find eternal rest (Isa 2:3–4).

Paul also indicates in Rom 11:26 that he believes "all Israel will be saved." After the time of hardening and once the gentiles have received salvation, God's eschatological purposes for Israel will continue.[14] There is disagreement over what Paul means by "Israel" in this passage, for he could be speaking only of people who believe in Jesus as Messiah, called "sons and daughters of Abraham" (Gal 3:7–9), the true circumcision (Phil 3:3), and the "Israel of God" (Gal 6:16).[15] Thus, it is possible that Paul is including gentile believers, but because of his discussion on the gentiles being grafted into Israel and Israel's lack of faith regarding Christ, it is plausible that Paul speaks of Israel in Rom 11 as ethnic Jews distinct from gentiles.[16] However, James Dunn articulates a distinction between Paul's usage of "Jew" and "Israel," noting that Paul's use of "Israel" in Rom 9–11 allows him to include the elect gentiles, since "Israel" denotes God's spiritual election of the people.[17]

That "the Deliverer will come from Zion" reminds Paul's audience of Zion's role in God's eschatological kingdom and a singular figure who would arise from there as Ps 2, Isa 11, and Zech 9 prophesied. The time of Israel's disbelief would be temporary, according to Paul, because the promises recorded in the Prophets would not be forsaken. Israel becoming a light to the nations (Isa 42:6; 60:3–4) was fulfilled in Christ, but not at the exclusion of Israel as a nation.[18] Dunn states that Israel appears "caught between present failure and future fullness," and the Zion symbol along with it.[19] While Christ had opened the door for salvation for God's elect, both Jew and gentile, God's eschatological purposes for Israel were not yet complete. Leon

13. Mounce, *Romans*, 224.
14. Schreiner, *Romans*, 614.
15. Schreiner, *Romans*, 614.
16. Schreiner, *Romans*, 614.
17. Dunn, *Theology of Paul*, 506.
18. Dunn, *Theology of Paul*, 523.
19. Dunn, *Theology of Paul*, 523.

Morris notes that Christ coming from Zion in Rom 11:26 could either be a reference to the incarnation and its resulting salvation coming out of Zion or to Christ's return as the Savior comes to glory in Zion.[20] Paul may also use the allusion to Isa 59:20 as a way of appeasing the Jews who were denying Christ, reminding them that Israel's hope rested in one who would deliver his people from Zion.[21] Either way, Rom 11:26 points to Zion as the place from which the Messiah will deliver his people, resulting in the removal of sins in both a present and future sense for Israel.

If Paul understands Zion in this passage in a spiritual sense as the heavenly city of God, then it follows that Zion represents the place from which righteousness is made available to all who "go up to the mountain of the Lord," as Isa 2:3 foresaw. Paul held the identity of Israel in tension as he longed for his brethren to be saved, for "Israel" appears to represent both the spiritual children of Abraham and the ethnic Jews who are still blessed under God's covenant promises.[22] Although Christ had fulfilled the hopes that a "Deliverer will come from Zion," the promises that Zion would be filled with the redeemed of Israel and become a light to the nations remained a future fulfillment. Furthermore, "all Israel" in Rom 11:26 does not contradict the salvation of the remnant in Rom 9, for Paul is speaking of "all Israel" at the end of history, not throughout its entire history.[23] In passages such as Isa 35:8–10, the prophet foresees a time when the "ransomed of the Lord shall return and come to Zion with singing" (Isa 35:10). The imagery of the redeemed returning to Zion on "the Way of Holiness" envisions a future remnant, not all ethnic Jews, returning to God and his presence. For Paul, these images of Zion are revealed in Christ but are still pointing to a future redemption for the chosen people of God. In the meantime, Christ's salvation comes to all whom God has chosen, so that "he may have mercy on all" (Rom 11:32).

The Jerusalem Above in Galatians 4:21–26

Another example of Paul's theology regarding Zion's transformation through Christ occurs within his allegorical teaching of Sarah and Hagar in Gal 4. While there are numerous interpretive opinions regarding this portion of Galatians, within Paul's discussion of Sarah and Hagar, he says, "The Jerusalem above is free, and she is our mother" (Gal 4:26). The core

20. Morris, *Romans*, 421.
21. Dunn, *Theology of Paul*, 529.
22. Dunn, *Theology of Paul*, 532.
23. Schreiner, *Romans*, 622.

argument from Paul is that there are two separate communities: one is under the law, and the other is free.[24] In the present situation, the community based upon the law is persecuting the free, yet ultimately, this will be reversed because the free people belong to the heavenly city of God. The concept of two cities, or an earthly and a heavenly Jerusalem, is unique to Paul in this passage, yet the way in which he writes suggests that this is not a new concept to him or his audience.[25] Hebrews and Revelation make use of the duality between the heavenly and earthly cities, but for Paul, it primarily relates to the theological purposes he has concerning the Galatians' struggle between the law and grace. Nonetheless, the presence of this "Jerusalem above" indicates that Paul understood an inaugurated eschatology in which Christians, belonging to the "free" community, are citizens of the heavenly city of God. This heavenly city is not bound by the rituals of the temple or by the Law of Moses but is the perfected city of the saints, who have been set free through faith in Christ.[26] The future home of believers was also something experienced in the present: by the Spirit, the Galatian believers are citizens of heaven as if they had been born there.

The imagery of Zion or Jerusalem being "our mother" in Gal 4:26 may be an allusion to Ps 87:5, which, in the Septuagint, could be interpreted as saying, "Mother Zion, a person will speak."[27] This psalm speaks of Zion as the center of life, eventually, for all the nations of earth.[28] Envisioning Zion as the center of worship and the home for many peoples, Ps 87 relates to Paul's concept of the heavenly Jerusalem as the eternal home for the true people of God set free in Christ. Psalm 87 focuses on gentiles who one day will make Zion their home because of the presence of Yahweh in the city; thus, the concept of being "born" in Zion creates a spiritual kinship among believers, which Paul expresses in Gal 4.[29] In a broader sense, Jerusalem is the "mother" city because it is through God's chosen people that the nations have come to salvation.[30] Since salvation in Christ originated with his death and resurrection in Jerusalem, all those who are chosen for salvation belong to the city, since it is the birthplace of their salvation. The hope of a remade city of God is fully realized in Christ, who has now made his followers part

24. Siegal, "Hebrew-Based Traditions," 406.

25. Bruce, *Epistle to the Galatians*, 221.

26. Dunn, *Theology of Paul*, 543.

27. Brannan, *Lexham English Septuagint*. Ps 87:5 (ESV) is equivalent to Ps 86:5 (LXX), which reads "Μήτηρ Σιων, ἐρεῖ ἄνθρωπος."

28. Tate, *Psalms 51–100*, 387.

29. Tate, *Psalms 51–100*, 390.

30. Perez-Gondar, "New Jerusalem as Mother," 546.

of the heavenly community. Galatians 4:26 also relates to the imagery of Isa 66:7–11 where, in the context of new creation, Zion is pictured as a mother who will give birth to sons as the fulfillment of God's promises concerning Israel's salvation.[31] Thomas Schreiner says this is an example of Paul's "already but not yet eschatology," meaning that the heavenly Jerusalem represents the inauguration of the covenant promises of new creation.[32] Believers, like Sarah gave birth to the son of promise Isaac, have become sons in God's heavenly kingdom through the Spirit's saving work.[33]

Paul mingles the temporal and spatial aspects of the present and eschatological cities in Gal 4:26 to portray the heavenly Jerusalem as a present reality to which true believers in Christ belong.[34] Ronald Fung notes this has also been called "the merging of temporal sequence and spatial gradation," or the way in which the present community of faith embodied the eschatological reality of their heavenly citizenship.[35] This aligns with the Old Testament and Jewish apocalyptic tradition that the world was not coming to an end but rather God's eschatological actions, including the coming of the Messiah, would result in a new creation.[36] Jerusalem, as the chosen city of God, was part of this remade creation; thus, the Galatian Christians experienced new creation through their entrance into the heavenly city. This further develops the already-not-yet reality of Zion, for even though new creation is expected in the future, the process has already begun in Christ.

Zion, as expressed in passages such as Ps 87 and Isa 62, is the beautiful, perfected city in which the people are called "the Holy People" because they are "the Redeemed of the Lord" (Isa 62:12). For Paul, this promise was both a present reality for those in Christ and a future expectation. Since Christians no longer belong to the earthly Jerusalem, which is ruled by the law, they are free to experience the spiritual blessings of a greater Zion, an eternal home filled with the presence of God. Hebrews 11:10 speaks to this new city being built by faith, a "city that has foundations, whose designer and builder is God" (Heb 11:10). Martin Luther understood this city "above" as representative not of the triumphant church in heaven but "of the militant Church on earth."[37] The spiritual blessings given to individual Christians were something experienced in the present, which would in turn

31. Schreiner, *Galatians*, 296.
32. Schreiner, *Galatians*, 296.
33. Schreiner, *Galatians*, 296.
34. Fung, *Epistle to the Galatians*, 210.
35. Fung, *Epistle to the Galatians*, 210.
36. Wright, *Paul and His Recent Interpreters*, 114.
37. Luther, *Commentary on Galatians*, 419.

provide believers the assurance they needed to hold fast to Christ. Luther also commented that this "spiritual Jerusalem . . . is dispersed throughout the whole world . . . in all places of the world where men dwell which have the Gospel and believe in Jesus Christ."[38] Therefore, Paul's depiction of the "Jerusalem above" in Gal 4:26 represents a remade city of God in which believers in Christ experience the eschatological presence of God in the present. Zion has then become the symbol of a new spiritual reality to be experienced through Christ in the present, not only of a future hope of new creation.

The Church as the Temple of God in 1 Corinthians 3:16–17

Paul taught the Corinthian church that they "are God's temple" and "God's temple is holy, and you are that temple" (1 Cor 3:16–17). Paul is speaking to a plural "you," indicating that the community gathered in Christ's name, not individuals, are the temple in which the Spirit dwells.[39] Since the Spirit dwells among the church as a corporate body in Paul's view, his writing is preoccupied with the threat of disunity caused by the dysfunctional relationships within the community of faith.[40] If the church, and specifically the community of believers in Corinth, was to be the new covenant community of Jer 31, then it would be defined by trustworthiness and unity as the evidence of the Spirit creating new hearts within each believer (Jer 31:33). Jeremiah proclaimed the result would be God's presence among them, as the Lord said, "I will be their God, and they shall be my people . . . for I will forgive their iniquity, and I will remember their sins no more" (Jer 31:34). This new temple community called the church, united by the renewed presence of God in the Spirit, reflects God's promises from Jer 31 and describes a people who would "come and sing aloud on the height of Zion, and they shall be radiant over the goodness of the Lord" (Jer 31:12). According to 1 Cor 3:16–17, Paul sees the community of faith in Corinth as a temple, or the place where God's presence dwells through the Spirit; thus, the hope of Zion and the restoration of God's people imbued with his Spirit is realized in the body of believers.[41]

Most non-Christian religion during Paul's day involved an image or statue of a deity, yet 1 Cor 3:16–17 transforms the typical temple imagery involving a structure or images into the presence of the Spirit indwelling

38. Luther, *Commentary on Galatians*, 420.

39. Garland, *1 Corinthians*, 120.

40. Hafemann, "Temple of the Spirit," 29.

41. Thiselton, *First Epistle to the Corinthians*, 316.

believers.[42] The idea that the gathering of Christians, likely in a small, cramped house compared to the grandiose temples elaborately constructed for Greek or Roman gods, serves to highlight Paul's theme of unity alongside his discussion of the world's perception of the gospel as foolishness.[43] This idea further enforces Paul's theology of the church as a temple due to the Spirit's indwelling, not any man-made structure or geographic location. If the Zion symbol's goal was for the presence of God to fill the earth with God's glory, then it follows that the Spirit's indwelling among a community of faith far from Jerusalem was fulfilling that mission. Therefore, Paul reprimanded the Corinthians for their divisions and factions, seeing this as a threat to the mission of God.[44]

In the Old Testament, the tabernacle and the temple were constant visual reminders of God's presence among the people, yet over time the concept of God's presence expanded. The eschatological expectation in the Psalms and Prophets envisioned one earthly temple, and the New Testament fulfills this through the Spirit's indwelling instead of a physical building.[45] Isaiah 66:1 says, "What is the house that you would build for me, and what is the place of my rest," indicating that God's goal was for the whole world to serve as a temple for his glory.[46] Paul's repetitive use of *soma* ("body"), appearing forty-six times in 1 Corinthians, indicates he views the "body" of believers, made up individual spirit-filled people, to be a new temple that houses the glory of God. This transfer from a physical temple to a body of believers still appears in a singular place, for the Spirit has unified all believers through Christ's own body.[47] The interplay with the words "body" and "temple" in 1 Cor 6:19 further indicates that, while an individual believer is in himself like a "temple," the collective of believers constitutes God's eschatological temple, displaying the glory of God outward to the world with the mission of covering the earth with the glory of God.

Paul's discussion of the Spirit as the renewed presence of God in the church also points to the prophets' hope of a restored Zion that would draw the nations toward God's presence in the temple. Ezekiel 37:27 echoes Jer 31:33 that God "will be their God and they will be my people." Malachi 3:1 also spoke to a time when "suddenly the Lord you are seeking will come to

42. Thiselton, *First Epistle to the Corinthians*, 317.

43. Garland, *1 Corinthians*, 120.

44. Garland, *1 Corinthians*, 120.

45. Piotrowski, "One Spirit, One Body," 738.

46. Fetherholf, "Body for a Temple," 93.

47. Fetherholf, "Body for a Temple," 96.

his temple," yet the Second Temple did not live up to these expectations.[48] Thus, Paul recaptures temple imagery through the presence of the Spirit and the indwelling of those belonging to Christ's body. Gordon Fee states, "For Paul the Spirit is how God presently dwells in his holy temple."[49] James Dunn adds, "With Paul at least the implication is that of a temple constituted by the immediate indwelling of God in individual people . . . and of such a direct indwelling that it made redundant any continuing loyalty to the Jerusalem temple."[50] Therefore, Paul was concerned for the unity of believers in Corinth because they were this new temple of God, and by the Spirit's work in salvation and indwelling the hearts of individuals, the church had become the eschatological temple. The prophetic hope of a restored Zion was realized through the Spirit's work in the church, though there remained an eschatological component yet to be fulfilled in Christ's return. Until "the Day will disclose it," Paul urged the Corinthian believers to pursue unity in the Spirit because of this new identity and, ultimately, because "you are Christ's, and Christ is God's" (1 Cor 3:13, 23). If the temple represents God's task originally given to Adam to fill the earth with his glory, Paul now sees the church as the vehicle to deliver it to the nations.[51]

THE HEAVENLY ZION IN HEBREWS

In what is perhaps the most striking example of Zion symbolism's transformation through Christ, the author of Hebrews encourages the church that "you have come to Mount Zion and to the city of the living God, the heavenly Jerusalem" (Heb 12:22). Hebrews 12:18–24 serves as the rhetorical climax to the author's exhortation to the church, providing a powerful visual of the stark contrast between choosing either the path of fear or the joyful celebration of those remaining faithful to Christ.[52] In its broader context, the passage serves as the author's final lesser-to-greater argument in the letter, reminding the church of the wilderness generation's disobedience while pointing to the reward for faith, which is eternal joy in God's presence. In Heb 12:18–21, the author recounts the fearful and awesome experience of God's presence upon Mount Sinai, which even led Moses to "tremble with fear" (Heb 12:21). Yet, Heb 12:22–24 beautifully depicts the result of faithfulness to Christ, which brings joy, peace, and eternal rest. Through this

48. Fee, *Paul, the Spirit*, 14.

49. Fee, *Paul, the Spirit*, 15.

50. Dunn, *Theology of Paul*, 545.

51. Beale, *New Testament Theology*, 631.

52. Ellingworth, *Epistle to the Hebrews*, 669.

imagery regarding the two mountains, it becomes clear that Mount Zion is no longer a hill where a man-made temple stands; rather, Mount Zion is the eternal home of the saints of God who have been blessed through the blood of Jesus under his new covenant.

Eschatology of Zion in Hebrews

One of the major themes in Hebrews is the comparison between the heavenly and earthly temples as support for Jesus's superior ministry in the heavenly realm. However, the scholarly debate often centers on how this is presented, from either the perspective of cosmological dualism or Jewish future-oriented eschatology.[53] The Platonic, dualistic view focuses heavily on the spatial contrast between the earthly temple and its ministries as opposed to Jesus's superior priesthood and ministry from heaven. Yet, from an eschatological perspective, there is more interest in the present ministry of Jesus and its future implications, which the church is anticipating.[54]

Since Hebrews is filled with Jewish messianic theology and repeatedly builds its arguments through a lesser-to-greater model, it is better to understand the Zion motif and its related symbolism through an eschatological lens. Jesus is the centerpiece of the letter, and he is labeled as the "Son of God," the "pioneer" of faith, and as the "high priest" over those faithful to God. The christological focus of the author through these titles depicts Jesus as the one leading his people or going before them to prepare the way.[55] While the Greek rhetoric and style of Hebrews has led some toward an interpretation based upon Philo of Alexandria, who often opted for Platonic interpretations, the focus on the Jewish tradition of the Old Testament reveals that the author is primarily writing from an eschatological perspective.[56] Therefore, Jesus, the mediator of a better covenant and the one who leads his people to a new Zion, is the fulfillment of the prophets' vision and is himself the way to the restored Zion. As the author builds this argument, he reflects upon the incomplete nature of the former covenants in comparison to Christ, who completed his work, sat down at God's right hand, and now ministers as the high priest for the church. There are numerous examples of how Zion symbolism plays a key role in the author's arguments, but in chapters 8, 9, and 12, there are distinct pictures of Jesus as the one who has not only established eternal salvation through his own sacrifice

53. Son, *Zion Symbolism*, 170.

54. Son, *Zion Symbolism*, 170.

55. Mason, "You Are a Priest Forever," 12.

56. O'Brien, *Letter to the Hebrews*, 37.

but has inaugurated a new, heavenly Zion allowing free access to the throne of God to all those who enter by faith.[57]

The Priest of a Greater Temple in Hebrews 8:1–6

One such example of the duality between heaven and earth is presented in Heb 8:1–6, where Jesus is described as a heavenly high priest, and the earthly temple is described as "a copy and shadow of the heavenly things" (Heb 8:1, 5). The theme of the heavenly sanctuary is present in this passage, for Jesus, in his role as high priest, is sitting down, having accomplished his work in making purification for sins.[58] Psalm 110 reflects this imagery, as the Lord invites the messianic figure to "sit at my right hand," proclaiming, "The Lord sends forth from Zion your mighty scepter" (Ps 110:1–2). However, in Heb 8:1 Jesus is depicted as a priest, or the one who stands between God and people as their mediator, since he has offered himself as atonement. Jesus, then, cannot be an earthly priest but must be a heavenly priest because the earthly temple is but a "copy" of the heavenly reality.[59] This passage hints at Jesus's role in transforming the earthly hopes of Zion into a heavenly reality, which then brings blessings to those remaining faithful to Christ while still on earth. Since the heavenly tabernacle is the "true tent," then the desert sanctuary and the Jerusalem temple were foreshadowing Christ's ministry, which established a permanent, perfect temple in heaven from which forgiveness is extended.[60] The Zion God had chosen in Jerusalem was a shadow of a better, complete sanctuary now that Jesus has offered himself as the perfect sacrifice.

Jesus is depicted as the exalted Son, first in Heb 1:13 and again in 8:1, as he is described as sitting at the right hand of God. The allusion to Ps 110:1 is an important aspect of the author of Hebrew's usage of Zion symbolism, for it describes Jesus as the king of the heavenly Zion in spatial terms.[61] Zion has been exalted to the heavens and is now a symbol of the perfect sanctuary because of Christ's atonement for sin. The purpose of this imagery is not necessarily to present a Platonic duality, for it adopts both the Jewish hope for a new age and the distinction between two spheres of reality.[62] James Thompson adds, "Because of his Christian confession, he parts company

57. Son, *Zion Symbolism*, 198.
58. Cockerill, *Epistle to the Hebrews*, 229.
59. Ellingworth, *Hebrews*, 399.
60. Attridge, *Essays on John and Hebrews*, 277.
61. Son, *Zion Symbolism*, 176.
62. Thompson, *Hebrews*, 169.

with both the apocalyptic and the philosophical traditions at significant points, using them for his own purposes."[63] The heavenly Zion is not the result of the author's philosophical perspective but rather it represents his Christology, seeing Christ as the fulfillment of the Old Testament hope and the reason for the church not to turn away from faithfulness to Jesus. By picturing the heavenly Zion as God's dwelling place, the author of Hebrews portrays Jesus as the Son who has fulfilled what was left incomplete in the former sanctuaries.[64]

Inaugurated eschatology shapes Jesus's role in Hebrews, for in chapter 8, it is apparent that Christ's heavenly ministry was a present reality experienced by the author and his audience. Furthermore, the author's repeated use of *teleioō*, for "to make perfect," enhances his understanding that, in Christ, the incomplete or imperfect previous covenants were fulfilled, or were being fulfilled, in Christ's present and future ministry as high priest.[65] The contrast between the incomplete Mosaic covenant and Christ's better covenant, which is "enacted on better promises," also highlights the way in which Christ has brought the eschatological hopes in the Old Testament to their fulfillment (Heb 8:6).

The Greater Tabernacle in Hebrews 9

Throughout Hebrews, the theme of sacred space, especially in terms of the heavenly realm where Christ is seated and to which believers belong, connects the Old Testament hope of a restored Zion upon a renewed earth with the present reality experienced through faith. Salvation is often described in spatial terms, such as a resting place, throne room, or sanctuary, and Christ is depicted as serving as high priest in the heavenly realm.[66] Hebrews 9:1–10 recalls, in primarily spatial terms, the earthly tabernacle, its physical

63. Thompson, *Hebrews*, 169.

64. Son further argues that "the conceptual background of the antithesis between the superior heavenly temple and its earthly counterpart is derived neither from Platonic metaphysical dualism nor from the architectural language of a sketch plan on the basis of the temporal eschatology. The contrast . . . is developed from the Jewish apocalyptic tradition which views the earthly tent of Sinai as built by Moses according to the pattern of the true heavenly dwelling place of God." The heavenly Zion, then, is the true temple of God, and the earthly tabernacle or temple is based upon it. Yet, the emphasis is still primarily theological, not spatial, for the reality of the heavenly Zion leads to the blessing of salvation in Jesus, which all believers experience in the present. Son, *Zion Symbolism*, 175.

65. Blomberg, *New Testament Theology*, 499.

66. Jon Laansma, "Cosmology of Hebrews," in Pennington and McDonough, *Cosmology and New Testament Theology*, 127.

properties, and ritual significance for the Israelites. Despite the importance of the holy of holies, verse 8 says, "By this the Holy Spirit indicates that the way into the holy places is not yet opened as long as the first section is still standing (which is symbolic for the present age)" (Heb 9:8–9). These verses reveal that, before Christ, there was no free access to the presence of God and that, if "the first section is still standing," the sacrifices offered "cannot perfect the conscience of the worshiper" (Heb 9:9). As long as this outer tent served as a sanctuary, it prevented the people from even seeing, let alone entering the presence of God.[67] Ellingworth notes that this portrays "the mutual exclusiveness, in theological terms, of the old and new dispensations."[68] Thus, the former symbolism of the sanctuary, which limited people's access to the presence of God, was waiting to be remade through one who would enter into the holy of holies and offer himself as a perfect sacrifice.

One of the primary images related to the future-oriented hopes of a restored Zion was the presence of God among the people without restrictions or fear. If the goal was to return to an Edenic paradise where God and man walked together, then the separation created by sin must be resolved. In Heb 9:11–14, the author says that Christ appeared "through the greater and more perfect tent (not made with hands, that is, not of this creation)," reaffirming that the temple symbolism involving the holy place and sacrifices was indeed a shadow of what was to come in Christ (Heb 9:11). This verse does not speak to a rebuilt temple but a new institution created by Christ himself, described in terms similar to the old but one that is "not made with hands" (Heb 9:11).[69] In dramatic fashion, this verse takes Zion symbolism involving the temple and the glory of God and shows that it was recreated in Christ. Isaiah's suffering servant, who "poured out his soul to death" and now "makes intercession for the transgressors," is fulfilled in Christ, yet not in remaking a Jerusalem temple but through entering the "more perfect tent" in heaven, so that his sacrifice would secure eternal redemption (Isa 53:12; Heb 9:11). Since Jesus "passed through the heavens," he is able to intercede for those in need from his priestly position in heaven (Heb 4:14).[70]

Harold Attridge notes that this "tent" in Heb 9:11 has been variously interpreted as "Christ's human body, his whole human life, his glorified body, his sacramental body, the liturgy of the new covenant, or the church."[71] Allegorical interpretations detract from the significance of

67. O'Brien, *Letter to the Hebrews*, 313.

68. Ellingworth, *Epistle to the Hebrews*, 439.

69. Attridge, *Essays on John and Hebrews*, 245.

70. Johnson, *Perfect Priest for Weary Pilgrims*, 110.

71. Johnson, *Perfect Priest for Weary Pilgrims*, 246.

this tent, which ultimately symbolizes the place of God's presence, for the language of the temple is used typologically to show the contrast between the old, incomplete system and Christ's new, perfect sacrifice.[72] Attridge further relates that this "tent" is "the heavenly or spiritual archetype of the earthly tabernacle."[73] The sacred space of the previous sanctuaries pointed forward to a time when God himself would make his presence available to all, and in Hebrews, this was accomplished through the Son. Whereas, in the ancient world, the concept of sacred space often involved the model of concentric circles, where the holiness of the space increased as one moved toward the center; Jesus's atoning sacrifice removed the barriers that inhibited people from approaching God.[74] The holy of holies was understood to be the intersection of heaven and earth, the center of Israel and of all creation. Zion's future in Isa 2:2–4, Jer 31 and Ezek 40–48, in broad, global terms, pictured God himself remaking creation, including humanity, so they can rest eternally in his holy presence. The author of Hebrews attaches these hopes to Jesus, who through his own sacrifice, secured eternal redemption, making the sacred space of God's presence accessible to those who enter by faith. In other words, the sacred space once attributed primarily to Mount Zion is now alive within and among the faithful community of the church because of Christ's atoning sacrifice.

Hebrews 9:23–28 further reveals that the ultimate hope of a restored Zion could not rest in any man-made temple but would be a perfect, heavenly place where God dwells. The Christian hope of heaven is not that the copies, or shadows, of the present will be repaired or purified but that a new reality will come through Christ.[75] Phillip Church offers a different perspective, concluding,

> In Hebrews the heavenly temple is not an eternal heavenly archetype of which the wilderness tabernacle is a copy. Rather, the wilderness tabernacle, Solomon's temple and the Second Temple still standing in Jerusalem prefigured the heavenly temple, which is to be understood as the eschatological dwelling of God with his people.[76]

In this sense, the older sanctuaries were valid in their time, but with the exaltation of Jesus, all the eschatological hopes the former things represented

72. O'Brien, *Letter to the Hebrews*, 321.

73. Attridge, *Essays on John and Hebrews*, 247.

74. Jon Laansma, "The Cosmology of Hebrews," in Pennington and McDonough, *Cosmology and New Testament Theology*, 132.

75. Beale, *New Testament Biblical Theology*, 634.

76. Church, *Hebrews and the Temple*, 433.

have become a new reality.[77] The symbols which anticipated a perfect, heavenly temple, are now left behind because Christ has entered "once for all at the end of the ages," transforming the sacred space of Mount Zion and the temple into an experienced reality within the life of individual believers in Jesus (Heb 9:26). Therefore, Christ himself is the new Zion, for he is the intersection of heaven and earth and the place from where God's glory will extend to the nations.

The Inaugurated Zion of Hebrews 12:18–24

The letter to the Hebrews reaches a climactic scene involving a vivid contrast between the terrifying imagery of Sinai and the perfection of the heavenly Zion in Heb 12:18–24. By summoning the audience to visualize the events of Sinai in 12:18–21, the author heightens his theological emphasis on Christ as high priest of the heavenly Zion. "You have not come" in verse 18 contrasts with "you have come" in verse 22, establishing the stark contrast between the old, incomplete covenant and the new, perfect covenant in Christ. The perfect tense verb indicates that the believers had already obtained the spiritual blessing of their pilgrimage and were receiving the benefits of it even though they still needed to stay the course.[78] Because they belong to Jesus, Christians stand in an even holier place than what the Israelites experienced at Sinai.[79] Mount Sinai is not named in this passage but is called "what may be touched," conveying the impersonal, earthly nature of that experience instead of the personal, heavenly reality for those with faith.[80] Through this contrast, the author is able to paint a beautiful image of the heavenly Zion, the dwelling place of God and the home for all the saints in Christ.

The Antithesis of the Heavenly Zion in Hebrews 12:18–21

To facilitate his climactic exhortation, the author of Hebrews recounts the events experienced by the Israelites at Mount Sinai as recorded in Exod 19–20 and Deut 4. By beginning with the negative, the author amplifies the perfection of the heavenly Zion and prepares his audience to be awed by the contrast between the two realms. Sensory language in 12:18–19 enhances

77. Church, *Hebrews and the Temple*, 433.

78. Johnson, *Hebrews*, 328.

79. Ellingworth, *Epistle to the Hebrews*, 670.

80. Cockerill, "Hebrews 12:18–24: Apocalyptic Typology," 225.

the retelling: "blazing fire," "darkness and gloom," and "tempest" were terrifying sights, while the "sound of a trumpet" and a "voice" from heaven were the accompanying sounds.[81] William Lane notes that these terms "combine to create a verbal impression of the awesome majesty of the God who made his presence known at Sinai."[82] The holiness of God was on display, for Sinai functioned as a precursor to the tabernacle, as God's presence created a holy place where "if even a beast touches the mountain, it shall be stoned" (Heb 12:20). The people felt an overwhelming sense of fear, for even though they knew the boundaries to God's presence on the mountain, they were afraid the boundary was dissolving as the voice thundered from Mount Sinai.[83]

The feeling of fear in God's presence is even attributed to Moses, who, in Heb 3:2, is described as "faithful in all God's house." Yet in Heb 12:21, Moses is described as trembling, likely recalling his own account from Deut 9:19 where he lay before the Lord in fear because of the people's disobedience.[84] This fear does not discredit Moses but, rather, such fear acknowledges the truth about God and enables people of faith to trust God instead of people.[85] The author revisits his earlier discussion in chapter 9 by highlighting the separation between God and people that existed under the old covenant. Sanctity was preserved by exclusion under the old model, for only Moses was allowed to approach God, and even he shook in fear.[86] The situation under the new covenant is vastly different, but the contrast is the author's point. The material, touchable elements of Sinai are inferior to the immaterial, spiritual nature of the heavenly city of God.[87]

Theologically, the author's exhortation is intended to prevent the church from reenacting the events of Sinai because they already belong to the blessing of the new covenant. For the church to understand that turning away from Christ would be a devastating decision, the author dynamically portrays the inferiority of the earthly, old covenant thinking in light of the heavenly reality in Christ they already obtained through faith.[88] The results of Sinai, such as the tabernacle, priesthood, and sacrificial system, were established so that Israel would become a holy nation, set apart for God's glory

81. Ellingworth, *Epistle to the Hebrews*, 671.

82. Lane, *Hebrews 9–13*, 297.

83. Guthrie, *Hebrews*, 418.

84. The source for Heb 12:21 has been debated as either Deut 9:19 (LXX), Stephen's account of Exod 3:3 in Acts 7:32, or possibly Jewish homiletical tradition, which elaborates on Moses's experience at Sinai. Lane, *Hebrews*, 299.

85. Johnson, *Hebrews*, 330.

86. Attridge, *Essays on John and Hebrews*, 374.

87. Thompson, *Hebrews*, 262.

88. Schenck, *Cosmology and Eschatology in Hebrews*, 123.

in the world; yet, that covenantal system was a shadow of what was fulfilled in Jesus.[89] The discontinuity between Sinai and Zion is another piece of evidence within the author's greater theological argument that Jesus entered into a new covenant, so "he makes the first one obsolete" (Heb 8:13).[90] However, the purpose is not that the Old Testament itself is obsolete but rather Jesus has made the old covenant between God and Israel obsolete, because through his sacrifice, he has established a new, better covenant sealed with his blood, which offers eternal redemption. Thus, Sinai represents the antithesis of the heavenly city of God, for the people were not allowed to approach God's presence due to their sin and rebellion, but through Jesus, those with faith "have confidence to enter the holy places by the blood of Jesus" (Heb 10:19).

"You Have Come to Mount Zion" in Hebrews 12:22–24

The experience of the presence of God for the community of faith is radically different from the wilderness generation, for Christians "have come to Mount Zion and to the city of the living God, the heavenly Jerusalem" (Heb 12:22). The themes of faith and perseverance point to the greater mountain, the eternal home of those who have not turned back and who have fixed their gaze upon Jesus.[91] The perfect tense of "you have come" indicates the effect of a present reality the believers were currently experiencing; thus, the seven descriptions listed are intended to encourage the church as present blessings to be further enjoyed in the future. Since Sinai also had seven descriptions alongside references to a voice speaking, the author is viewing the two mountains as symbols of two revelations, with Zion being the goal for those who are faithful.[92] What Zion was meant to be in the past has now become a present reality because of Jesus, who mediates for his people in a perfect, heavenly temple.

Hebrews 12:22, along with Rev 14:1, are the only occurrences of "Mount Zion" in the New Testament that are not within Old Testament citations. Since this is the only mention of Zion in Hebrews, the author may have considered that his audience was thinking of the earthly Temple Mount, so the additional descriptors of "the city of the living God" and "the heavenly Jerusalem" prevent such a thought.[93] Although he previously

89. Peterson, *Hebrews*, 257.

90. Guthrie, "Hebrews' Use of the Old Testament," 275.

91. Blomberg, *New Testament Theology*, 526.

92. O'Brien, *Letter to the Hebrews*, 478.

93. Church, *Hebrews and the Temple*, 347.

spoke of heavenly tents and Jesus's role as a priest in the heavenly realm, the insertion of Zion in verse 22 recalls the rich imagery of the Psalms and Prophets describing the central place of God's interaction with his chosen people on earth. Attridge states that this mountain "is the ultimate point of God's manifestation" because it represents the eschatological city of God or the final home of the faithful.[94] No longer is Mount Zion the earthly Jerusalem that God protects as Ps 48 proclaimed; rather, Zion is now exalted to the heavens, yet the focus is the same because it is the place where God dwells among his people. The mention of Zion also connects to the Davidic dynasty and God's covenant promises in 2 Sam 7 as well as Ps 110:1–2; however, Zion here is not the seat of rule for a king in Israel but the seat of God's eschatological rule through Christ.[95]

The description "city of the living God" evokes the imagery of God dwelling among his people, assuring the community of faith that the goal of their perseverance is God's presence. Eden, the tabernacle, and the temple were forerunners to what Christians presently experience. God's incarnational presence in Jesus has now opened the way for God's revelatory presence to become reality for the believer.[96] Zion symbolism had been a source of hope for Israel as a reminder of God's covenant promises and the vision he gave to the prophets of a new creation; yet, now this vision is fully realized through Jesus, who is "the mediator of a new covenant" (Heb 12:24). The heavenly Zion is greater than any form of an earthly Zion, so the hope for the Christian now rests in their identity as a citizen of this city.

The "city of the living God" is synonymous with "the heavenly Jerusalem," which recalls the author's previous discussion about Zion's exaltation to the heavenly realm and Jesus's high priesthood within it (Heb 12:22). Jerusalem had been a central religious city for centuries, and even when it was no longer the royal residence, it maintained a key role in Jewish eschatology, much in part because of the Zion theology presented in the Prophets.[97] Even where the Second Temple failed, the belief in a future, heavenly temple remained.

The approach toward the heavenly city relates to the corporate life of the believers, especially in the context of Heb 12–13, for concepts such as "acceptable worship," "brotherly love," and "hospitality to strangers" were trademarks of their earthly transformation in Christ while already citizens

94. Attridge, *Essays on John and Hebrews*, 374.

95. Johnson, *Hebrews*, 331.

96. Duvall, *God's Relational Presence*, 272.

97. Lohse and Fohrer, "Σιών," in *TDNT* 7:308.

of the heavenly Zion.[98] In this sense, Zion exists in heaven, yet by their identity with it, the believers now represent the heavenly city in their daily lives and through their confident expectation in Christ. This picture is distinct from Jewish eschatology, where passages such as Isa 2:2–4, Mic 4:1–3, and Zech 1:12 envisioned a remade earthly Jerusalem.[99] Yet, this furthers the purpose of Christ in transforming Zion symbolism: through him, the church has become a reflection of the heavenly realm through their worship, love, and confident hope. "Mount Zion . . . the heavenly Jerusalem" in Heb 12:22 is less about a geographical location or religious site and more about the identity believers in Christ receive through faith. This heavenly Jerusalem presupposes the apocalyptic tradition of a transcendent Zion; thus, there is nothing abstract about this city but rather it represents the spiritual reality inaugurated by Jesus.[100] While there has been a tendency to steer this imagery toward the Platonic tradition put forth by Philo, there is no concept in Heb 12 that a heavenly Jerusalem will be made visible in the new age; rather, it signifies the spiritual reality already accessible by those who are faithful to Jesus.[101] The new Zion hoped for in the Prophets and in the Jewish apocalyptic tradition has been fulfilled in Christ, who has now opened the way for believers to enjoy the presence of God.

The book of Hebrews speaks to a shift in holiness, which can be misinterpreted through a lens of material versus immaterial, because the heavenly reality of Christ's priesthood intersects with the life and faith of believers on earth. When the concept of God meeting with people is stressed, often in the New Testament, the writers prefer temple symbolism to convey this idea.[102] Even though the physical temple had faded from centrality, the imagery nonetheless continued as a primary way of communicating the theological reality of God's presence among his people. The heavenly is superior because that is where God dwells, and it is the destination for those who

98. Ellingworth, *Hebrews*, 678.

99. Ellingworth, *Hebrews*, 678.

100. O'Brien, *Letter to the Hebrews*, 484.

101. Lane, *Hebrews 9–13*, 302.

102. Lane points out that "in Hebrews the heavenly city is a transcendent reality that faithfully reflects the realism of the Jewish apocalyptic tradition as represented in *4 Ezra* and *2 Apocalypse of Baruch*. There is nothing abstract or contingent about the heavenly city in v. 22, which differs fundamentally from the philosophical concept in Philo." This concept is significant to the transformation of Zion symbolism as a present reality already experienced through faith, not only a future heavenly city that will become realized in a new age. Platonic interpretations fail to see the book's emphasis on holy living precisely because the new Zion has already come. Lane, *Hebrews 9–13*.

remain faithful to Jesus. The church is encouraged to approach God, as in corporate worship, as a reflection of their heavenly citizenship in Christ.[103]

The inhabitants of the heavenly Mount Zion include "innumerable angels," "the assembly of the firstborn," "God, the judge of all," "the spirits of the righteous," and "Jesus, the mediator of a new covenant" (Heb 12:22–23). The ordering of these terms, according to Ellingworth, suggests "rhetorical heaping rather than logical sequence," so the mention of angels ahead of the assembly of believers likely is insignificant to the overall picture.[104] The presence of angels in a festal gathering occurs in other literature contemporary to Hebrews, and in Jewish sects such as the Qumran community, the worship of the community of faith was seen as a reflection of heavenly worship given by angels.[105] This imagery further brightens the intensity of the beauty and joy that comes from the heavenly Zion, especially in contrast to the tangible, yet terrifying presence of God at Sinai.

The "firstborn" was mentioned in Heb 1:6 in reference to the Son's divinity, but in Heb 12:23, the term is plural, so these are the followers of Jesus, the ones redeemed through his sacrificial death and who are now enrolled as citizens of the heavenly city of God.[106] The assembly has gathered as siblings of Jesus, for in Heb 2:11, Jesus "is not ashamed to call them brothers," indicating their personal relationship with Jesus through faith.[107] The "assembly" is from *ekklesia*, often translated as "church," but this term is also used in the Septuagint in reference to the "congregation" of Israel in Deut 4:10. The heavenly Zion has become the home of God's people, now called "firstborn" and having their names "enrolled in heaven" (Heb 12:23). Calling the saints "firstborn" is uncommon, yet this designation contrasts with Esau who was mentioned in Heb 12:16 as a poor example of faith. Therefore, the "firstborn" are those who are not like Esau because they have remained faithful to God, whether under the old or new covenants.[108] This title may also recall the exodus story, where Israel, as God's firstborn son, is freed from Egypt while Pharaoh's firstborn died (Exod 12:29–32). This symbolism describes God's unique relationship to Israel, but in the context of Hebrews, it highlights the status of those who have faith in the Son and

103. Long, *Hebrews*, 167.

104. Ellingworth, *Hebrews*, 677.

105. Examples of references to angels involved in such gatherings can be found in Pss 89:6; 103:21; 148:2; Jub. 31; 1 En. 5–16. Church, *Hebrews and the Temple*, 349.

106. Cockerill, *Epistle to the Hebrews*, 395.

107. Cockerill, *Epistle to the Hebrews*, 350.

108. Grindheim, *Letter to the Hebrews*, 507.

have become like him by being enrolled in the book of life.[109] The heavenly Zion will be filled with redeemed, righteous children of God, seen now as having the rights of the firstborn. Isaiah said, "And he who is left in Zion and remains in Jerusalem will be called holy, everyone who has been recorded for life in Jerusalem" (Isa 4:3). What was envisioned by the prophet has now become both present reality and future expectation as the community of faith approaches the heavenly Zion through Christ.

God holds the central position as the third in the list of five persons or groups present in the heavenly Zion, and he is described as "the judge of all." While it is plausible to understand the title of judge in a positive sense, as a vindicator or redeemer, in this context, it more likely emphasizes that this joyful gathering is not to be taken lightly.[110] The salvation provided through the Son is only possible because of God, so it is with gratitude and awe that the believers are able to approach the throne of God with confidence. The "spirits of the righteous made perfect" are also present because God has judged them as righteous. While the "assembly" likely speaks to the triumphant church, these "spirits" are the faithful people of God who have died.[111] These spirits represent the faithful in chapter 11, the saints who died in expectation of the Lord's vindication. Abraham journeyed to the promised land, yet he "was looking forward to the city that has foundations" (Heb 11:10). One aspect of the heavenly Zion is that all who enter by faith, whether Abraham, Moses, or the unknown follower of Jesus in Rome, will equally enjoy the presence of God forever.[112] The heavenly Zion, then, is the home for both the faithful in Christ and those who died before Christ in faithful expectation. Their reward is God himself, made possible by Jesus, who has mediated a new covenant with his own blood.

In what forms the climax of this section and the whole epistle, Heb 12:24 says the final figure present in the heavenly Zion is Jesus, whose sprinkled blood has made a new covenant for those who enter by faith.[113] The heavenly temple and the access granted to those who approach in faith is only possible because of Jesus's sacrificial blood, described as "sprinkled" as a visual reminder of the heavenly temple and Christ's better, permanent sacrifice for sins. In the previous Zion, the priests offered countless sacrifices, and on the Day of Atonement, the high priest sprinkled blood on the altar for the sins of the people. Now, this imagery is complete in Christ and

109. Grindheim, *Letter to the Hebrews*, 507.

110. Cockerill, *Epistle to the Hebrews*, 396.

111. Cockerill, *Epistle to the Hebrews*, 396.

112. Duvall, *God's Relational Presence*, 274.

113. Ellingworth, *Hebrews*, 681.

is no longer a recurring event, so its function in Heb 12:24 speaks to the finality of Jesus's sacrifice (Heb 9:12). His sacrifice speaks a better word than the blood of Abel, for through faith, Abel continues to "speak," yet Jesus's sacrifice is the ultimate example of faith before God.[114] Jesus's blood does not cry out for justice, but rather, it purifies those who approach God in faith; thus, the heavenly Zion has become a more perfect temple, where the sacrificial blood offers permanent cleansing and reconciliation to God.[115]

Zion is now fully transformed into a glorious, joyful gathering of the saints of the Old Testament and the faithful in Christ still on earth. Because Jesus continues to minister as high priest, all who draw near to him in faith become citizens of the eschatological Zion in both a present reality and a future hope. The imagery of Heb 12:22–24 revolves around the presence of God, displaying what is both realized by Christians in the present and what is hoped for in the future. Zion has become a symbol of the new covenant through Jesus, and while the prophets saw a future day, believers in Jesus experience the blessing of belonging to Zion in the present.

THE DESTINATION OF ZION IN REVELATION

As the canon of Scripture comes to a close, Revelation includes two important visions regarding the destination of the Zion symbol. In Rev 14:1, Jesus is seen standing on Mount Zion, victorious with 144,000 saints; and in Rev 21–22, the heavenly Jerusalem descends in God's final act to permanently dwell among his people in paradise. The former speaks to the finality and completeness of Jesus's rule over the earth as the fulfillment of Pss 2 and 110, and the latter speaks to the hope of new creation, which the prophets foresaw. Through these final, powerful images, Zion has reached its destination as a symbol denoting the presence of God among his people. The Lord comforted the apostle John by saying, "Behold, the dwelling place of God is with man. He will dwell with them, and they will be his people, and God himself will be with them as their God" (Rev 21:3). From Eden to the tabernacle, to the temple, and through the church, God's mission to eternally dwell in peace with his beloved creation is complete as God himself brings forth the heavenly Zion into an eternal reality.

114. The allusion to Abel recalls Heb 11:4 and emphasizes his faith through his righteous sacrifice, not the fact that he was murdered or that his blood cried out as in Gen 4:10. McCruden, "Eloquent Blood of Jesus," 506.

115. McCruden, "Eloquent Blood of Jesus," 507.

The Victorious Lamb on Mount Zion in Revelation 14:1–5

Revelation 14:1 says, "Then I looked, and behold, on Mount Zion stood the Lamb, and with him 144,000 who had his name and his Father's name written on their foreheads." By naming Mount Zion, the text emphasizes the genuine nature of Jesus's victory because Zion is typically reserved as a name for the true city of God.[116] Out of the nineteen occurrences of "Mount Zion" in the Old Testament, over half refer to a remnant being saved, but this context also alludes to Ps 2's depiction of the messianic king who rules from Zion over the rebellious nations. This may be in preparation for Christ's return as King of Kings in Rev 19–20, establishing the dual imagery of the sacrificial lamb and the conquering king. Grant Osborne adds that the imagery of Zion is "blending past, present, and future aspects . . . it is an earthly scene but anticipates a future reality."[117] As the symbolism of Zion expanded through the Prophets, it became not only the Temple Mount but the city where the Messiah would deliver God's people and gather them in a new age. Therefore, Mount Zion represents the capital of the renewed kingdom of God, the place from which God's rule over earth extends through the Messiah.[118]

While Rev 14:1 draws from several Old Testament texts regarding the centrality of Mount Zion in the eschatological age, it also presents the fulfillment of those passages through Jesus. The symbolism of the 144,000 (12 x 12,000) standing with the Lamb affirms the complete regathering of God's people to Zion.[119] Because of Jesus, the prophecies concerning the regathering of true Israel on Zion are now complete, and those whom he has gathered are standing with the Lamb in victory over the beast. David Aune suggests that the image of Jesus standing on Mount Zion is dependent on 4 Ezra 13:35, which states, "He will stand on the top of Mount Zion."[120] However, if this Zion is symbolic of the heavenly temple, where God resides with his people, then Zion in Rev 14 is not the earthly city from which the Messiah conquers his enemies but rather the focus is on the righteous saints who now stand with the Lamb, eternally victorious over their enemies. Aune also suggests that the scene may be based upon Isa 40:9–11, where Zion is described as the herald of good news for the people.[121] In any case, in Jewish

116. Beale, *Book of Revelation*, 731.

117. Osborne, *Revelation*, 525.

118. Osborne, *Revelation*, 525.

119. Fanning, *Revelation*, 388.

120. Aune, *Revelation 6–16*, 476.

121. Aune, *Revelation 6–16*, 476.

apocalyptic literature, Zion is often the place from which the Messiah will defeat his foes and judge them.[122] While that imagery is in view in Rev 14:1, the primary emphasis of this verse points forward to the heavenly Zion, to which the saints belong.[123] Zechariah prophesied the Lord's return to Zion (Zech 8:3), Joel saw a day when Zion would be Israel's refuge (Joel 3:16), and Isaiah spoke of a time when Israel's exile would end, bringing a time of singing and joy (Isa 51:11).[124] The earthly Zion did not live up to these expectations, but because of the Lamb's victory, it has been accomplished in heaven. The prophets were pointing to an eternal day of salvation and victory, and through Jesus, this has been accomplished in the spiritual realm and will one day be fully realized upon the new earth.

Jerusalem appeared in Rev 11 in a negative light, as "the great city that symbolically is called Sodom and Egypt, where their Lord was crucified" (Rev 11:8). Yet, Rev 14:1 points forward to the moment when the Lamb returns victoriously with those who refused to follow the beast and instead were faithful to him. The imagery from Ps 2 regarding the nations raging against the Lord's anointed also comes into view in this passage, for the beast's efforts to defeat the Lamb ultimately fail, resulting in the Lamb standing victorious atop a new Mount Zion. The dispensational view places this Zion on the old earth where Christ's millennial reign is centered, and a more figurative view understands it to be the new Jerusalem of Rev 21.[125] However, a more balanced view suggests that John is depicting Zion within the already-not-yet framework, which is more focused on the saints overcoming the beast by faith in the Lamb than placing this moment in a historical timeline.[126] Thomas Schreiner offers still another viewpoint, stating that "the Lamb standing on Mount Zion refers to Jesus as the risen and exalted Lord, reigning and ruling in heaven. The 144,000, which indicates the people of God, are with him in the heavenlies."[127] Therefore, John is anticipating the heavenly reward coming for the faithful in the new Jerusalem. Schreiner's view is also consistent with Paul's view of the saints having citizenship in heaven in Phil 3:20 and his view of the church as the "Jerusalem above" in Gal 4:26. This concurs with Heb 12:22, speaking of Zion as both the present reality experienced by the faithful in Christ and the anticipated final state where all believers will dwell victoriously with Christ.

122. Aune, *Revelation 6–16*, 477.

123. Schreiner, *Revelation*, 663.

124. Schreiner, *Revelation*, 663.

125. Beale, *Book of Revelation*, 732.

126. Beale, *Book of Revelation*, 732.

127. Schreiner, *Revelation*, 663.

Further evidence that Zion has been transformed through Jesus in Rev 14:1–5 comes from the description of the saints, who "had his name and his Father's name written on their foreheads" (Rev 14:1). In contrast to those who follow the beast in chapter 13, these saints belong to God and to the Lamb, since the name on their foreheads symbolizes God's recognition of them.[128] Furthermore, these saints produce a deafening sound of praise to God, loud like thunderous water yet beautiful like music played by skillful harpists. This worship demonstrates that this scene depicts the heavenly Zion as the final home for God's faithful people, for they now are at peace in his presence and sing his praise joyfully.[129] In Rev 22:4, the saints are again described as having the name of God on their foreheads, symbolizing God's divine election and protection over them. Therefore, John is likely portraying the same group of people under the same circumstances in Rev 14:1 and 22:4. They are the redeemed of God, forever worshiping in God's presence in a new Zion without a temple, for no longer does the symbol point to something coming but rather, it has become a new, eternal home in which the presence of God fills all of creation. In this sense, John portrays Zion or the new Jerusalem as a symbol of the saints themselves: a temple is not needed because the relationship between God and man is restored.[130]

In the broader context of Rev 12–14, the imagery of Mount Zion in 14:1 reinforces John's contrast between the earth-dwellers and those who belong to Lamb. The heavens, the earth, and the sea are three distinct regions in this section, and while those who follow the beast are labeled as inhabitants of the earth, God's people are symbolized as "those who dwell in heaven" (Rev 13:6).[131] Alongside these symbols are universal terms, such as in Rev 13:8, which says that "all who dwell on earth will worship it." Thus, John's contrast between the earthly rule of the beast and the heavenly rule of the Lamb are intended to encourage the church to overcome, through faith in the Son, not expecting a physical kingdom to appear but rather having confidence in the eternal promise of God's presence. Zion's appearance in Rev 14:1 pulls together symbolism from Rev 7's depiction of an uncountable number representing true Israel with the prophets' expectation that Zion would be the sacred space where the Messiah would return and establish his rule. That the redeemed saints are singing a heavenly song from Zion reflects the picture in Isa 51:11 that the ransomed will "come to Zion with

128. Beale, *Book of Revelation*, 737.

129. Schreiner, *Revelation*, 665.

130. Gundry, "New Jerusalem," 255.

131. Bauckham, *Climax of Prophecy*, 240.

singing; everlasting joy shall be upon their heads."[132] While some suggest the 144,000 represent ethnic Israel, the presence of God's name on their foreheads suggests that the number is symbolic of all those who are faithful to God and belong to the Lamb, for the heavenly Zion is a place for true Israel, God's chosen and faithful.[133] The ransomed people of Isaiah's prophecy have become citizens of the new Zion, and they now rejoice in the presence of God forever, victorious because they "follow the Lamb wherever he goes" (Rev 14:4).

Whereas Israel's prophets foresaw a new creation, including a remade and perfected Zion to which the Messiah would gather the nations, the New Testament, especially Revelation, reveals that the heavenly Zion is that goal. Until Christ returns and the new heavens and earth appear, the goal for the Christian is to come to Mount Zion as Heb 12:22 describes it. Mount Zion in Rev 14 is not the earthly city, nor should it be understood as the seat of Christ's reign in an earthly millennial kingdom.[134] Premillennial dispensationalists typically locate this Zion on the old earth as the center of Christ's reign during his thousand-year kingdom, yet the emphasis is not as much on location as it is on the victory Christ and his followers have won over the beast.[135] The eschatological Zion is repeatedly associated with the concept of a new name in Isaiah (Isa 56:5; 62:2–4; 65:15); thus, the Old Testament background suggests that the divine name written on believers, and their new song, is a figurative way of describing God's presence with them.[136] If God's presence, strongly contrasted to the beast's satanic rule, is the focus of Rev 14:1–5, then it follows that Zion is symbolic of God's cosmic throne, the place from where Christ reigns eternally. It is because of Christ that Zion represents God's rule over all creation, for through him his followers experience eternal salvation in the present and await his coming when he will make all things new.

132. Osborne, *Revelation*, 528.

133. Schreiner, *Joy of Hearing*, 125.

134. The premillennial viewpoint typically views a first return of Christ and a resurrection, followed by a second resurrection after a thousand-year kingdom of Christ. Under this view, it is sensible to see Rev 14:1 as an earthly reign of Christ with his saints. However, every other mention of the Lamb in Revelation is in heaven, and Rev 7 equates the 144,000 with the great multitude worshiping in heaven. Ladd, *Gospel of the Kingdom*, 42.

135. Beale, *Book of Revelation*, 732.

136. Beale, *Book of Revelation*, 733.

The New Jerusalem of Revelation 21–22

In the final two chapters of the canon, the apostle John receives a vision of "a new heaven and a new earth" and "the holy city, the new Jerusalem, coming down out of heaven from God" (Rev 21:1–2). These final chapters are imbued with symbolism, filling John's original audience with a sense of wonder, yet bolstering their confidence that remaining faithful to Christ would be worth the suffering they may endure on earth. The "new" heavens and earth, from *kainos*, typically indicates newness in quality, not time.[137] The first creation was temporary and became corrupted, but the new is intended to be perfect. From the beginning of the Bible, from the time of Eden, the storyline of Scripture has been moving toward this moment when all things will be made new.[138] Brian Tabb says, "The syntax of 21:5 signals that God does not simply make new things to replace the old but makes all things to be new."[139] Not only have the saints been redeemed and granted access to God's presence, for they also will live eternally upon a new earth, not a cleansed or repaired earth. The symbolic function and meaning of this new creation, and the new Jerusalem, has been variously interpreted, but its relationship to the theological purpose of Zion symbolism provides a beautiful picture of the goal of Zion, which is the eternal presence of God among his people.[140]

The New Jerusalem: A People, a City, or Both?

Isaiah provides the background for much of the language and imagery regarding the new Jerusalem, for Isa 52:1 calls it a "holy city" that has been cleansed and Isa 62:1–2 speaks of the city receiving "a new name that the mouth of the Lord will give." Combined with the marriage metaphor, this expresses a new, intimate relationship between God and true Israel, his redeemed people from the earth who conquered through the Lamb.[141] Isaiah's vision is fulfilled in the new creation and its city, but it is only possible because the Lamb has conquered death. Thus, Isaiah's imagery is transformed through Christ, because now the new city belongs only to true Israel, or those whom the Lamb has redeemed. What Isaiah saw in part, Christ has completed.

137. Beale, *Book of Revelation*, 1040.

138. Osborne, *Revelation*, 726.

139. Tabb, *All Things New*, 188.

140. Schreiner, *Joy of Hearing*, 158.

141. Beale, *Book of Revelation*, 1044.

One view regarding the theological purpose of the new Jerusalem, defended by Robert Gundry, is that the imagery in Rev 21–22 is a symbol describing the saints themselves: that is, the new Jerusalem is the church.[142] Under this view, John takes the Jewish traditions and imagery surrounding the renewal of Jerusalem and applies them directly to the saints. Gundry states, "The New Jerusalem is a dwelling place, to be sure; but it is God's dwelling place in the saints rather than their dwelling place on earth."[143] This view is significant in terms of Zion's transformation in the New Testament, for as Heb 12:22 envisioned Mount Zion as the already-not-yet home of the saints, Gundry's view places the emphasis of the heavenly city onto the converted believer instead of a future location. John does not describe the new heavens or earth, but he spends much time describing the dimensions, inhabitants, and rewards of the new city of God. In light of persecution and the threat of martyrdom, John's description of the saints in the new Jerusalem is sharply contrasted to the "cowardly, faithless," and "liars" who are unwelcome in the new city (Rev 21:8).[144] The city's invulnerability, massive walls, and ornate materials are symbolic of the saint's protection against the devil and the beast and are thus designed to encourage the saints to be overcomers in the present life.

While Gundry's perspective heightens the present blessing of belonging to the new city and experiencing the presence of God during times of earthly suffering, the content of Rev 21–22 is better understood through a lens of seeing the new Jerusalem as descriptive of both the believers and a future, physical new earth, yet to be realized.[145] It is certain that the reality of the new city and the new creation instills confidence in believers and provides a deeper sense of hope beyond the present, yet the sacred space of God's presence still speaks to an eternal home upon a new earth. The notion that the physical world is looking forward to a glorified, future state is true, but it is more than a model for how Christians should live until that day or a beautiful depiction to instill courage in the face of persecution.[146] From the perspective of inaugurated eschatology, the new Jerusalem has begun through Christ's resurrection but awaits its final consummation in Christ's return. Revelation 3:12 indicates that the overcomers already belong to the new Jerusalem, and Jesus calls himself "the beginning of God's creation" in Rev 3:14. Thus, John's descriptions of the new Jerusalem in Rev 21–22

142. Gundry, "New Jerusalem," 254.

143. Gundry, "New Jerusalem," 256.

144. Gundry, "New Jerusalem," 258.

145. Schreiner, *Joy of Hearing*, 258.

146. Erickson, "New Jerusalem Is No Heaven," 178.

describe both the glorified community of believers and the eternal home for all saints, past and future.[147] The imagery of the city is likely figurative, but it represents God's fellowship among his people in a real, new creation.[148]

Zion, according to Heb 12:22 is not only a future destination but is something already experienced because Jesus has opened access to God's presence. In a similar way, John's descriptions speak to the final home of Christians, but its theological purpose is to strengthen believers, as persecution was increasing in that day. However, the new creation described in the Prophets and by John is deeper than a metaphor describing the saints, for it is both a new spiritual state in Christ and the promise of a future, eternal home. The presence of God experienced through the Spirit now is the beginning of what will be fully realized after a final resurrection.

J. A. du Rand provides another perspective on the new Jerusalem as the "pinnacle of salvation."[149] Within this framework, the dramatic narrative of Revelation and the climax of the new Jerusalem are filtered through the soteriological purpose of the book. The heavenly temple imagery serves as a functional metaphor to represent the individual Christian's salvation, which is complete in the new Jerusalem.[150] In this sense, the new Jerusalem is "the consummation or pinnacle of God's macro-narrative of salvation," meaning that beyond the scope of Revelation, John's description of the city and its inhabitants completes the thread of salvation woven through God's redemptive history beginning in Eden.[151] Furthermore, du Rand points out that John's description of the new Jerusalem shows how the prophets' depiction of new creation has been transformed. For instance, Isa 65 saw the new Jerusalem or Zion as the center of new creation, offering longevity, fertility, and restored relationship with God, and Isa 66 spoke to the gathering of the nations into the new city.[152] The spiritual renewal and rebuilding of the temple emphasized in Ezek 36–48 also points to the blessings coming from a time when God would bring salvation to his people. All these images speak of a new creation that God himself brings to humanity; thus, Jesus transforms the prophets' expectation for ethnic Israel into a hope experienced by those who have faith in him.

The new Jerusalem is certainly the eternal destination of all saints who have been redeemed by the blood of Jesus, but the Zion motif in Rev 21–22

147. Beale, *Book of Revelation*, 1041.

148. Beale, *Book of Revelation*, 1041, 1045.

149. du Rand, "New Jerusalem as Pinnacle," 275.

150. du Rand, "New Jerusalem as Pinnacle," 275.

151. du Rand, "New Jerusalem as Pinnacle," 277.

152. du Rand, "New Jerusalem as Pinnacle," 282.

goes beyond this to encompass the fullness of God's glory upon the whole earth. The city-temple described in this passage appears to equate the new earth with this city, meaning that the new earth itself has become the heavenly temple of God's presence.[153] The new Jerusalem descends from heaven as a bride prepared for her wedding because the contrast between heaven and earth disappears in the new creation.[154] Therefore, those saved by God enjoy the blessings of new creation and the eternal peace offered by God in the new city, but ultimately, it restores what began in Eden—God's glory filling all of creation. Zion's destination is not only the final place of God's salvation, but it is also the sacred space in which the glory of God fills all creation.

One aspect of Zion symbolism in the Psalms and Prophets was Zion's inviolability because it is the place of God's presence. Zion was a protected fortress not because of military strength but because Yahweh inhabited the holy mountain. Since Israel's apostasy led to the Assyrian and Babylonian incursions and resulting exile, the prophets began to interpret this through a future-oriented lens, and Rev 21 depicts the final state of the place of God's sacred presence. Revelation 21:3 states, "the first earth had passed away, and the sea was no more." This indicates that those who belong to the new city will be forever safe from any threat. Beale lists five significant meanings for the lack of a sea in the new creation: no threat from Satan; no threat from rebellious nations; no more death; no more idolatry; no more fear.[155] Psalm 48 contained these themes, describing Zion as the highest summit from which God expels Israel's enemies and brings peace to his people. Therefore, the new Jerusalem represents the fullness of these hopes, because never again will God's people fear that his presence will leave. Evil and death are no more, and there is no longer the threat of foreign invasion.[156]

The new Jerusalem in Rev 21 also completes the expanding theological concept of God's sacred space that began in Eden and was gradually revealed as God's plans for salvation unfolded. The tabernacle and Solomon's temple were reflections, or shadows, of God's heavenly temple, but through Jesus's death on the cross, the temple curtain was torn, symbolizing access to God through faith in Jesus. Sacred space is transformed from a localized area, such as the Jerusalem temple, to a mobile, expanding group of people called the church. Isaiah 4:2–6 foresaw the glory of God's presence filling the new city, and Rev 21:22–24 describes a city with no temple because God's

153. Beale, *Temple and the Church's Mission*, 409.

154. du Rand, "New Jerusalem as the Pinnacle," 291.

155. Beale, *Book of Revelation*, 1042.

156. Beale, *Book of Revelation*, 1042.

presence fills it. God's sacred space is no longer in conflict with a corrupted creation, for now it fills the entirety of this new world.[157]

Glory to God and to the Lamb—Revelation 21:22—22:5

In the final chapter of the Bible, the redeemed people of God find themselves in the garden of his presence, for "they will see his face" (Rev 22:4). The barriers of sin and death are gone, and instead of hiding from God's face, people will see him and enjoy him forever. No priest is needed, and no sacrifice is necessary, because the Lamb has covered the saints by his own blood and washed them clean.[158] The temple is no longer a stone structure with restricted access, for the Lord himself has become the temple, spreading his divine presence across the new creation so that all his children can dwell with him in peace.[159]

Much of the imagery of the new Jerusalem resembles Ezekiel's vision of a new temple, yet in this instance, John diverges from Ezekiel, for there is no physical temple. God's presence is no longer limited because sin and death have been forever banished from this place, and what was once veiled in the holy of holies is now experienced by all the inhabitants of the new city.[160] Zion had begun as a symbol of God's presence upon earth, and specifically, his choice of David and the place in which his presence would dwell (Ps 132:13–14). By the end of the canon, the motifs associated with the divine presence have expanded into a symbol denoting God's eternal presence within and among all those who have been redeemed and now rest upon the new earth. The continuity between the Old and New Testaments is significant in Rev 21–22, for it allows the original audience and readers in the present day to visualize the new Jerusalem as the reality awaiting all those who are faithful to God. This process began in Genesis when God created humans in his image with the purpose of expanding beyond Eden to fill the earth.[161] The remainder of Scripture contains God's rescue plan to restore humanity by freeing them from Satan's control, and this unfolds in the final chapters of the Bible as Satan and all evil are forever banished from God's new creation. The tabernacle and the Jerusalem temple, as well as the church established by Jesus, all point to this moment when God finalizes his rescue

157. Beale, *Temple and the Church's Mission*, 411.

158. Koester, *Revelation and the End*, 196.

159. Tabb, *All Things New*, 196.

160. deSilva, *Discovering Revelation*, 256.

161. Alexander, *From Eden*, 103.

plan in an eternal rest given to those who have been redeemed.[162] Thus, the imagery associated with Zion weaves through Scripture, reminding God's people that his presence is the goal, that salvation is completed not merely in a heavenly realm but in the eternal presence of God. More than an absence of evil, the temple of God's presence is life-giving, ultimately bringing all the redeemed into unity with Christ as God's eternal priests over all creation.[163]

Another image related to Zion is the "river of the water of life . . . flowing from the throne of God and of the Lamb" in the new Jerusalem (Rev 22:1). A life-giving river flowed through Eden outward toward the rest of creation, and Zion is depicted as having "a river whose streams make glad the city of God" in Ps 46:4. Ezekiel's vision of a new temple included a river flowing from the temple and gaining strength as it flowed outward, indicating that God's presence will bring life to all creation.[164] Joel 3:18 foresaw a time when "a fountain shall come forth from the house of the Lord," bringing forth life and blessing to Jerusalem and the defeat of the Lord's enemies. In all these images, the focus is the same: the presence of God flows outward from his dwelling place to bring life and blessing to his people. These images come together in Rev 22:1 in God's final, eternal dwelling among his people. If Rev 22:1–5 serves as a climax to the descriptions of the new city in chapter 21, then the centrality of the throne of God, from which the river of life flows, shows this to be the finality of salvation.[165] The river flowing from God's throne is not merely a source for eternal life, for it represents the culmination of God's salvation to those believe. They will be forever nourished and at peace because God has saved them and is dwelling among them. Zion is symbolic of God's protection over his people but also as the place from which the Messiah would regather Israel; thus, this final imagery of God's throne conveys completeness. No longer will people thirst for God, for the river of life will forever be available to them: the hunger for the knowledge of the Lord desired by the nations in Isa 2:3 is now forever satisfied through God's abundant blessing.[166]

Just as Zion was the symbolic center of creation, the place where God's divine presence intersected with the earth, so, too, is the new creation the place of God's presence, except it now fills the cosmos. This is Zion's destination, that what began in the garden would fill the cosmos, making all creation a temple where God's presence is enjoyed. All the predecessors, such

162. Alexander, *From Eden*, 103.

163. Beale, *God Dwells Among Us*, 140.

164. Schreiner, *Revelation*, 986.

165. Gallusz, *Throne Motif*, 167.

166. Koester, *Revelation and the End*, 823.

as the tabernacle, temple, and even the church, were symbolic of the cosmos of God's creation, pointing to a time when the task to extend God's glory throughout the earth would come. Revelation presents the culmination of this process in the new Jerusalem, a city that in fact is a worldwide temple, because God's presence is now everywhere.[167] This is the reason Zion expanded outward as a symbol of God's presence through the Psalms, Prophets, and New Testament, culminating in a vision of God's glory filling all creation. Zion was never meant to remain on a small hill in Jerusalem, but rather, its purpose was to remind the people of God that their ultimate satisfaction would come only in the presence of God their Creator. Revelation serves as the capstone to the canon of Scripture because it weaves together numerous symbols from the Old Testament, creating a tapestry which reveals God's final plans for those chosen as citizens of his eternal city.[168] None of this is possible without Christ, for John is clear that the "throne of God and of the Lamb" is the centerpiece of the new Jerusalem. Christ is the Messiah who reigns from Zion (Ps 2:7–9), the "branch" who nourishes and protects his people (Isa 4:2; 11:1–9; Zech 3:8–10), the one who released the Spirit to indwell his body the church (1 Cor 3:16), the great high priest who made atonement by his own blood (Heb 9:12), and the Lamb who reigns victorious on Mount Zion with his faithful saints (Rev 14:1). Each of these images contribute to a beautiful painting depicting Christ as the fullness of God's presence, making the way for all who enter by faith to live forever in the warmth of his presence.

CONCLUSION: THE CHURCH AS THE CITY OF GOD

Zion, a theological symbol representing God's presence, was developed and expanded through Scripture until it reached its destination in the new Jerusalem, where God and the Lamb reign eternally with the redeemed people from "all tribes and peoples and languages" (Rev 7:9). Through an expositional study through key biblical texts, Zion emerges as a symbol that expands beyond a hill in Jerusalem to a symbol of God's eternal presence upon a new creation. However, along this journey, an image of the Messiah is born out of the separation caused by sin and through God's progressive revelation of his heart and purpose for mankind. Zion's transformation through the Prophets and within the New Testament is fulfilled in Jesus Christ, for through his sacrificial death, the temple veil was torn (Matt 27:51), symbolizing access to the holy of holies through faith in the Son

167. Beale, *Temple and the Church's Mission*, 428.

168. Tabb, *All Things New*, 196.

(Heb 9:12). Because of this great salvation (Heb 2:3), the New Testament reveals Jesus as the fulfillment of the prophetic hope that one day God would remake creation, gathering the nations for his own glory to enjoy his presence forever (Isa 2:3–4; 66:18–19).

FROM TEMPLE MOUNT TO ETERNAL KINGDOM

Theological symbols are multivalent vehicles, carrying specific meanings and collecting newer and deeper meanings as they expand and develop through the canon of the Bible. Because of this, the full meaning of Zion as a symbol is not limited only to texts that explicitly mention Zion by name; rather, various texts develop a web of related meanings that interact to create a fuller picture.[169] Chapter one of this study demonstrated that Zion symbolism was not created by enthusiastic Jerusalemites who were celebrating the arrival of Yahweh and his anointed king in the capital city of the Israelites; rather, the symbolism that emerged out of the Temple Mount during the united monarchy was the product of centuries of compounded history and revelation from Eden until Solomon's dedication of the temple. While the term "Zion" originally indicated the topographical location within the greater city of Jerusalem, it never again refers only to the physical city after the period of the later monarchy.[170] Instead, Zion becomes the primary theological symbol for the presence of God among his people, representing Yahweh's reign on earth and the subsequent blessing given to the Israelites. Therefore, Zion still refers to a place throughout the Old Testament, but it is the sacred space of God's presence.

Building upon the established tradition of the tabernacle and the holy of holies within it, the presence of God in the Jerusalem temple represents the moment when God chose a permanent dwelling for his name. After the presence of God terrified the people at Mount Sinai, God initiated a new arrangement, saying, "And let them make me a sanctuary," revealing God's desire to dwell among the Israelite community in a personal, approachable way (Exod 25:8).[171] In Deuteronomy, Moses looked forward to "the place that the Lord your God will choose, to make his name dwell there," indicating the divine election of a then unknown place (Deut 26:2). However, to David, God denies the need for a permanent house and instead blesses David as the anointed king, saying, "And I will make for you a great name" (2 Sam 7:9). In this pivotal moment, God's primary concern for David is that

169. Ollenburger, *Zion, the City*, 20.

170. Lohse and Fohrer, "Σιών," in *TDNT* 7:295.

171. Merrill, *Everlasting Dominion*, 533.

he and his kingly line are committed to him, resulting in the promise that "I will establish the throne of his kingdom forever" (2 Sam 7:13). God affirms David's desire to construct a permanent dwelling place, yet his primary desire is that his name be glorified throughout the earth through the righteous and prosperous rule of his anointed king. Isaiah saw the heavenly throne room of God as vast and glorious, far beyond what the temple of stone could contain (Isa 6:1–2). Isaiah's vision depicts the Holy One of Israel as the creator of all things, for as the book of Isaiah closes, the Lord says, "Heaven is my throne, and the earth is my footstool; what is the house that you would build for me, and what is the place of my rest" (Isa 66:1). Thus, God's presence was never truly confined to any tabernacle or temple, but rather, God, in his mercy toward Israel, revealed himself to them in a way that was approachable. The point of God's "house," whether in a tent or temple, was that it represented the place where people were invited to meet with him.[172] The furnishings, bread, and lampstand were symbolic of God's desire to "dwell in their midst" (Exod 25:8), and the priesthood was consecrated because "I will dwell among the people of Israel and will be their God" (Exod 29:45). These pivotal moments in Israel's history build toward the goal of Zion as the permanent place of God's holy presence among his people.

Chapter 2 researched the role of Zion in Psalms as a significant theological motif, especially as the psalmists reflected upon Israel's unique relationship with Yahweh and its place among the nations. The Psalter has an intentional structure that builds toward a growing anticipation of the Messiah, and alongside this is the role of God's chosen sacred space on earth called Zion. Zion can be a reference to the Temple Mount or to the city of Jerusalem and even its inhabitants, and through the Psalms, many descriptions of Zion emerge. Zion is invincible in Pss 46 and 48, and even from exile, the Israelites long for God's justice as Ps 137 laments. God is the King enthroned in Zion, and from there, he subdues Israel's enemies and has conquered chaos, giving Israel salvation from its enemies and protection from future threat. Amid Zion's praise emerges a vision of the future, where people from various nations will claim Zion as their home. Psalm 87 says, "And of Zion it shall be said, this one and that one were born in her; for the Most High himself will establish her" (Ps 87:5). Zion, God's chosen dwelling place and the place where he has anointed his king, is also the home of the nations as God brings people from across the earth toward his presence. Zion in the Psalms is a testament to God's faithfulness in establishing Israel's kingdom in Jerusalem but also a symbol depicting God's plans for the city in a future day when the nations will experience the fullness of his presence.

172. Merrill, *Everlasting Dominion*, 22.

Chapter 3 examined the Prophets, the section of Scripture with the most use of the Zion symbol and the place where its symbolism greatly expands through Israel's history and God's progressive revelation. Psalm 132:13–14 celebrates Yahweh's choice of Zion as his "resting place forever," yet within the Prophets, a new picture emerges of God's judgment and future restoration upon Zion, even if his presence is no longer in the temple. It becomes evident in the Prophets that, while God maintains his sacred space in Zion, that is not the goal, but rather, Zion is the beginning of God's mission to spread his glory upon the whole earth. Thus, Isaiah prophesied that Yahweh was returning to comfort his people (Isa 40:1–5), implying that the Lord's holy presence had left Zion during its time of cleansing and punishment. After exile, Israel's "iniquity is pardoned" because "she has received . . . double for all her sins" (Isa 40:2). Intertwined with God's sacred space is the covenant God made with Israel, for even in times of exile and destruction due to Israel's apostasy, God did not forget his promises. He would return, he would make Zion holy, and he would deliver his people through a coming servant.[173] The messianic expectation building in the Prophets arises from the Davidic covenant and the belief that God would not forget his promises to David, which provided Israel with the hope that the righteous "branch" would indeed arrive, bringing peace and holiness once again to Zion (Isa 11:1–2; Jer 23:5–6). Zion exists between judgment and salvation, representing God's presence, yet incomplete because of the people's sin.[174] For Zion to become a holy city, drawing the nations to learn from God and extending peace across the earth (Isa 2:2–4), God's sacred space must be cleansed of its sin and idolatry.

Ezekiel receives further insight into this dilemma, seeing the glory of God established in a new temple containing a river of life and fruit-bearing trees. The former Zion has passed away, along with its leaders, but a new temple that is eternal and glorious will replace it. Ezekiel's vision portrays a perfect, even heavenly temple as God's dwelling place among people. By the time of Zechariah, the Lord is rebuilding the place of his presence, saying, "I have returned to Zion and will dwell in the midst of Jerusalem, and Jerusalem shall be called the faithful city, and the mountain of the Lord of hosts, the holy mountain" (Zech 8:3). God reaffirms that "they shall be my people, and I will be their God," but the way for this to be accomplished must include the return of God's anointed king (Zech 8:8; 9:9). However, through the Second Temple era, the sentiment that these promises were unfulfilled

173. Abernethy, *Book of Isaiah*, 57.

174. Poulson, *Representing Zion*, 25.

began to grow, leading to an increasing interest in the arrival of the Messiah, the one through whom Israel's salvation would come.

Zion's developing symbolism was pointing toward the Messiah's entrance into God's redemptive history. The prophets foresaw a coming king who would usher in a time of salvation for God's faithful remnant, and it would be in God's chosen city that he would draw the nations and establish eternal peace. The Gospels clarify this in Jesus Christ, showing him to be the fulfillment of the prophets' expectation and the only Son of God who would bring true salvation to Israel and the world. Jesus, as he reenacts Israel's history and teaches about the true kingdom of God, reveals himself as the new temple. The primary symbolic function of Zion is the presence of God among his people, and Jesus was that very presence in himself. The longing for Zion's restoration is not forgotten in the Gospels, but rather Jesus presents himself as the fulfillment of those hopes as the "place" of God's presence on earth.[175] In Matthew 16, Jesus states that he will "build my church" upon "this rock," meaning believers like Peter would constitute God's heavenly temple, built upon the true cornerstone and foundation of Christ (Matt 16:18). Thus, those who confess Jesus as Peter did are welcomed as part of this spiritual temple, like individual blocks that form a temple inhabited by God's presence.

Jesus is the turning point between the old and the new temples: Jesus claimed in Luke 21:6 that the temple structure in Jerusalem would be completely destroyed, making way for a new temple community to be formed by faith in him. Furthermore, Acts showed that, as the disciples gathered in the temple courts, they were representing the true temple, people filled by God's presence through the Spirit. All these moments in the Gospels and Acts point to the same premise, that God, in Jesus and through the Holy Spirit, was creating a new Zion. This, in fact, was the goal all along, for the vision of Isa 2:2–4 concerning Zion and the new covenant of Jer 31:31–34 could not be fulfilled unless the hearts of individuals were transformed. Jesus, the one who purchased atonement through his sacrifice (Heb 9:12), the mediator of a better covenant (Heb 12:24), and the victorious Lamb (Rev 14:1), was the only one who could fulfill all these prophecies and transform individual hearts to create a new community of redeemed saints as Isaiah envisioned. Thus, Zion's symbolic journey is transformed through Jesus's life and death, because he is the new Zion to which people come in order to receive salvation and be forever at peace in the presence of God.

Beyond the Gospels, the New Testament further develops the transformation of the Zion symbol through Paul's theology, the teaching of

175. Lister, *Presence of God*, 133.

Hebrews, and Zion's final role as depicted in Revelation. Paul understood that the church, as the body of Christ, was the heavenly temple on earth. He admonished the churches to consider their calling as God's temple as a sacred space, despite its humble circumstances. Whether the churches met in cramped homes or in secret gatherings, they had become a new temple through the indwelling Spirit. Zion was not left behind in Paul's thinking, but rather its symbolism plays a unique role as he teaches the churches to live as though they are citizens of "the Jerusalem above," which "is free" (Gal 4:26).

Because of the Lamb's victory in bringing salvation, the New Testament reveals the final picture of Zion as the city of God in an unending, peaceful paradise called the new Jerusalem. Zion represents this hope from Israel's historical pinnacle in the time of David and Solomon but persists through exile and devastation because the faithful remnant of Zion would not only be saved but God would "make her wilderness like Eden" (Isa 51:3). Hebrews argues that Jesus ministers in the superior, heavenly temple, which is already accessible to believers, for he is continually making "intercession for them" (Heb 7:25). However, the prophets' hope of new creation is not found in a heavenly temple descending to the present earth, but rather all creation must be remade. For God's presence to fill the earth as originally intended, a new city of God in a new creation would come. Revelation 21:22 says, "And I saw no temple in the city, for its temple is the Lord God the Almighty and the Lamb." John saw the glory of God filling the new city, which has now become symbolic of both God's eternal presence and those who fill it. What began on Mount Zion will be complete in the new Jerusalem, which will fill the new creation and be an everlasting home for God's people.

Theological symbolism plays a significant role in the Bible, connecting the truth of God's character and divine will with the hopes and expectations of people. Furthermore, symbols such as Zion reflect the Bible's cohesive theology, drawing together hundreds of years of revelation toward a common center: God's presence.[176] Zion not only captured Israel's attention and focused the people's prayers on a physical intersection between heaven and earth, but it also refocused the people upon God himself. God chose Zion (Ps 132:12), he would return to restore it (Isa 40:1–4), and he would be the one to send the "branch" to bring salvation (Isa 11:1–2). All this is fulfilled in Jesus Christ and the salvation he brings, culminating in the saints' eternal dwelling with God and the Lamb upon the new earth. Zion, then, is a powerful symbol that denotes God's presence, yet it was transformed through Jesus and its promises were transferred to all who are redeemed by

176. Duvall, *God's Relational Presence*, 5.

the Lamb, the true Israel who are Abraham's "seed" (Gal 3:29). John saw the faithful saints standing victorious on Mount Zion (Rev 14:1), representing both their victory in Jesus and their eternal status as the redeemed brothers and sisters of Jesus. This was the goal of Zion, that one day God would eternally dwell among his most beloved creation. Zion returns the hopes of men to Eden, but then it envisions an eternal future where man's broken relationship with God is finally and fully restored.

Zion symbolism transforms as it develops through the canon of Scripture: what originally began as a symbol of God's presence and the permanent dwelling of God in Jerusalem expanded to represent God's divine activity on earth. Zion became the place where God would purify a remnant and subsequently draw the nations of the earth toward his presence, leading to a time of peace. However, Zion's ultimate fulfillment comes through Jesus, who created permanent access to God through his own sacrificial offering in the heavenly, eternal temple of God (Heb 9:11–12). Therefore, Zion's development in the Old Testament made way for its transformation in Jesus. Ultimately, Zion is depicted as the eternal resting place of the saints in a new Jerusalem, bringing to fruition the prophets' hope and the longing of all those who remain faithful to God.

BECOMING THE NEW ZION TODAY

Zion represents much more than an Old Testament symbol or the place where Yahweh's temple sat, for through its theological symbolism, it bears application for Christians and the churches they represent. An essential text in this study is Heb 12:22–24, which states that Christians "have come to Mount Zion . . . and to the assembly of the firstborn," meaning they have a new identity as citizens of the heavenly Zion. This text portrays the blessing of this citizenship in a heavenly Zion as both something already experienced in Christ and as something to be fully realized in the future. The church, then, is the city of the living God in the present and future. In the present, the Church is like Zion because it has become the place of God's presence on earth. Paul captured this in 1 Cor 3:16, saying, "Do you not know that you are God's temple and that God's spirit dwells in you?" The church inhabits the presence of God in a corporate sense, meaning that the congregation functions as a temple. No longer does the world need to see a structure representing a deity; rather, they can approach the presence of God through the life and witness of the members of Christ's body. This "temple is holy," meaning that God has purified it so that his presence can dwell within it through the Holy Spirit (1 Cor 3:17).

Worship Gatherings

The truth that the temple of God's presence now exists in the church is significant for the weekly gatherings of a local church. Worship, communion, baptism, and the preaching of the word are testimonies of God's faithfulness and presence among individuals and the corporate gathering. Zion represents the place where God intersects with earth, a sacred space where his holiness is on display, which draws the nations toward it. Worship, then, is deeper than a gathering to sing, pray, and hear the word taught; rather, it is a sacred space where God's presence shines brightly to the world. Since individual believers make up the eschatological temple, the collection of believers in a worship service is a bright, beautiful picture of God's divine presence resting on earth in an accessible way. No curtain, no restriction, only the invitation to enter into the presence of God through Jesus. In this context, singing songs of praise reflects the heavenly praise of God's name, and rejoicing in God's presence echoes the words of Ps 48: "Walk about Zion, go around her . . . go through her citadels, that you may tell the next generation that this is God, our God forever and ever" (Ps 48:13–14). Worship is a testimony of God's redemptive actions in the past, which leads to an anticipation of future works.

Psalm 122 opens by saying, "I rejoiced with those who said to me, 'Let's go to the house of the Lord'" (Ps 122:1 CSB). This song, possibly sung or spoken by a traveler visiting Jerusalem for a festival, rejoices in the nearness of God's presence and gratitude the pilgrim experiences as part of celebrating Yahweh's goodness toward Jerusalem.[177] Seeking the presence of God together as the church should be a joyous occasion. The concept of personalized worship, preferences regarding musical styles, or even finding a place where one "feels comfortable" are insignificant compared to the joy of being able to worship the Lord together with other believers. In a me-centered, individualized society, church has often become more about singing the songs that trigger emotional responses, creating an atmosphere that helps people "feel" something, or even manipulating people through emotional language to increase giving or secure brand loyalty. These are failures to recognize the simple beauty of those who "go up to give thanks to the name of the Lord" (Ps 122:4 CSB). As the new Zion, local churches should primarily be a place of heartfelt joy, created within the individual heart but strengthened by the collective gathering. Psalm 122 ends by stating, "For the sake of the house of the Lord our God, I will seek your good" (Ps 122:9). This verse indicates that the author's contribution to the city and the prayers offered for it are

177. Allen, *Psalms 101–150*, 213.

directly linked to the Lord's presence there. Likewise, worship in the local church needs to be centered upon the glory of God, and a Savior who has redeemed faithful saints and offered them eternal life. If the church is the new Zion already, then through her singing, prayers, and joyful gatherings, a watching world sees a glimpse of the new Jerusalem.

A vertical-oriented worship service is the primary way in which worship gatherings reflect the church's identity as the new Zion. This means that prayers, Scripture readings, songs of praise, and the preaching of the word are each aligned with God as the central focus. Prayers are less about the problems of people and more about the goodness and mercy of God. Songs are selected not based upon their popularity but upon their focus on God's character and covenant promises toward the people. The preacher's aim is to point the congregants' hearts upward as they grasp the truth of God's word and its applicability to their daily lives. For instance, many popular songs on Christian radio are filled with the words "me" and "my," which are acceptable for times of reflection and personal devotion; yet, in the corporate gathering, aiming praise upward with "you" and "your" (in reference to God) are more reflective of the church functioning in her role as the new Zion. Styles, loudness, and particular preferences for instruments are secondary; what is primary is the theological conviction that the local church's objective in corporate worship is to point upward to God.

The age of a song is less important than its doctrinal confession and emphasis upon the glory of God and gratitude toward him. Songs that veer toward a therapeutic emphasis or a heightened sense of one's personal journey may also be helpful for personal devotions but should be avoided during corporate worship. Songs of thanksgiving, centered upon the character of God, his good works, his glory, and his salvation in Christ ought to remain the primary focus of corporate worship.

If the final home for Christians is eternal life in the new Jerusalem; then, as present citizens of that place, they have the unique privilege of serving as ambassadors of Christ through their lifestyle (2 Cor 5:20). Through Christ, Christians are the new Zion, citizens of the heavenly Jerusalem in an already-not-yet way, meaning that their new identity has transformed the way they live on the current earth. Christians love the unlovable, serve the undeserving, and rescue the helpless because they belong to a better, enduring city. Hebrews states, "For here we have no lasting city, but we seek the city that is to come" (Heb 13:14). By focusing their attention on the heavenly reality already experienced and yet to be fulfilled, Christians have the opportunity to point others toward the city that endures. The weekly gathering for worship becomes a time of rejoicing, encouragement, and equipping, launching the saints back into a world where they live out their God-given calling in humility and gratitude toward the one who saved them and invited them into citizenship in the eternal kingdom of God. While many in the watching world long for meaning due to the brevity of life and the numerous daily worries and difficulties, the church can portray the glory of God to the nations through their peace, love, and worship of God despite present circumstances. This is the essence of Zion, that through the presence of God, the nations would draw near, learn God's righteous ways, and find peace (Isa 2:3–4). Zion is the eschatological place of salvation where God's Messiah would reign over the nations in peace, and through Jesus, the church extends that reign across the earth through service and through witness of the gospel.

Authentic Christian Community

If Christians already belong to the heavenly Zion, then another important application of its theological symbolism is authentic community centered on Jesus Christ. The church, and individual believers, become like a taste of heaven on earth, or like a glimpse into eternity, because of their unity in Christ. This was Paul's concern in 1 Corinthians and why he reminded the believers that the church was collectively like a temple (1 Cor 3:16), but also as individual members of that body, they housed God's presence (1 Cor 6:19). Therefore, Christians with various backgrounds who come together in unity and peace because of Christ create a preview of the new Jerusalem, where people from every nation and language will gather to worship the Lord forever (Rev 7:9). Furthermore, Rev 14:1–5 portrays the saints of God gathered in victory with the Lamb on Mount Zion, and they are described as "these who follow the Lamb wherever he goes" (Rev 14:4). This picture has been inaugurated through Jesus, meaning that the present community of believers are already experiencing the blessing of Christ's victory even though there is a greater fulfillment to come.[178] The same deception and temptation that entered the garden of Eden persist even after conversion; thus, the unity, fellowship, and dedication of the Christian community is an essential aspect of the church becoming a taste of the heavenly Zion on earth. God's word has the power to restore wayward believers, and authentic Christian community exists to keep believers unified and accountable to one another for the sake of God's glory.[179]

One way church leaders can model this approach to Christian community is through intentional small groups of believers who are bonded

178. Beale, *New Testament Biblical Theology*, 223.

179. Beale, *New Testament Biblical Theology*, 224.

through the word and common life experiences. While the culture of today finds common ground through hobbies or lifestyle preferences, believers have the unique privilege of bonding with other believers through their belief in Jesus and common experience of salvation. Honest conversations, rooted in grace, create a sense of belonging and community much deeper than common interest; rather, those belonging to the new Zion share in suffering, even share in material possessions, because they already belong to an enduring city. These kinds of community groups are deeper than a weekly Bible study: while the word is central, its application for the individual and communal life propels the group to care deeply for one another, seek advice and wisdom from one another, and worship freely together. Younger generations are especially hungry for this kind of community, and the church has the satisfying love of Christ and the welcoming invitation to those who long to find rest in the presence of God. Such a community of faith reflects the beauty of Ps 125, which says, "Those who trust in the Lord are like Mount Zion, which cannot be moved, but abides forever" (Ps 125:1).

Ultimately, Zion reflects God's desire to dwell among his people in peace and harmony. Until that day is fully realized, believers in Jesus who are indwelt by the Spirit have the unique opportunity of dual citizenship as they represent the new Jerusalem, awaiting that final day when the present earth will pass away and the new will come (Rev 21:1). The Christian hope is like no other, for it is not based upon one's own works or effort but is based solely upon the grace of God in Jesus Christ. Therefore, as citizens of the heavenly Zion (Heb 12:22), the Christian has the responsibility and privilege of reflecting that hope to the world, knowing that one day the glory of God will cover all creation and that all of Zion's hopes will be fully realized in the everlasting presence of God.

In his hymn "We're Marching to Zion," Isaac Watts captures the spirit of Zion symbolism well:

> Come, we that love the Lord
> And let our joys be known
> Join in a song with sweet accord
> And thus surround the throne
>
> *Refrain:*
> We're marching to Zion
> Beautiful, beautiful Zion
> We're marching upward to Zion
> The beautiful city of God
>
> The hill of Zion yields
> A thousand sacred sweets

Before we reach the heav'nly fields
Or walk the golden streets

Then let our songs abound
And every tear be dry
We're marching through Immanuel's ground
To fairer world on high

Bibliography

Abernethy, Andrew. *The Book of Isaiah and God's Kingdom: A Thematic-Theological Approach*. Downers Grove, IL: InterVarsity, 2016.

Adler, Joshua J. "The Historical Background of Psalm 24." *Jewish Bible Quarterly* 20 (1992) 268–78.

Alexander, Desmond. *From Eden to the New Jerusalem*. Grand Rapids: Kregel, 2013.

Alexander, T. D., and D. W. Baker, eds. *Dictionary of the Old Testament: Pentateuch*. Downers Grove, IL: InterVarsity, 2003.

Allen, Leslie C. *Jeremiah: A Commentary*. Louisville: Presbyterian, 2008.

———. *Joel, Obadiah, Jonah, and Micah*. New International Commentary on the Old Testament. Grand Rapids: Eerdmans, 1976.

———. *Psalms 101–50*. Word Biblical Commentary 21. Nashville: Thomas Nelson, 2002.

———. "The Value of Rhetorical Criticism in Psalm 69." *Journal for Biblical Literature* 105 (1986) 577–98.

Allen, Ronald B. "Psalm 87: A Song Rarely Sung." *Bibliotheca Sacra* 153 (1996) 131–40.

Alvarez, Francis D. "The Temple Controversy in Mark." *Landas* 28 (2014) 115–52.

Anderson, Arnold A. *2 Samuel*. Word Biblical Commentary 11. Grand Rapids: HarperCollins, 2015.

Attridge, Harold. *A Commentary on the Epistle to the Hebrews*. Minneapolis: Fortress, 1989.

———. *Essays on John and Hebrews*. Tübingen: Mohr Siebeck, 2010.

Aune, David. *Revelation 6–16*. Word Biblical Commentary 52B. Grand Rapids: HarperCollins, 2014.

Baer, David A. *When We All Go Home: Translation and Theology in LXX Isaiah 56–66*. London: Bloomsbury, 2001.

Balogh, Csaba. "He Filled Zion with Justice and Righteousness: The Composition of Isaiah 33." *Biblica* 89 (2008) 477–504.

Baltzer, Klaus. *Deutero-Isaiah: A Commentary*. Minneapolis: Fortress, 2001.

———. "The Meaning of the Temple in Lukan Writings." *Harvard Theological Review* 58 (1965) 263–77.

Balz, Horst R., and Gerhard Schneider. *Exegetical Dictionary of the New Testament*. 3 vols. Grand Rapids: Eerdmans, 1990.

Barber, Michael P. "Jesus as the Davidic Temple Builder and Peter's Priestly Role in Matthew 16:16–19." *Journal of Biblical Literature* 132 (2013) 935–53.

Barker, Kenneth L. *Micah, Nahum, Habakkuk, Zephaniah*. New American Commentary 20. Nashville: Broadman & Holman, 1999.

Barker, Margaret. *King of the Jews: Temple Theology in John's Gospel*. La Vergne, TN: SPCK, 2014.

Barry, John D., et al., eds. *The Lexham Bible Dictionary*. Accessed using Logos Bible Software. Bellingham, WA: Lexham, 2016.

Barton, John. *Joel and Obadiah: A Commentary*. Louisville: Westminster John Knox, 2001.

Batto, Bernard F., and Kathryn L. Roberts, eds. *David and Zion: Biblical Studies in Honor of J. J. M. Roberts*. University Park, PA: Pennsylvania State University Press, 2004.

Bauckham, Richard. *Climax of Prophecy: Studies on the Book of Revelation*. London: Bloomsbury, 2000.

Beale, G. K. *The Book of Revelation: A Commentary on the Greek Text*. New International Greek Testament Commentary. Grand Rapids: Eerdmans, 1999.

———. *A New Testament Biblical Theology*. Grand Rapids: Baker Academic, 2011.

———. *The Temple and the Church's Mission*. Downers Grove, IL: InterVarsity, 2004.

———. *We Become What We Worship: A Biblical Theology of Idolatry*. Downers Grove, IL: InterVarsity, 2018.

Beale, G. K., and Mitchell Kim. *God Dwells Among Us*. Downers Grove, IL: InterVarsity, 2014.

Beasley-Murray, George R. *John*. Word Biblical Commentary 36. Waco, TX: Word, 1987.

Behr, John. *John the Theologian and His Paschal Gospel: A Prologue to Theology*. Oxford: Oxford University Press, 2019.

Berges, Ulrich. "The Zion Theology of the Book of Isaiah." *Estudios Biblicos* 58 (2000) 167–98.

Berlin, Adele, and Benjamin Sommer. *Psalms 120–50*. JPS Bible Commentary. Lincoln, NE: University of Nebraska Press, 2023.

Blackburn, Ross. *The God Who Makes Himself Known: The Missionary Heart of the Book of Exodus*. Downers Grove, IL: InterVarsity, 2012.

Blaising, Craig, et al., eds. *Psalms 1–50*. Ancient Christian Commentary on Scripture 7. Grand Rapids: Baker Academic, 2007.

Blenkinsopp, Joseph. *Creation, Un-Creation, Re-creation: A Discursive Commentary on Genesis 1–11*. London: Bloomsbury, 2011.

———. *Essays on the Book of Isaiah*. Tübingen: Mohr Siebeck, 2019.

———. *Isaiah 1–39: A New Translation with Introduction and Commentary*. The Anchor Yale Bible Commentaries 19. New Haven, CT: Doubleday, 2000.

Block, Daniel I. *Beyond the River Chebar: Studies in Kingship and Eschatology in the Book of Ezekiel*. Cambridge: James Clarke, 2014.

———. *The Book of Ezekiel: Chapters 25–48*. New International Commentary on the Old Testament. Grand Rapids: Eerdmans, 1998.

Blomberg, Craig L. *A New Testament Theology*. Waco, TX: Baylor University Press, 2018.

Bock, Darrell L. *Luke 1:1—9:50*. Baker Exegetical Commentary on the New Testament. Grand Rapids: Baker Academic, 1994.

Boda, Mark J. *The Book of Zechariah*. New International Commentary on the Old Testament. Grand Rapids: Eerdmans, 2016.

Boda, Mark J., and J. Gordon McConville, eds. *Dictionary of the Old Testament: Prophets*. Downers Grove, IL: InterVarsity, 2012.

Boda, Mark J., et al., eds. *Daughter Zion: Her Portrait, Her Response*. Williston, VT: Society of Biblical Literature, 2012.

Bokhorst, Mirjam J. "Enoch's Vision of the Heavenly Temple (1 En. 14:8–25) Reconsidered." *The Biblical Annals* 14 (2024) 245–70.

Booij, Thijs. "Psalm 132: Zion's Well-Being." *Biblica* 90 (2009) 75–83.

Bos, Johanna W. H. "Psalm 87." *Interpretation* 47 (1993) 281–85.

Bosworth, David. "Daughter Zion and Weeping in Lamentations 1–2." *Journal for the Study of the Old Testament* 38 (2013) 217–37.

Botha, P. J. "The 'Enthronement Psalms': A Claim to the World-Wide Honor of Yahweh." *Old Testament Essays* 11 (1998) 24–39.

Botterweck, G. J., and H. Ringgren, eds. *Theological Dictionary of the Old Testament*. 17 vols. Grand Rapids: Eerdmans, 2003.

Brannan, Rick, ed. *The Lexham English Septuagint*. Bellingham, WA: Lexham, 2012.

Brown, Francis, et al. *Enhanced Brown-Driver-Briggs Hebrew and English Lexicon*. Oxford: Clarendon, 1977.

Brown, Raymond E. "The Messianism of Qumran." *The Catholic Bible Quarterly* 19 (1957) 53–82.

Bruce, F. F. *The Epistle to the Galatians: A Commentary on the Greek Text*. New International Greek Testament Commentary. Grand Rapids: Eerdmans, 1982.

Brueggemann, Walter. *Isaiah 1–39*. Louisville: Westminster John Knox, 1998.

———. *Isaiah 40–66*. Louisville: Westminster John Knox, 1998.

———. *The Theology of the Book of Jeremiah*. Cambridge: Cambridge University Press, 2006.

Calvin, John. *Commentaries on the First Book of Moses, Called Genesis*. Translated by John King. Edinburgh: Calvin Translation Society, 1847.

Carey, Holly J. "Teachings and Tirades: Jesus' Temple Act and His Teachings in Mark 11:15–19." *Stone-Campbell Journal* 10 (2007) 93–105.

Carson, D. A. *The Gospel According to John*. Pillar New Testament Commentary. Grand Rapids: Eerdmans, 1991.

Carver, Daniel E. "Biblical Prophecy in Its Ancient Near Eastern Context: A New Interpretation of Jeremiah 30–33." *Journal of Biblical Literature* 142 (2023) 267–87.

Chae, Young S. *Jesus as the Eschatological Davidic Shepherd: Studies in the Old Testament, Second Temple Judaism, and in the Gospel of Matthew*. Tübingen: Mohr Siebeck, 2019.

Charles, Robert H., ed. *Commentary on the Pseudepigrapha of the Old Testament*. 2 vols. Oxford: Clarendon, 1913.

———. *Pseudepigrapha of the Old Testament*. 2 vols. Oxford: Clarendon, 1913.

Childs, Brevard. *Isaiah*. Old Testament Library. Louisville: Westminster John Knox, 2001.

Church, Philip. *Hebrews and the Temple: Attitudes to the Temple in Second Temple Judaism and in Hebrews*. Boston: Brill, 2017.

Clark, David J., and Howard A. Hatton. *A Handbook on Zechariah*. UBS Handbook Series. New York: United Bible Societies, 2002.

Clifford, Richard J. *The Cosmic Mountain in Canaan and the Old Testament*. Cambridge, MA: Harvard University Press, 1972.

Cockerill, Gareth. *The Epistle to the Hebrews*. New International Commentary on the New Testament. Grand Rapids: Eerdmans, 2012.

———. "Hebrews 12:18–24: Apocalyptic Typology or Platonic Dualism?" *Tyndale Bulletin* 69 (2018) 225–39.

Cohn, Robert L. "The Mountains and Mount Zion." *Judaism* 26 (1977) 97–115.

Craigie, Peter C. *Jeremiah 1–25*. Word Biblical Commentary 26. Dallas: Word, 1991.

Craigie, Peter C. *Psalms 1–50*. Word Biblical Commentary 19. Grand Rapids: HarperCollins, 2016.

Culley, Robert C. "Psalm 102: A Complaint with a Difference." *Semeia* 62 (1993) 19–35.

Currid, John. *Against the Gods: The Polemical Theology of the Old Testament*. Wheaton, IL: Crossway, 2013.

deClaissé-Walford, Nancy, et al. *The Book of Psalms*. New International Commentary on the Old Testament. Grand Rapids: Eerdmans, 2014.

Delitzsch, Franz. *Commentary on the Psalms*. 2 vols. Edinburgh: T&T Clark, 1871.

Dempster, Stephen G. *Dominion and Dynasty: A Theology of the Hebrew Bible*. Downers Grove, IL: InterVarsity, 2003.

deSilva, David A. *Discovering Revelation: Content, Interpretation, Reception*. Grand Rapids: Eerdmans, 2021.

DeVries, Simon, and Bruce M. Metzger. *1 Kings*. Word Biblical Commentary 12. Grand Rapids: HarperCollins, 2015.

Dodson, Derek S., and Katherine E. Smith, eds. *Exploring Biblical Backgrounds: A Reader in Historical and Literacy Contexts*. Waco, TX: Baylor University Press, 2018.

Dumbrell, William J. *Covenant and Creation: An Old Testament Covenant Theology*. Milton Keynes, UK: Paternoster, 2013.

Dunn, James D. G. *The Theology of Paul the Apostle*. Grand Rapids: Eerdmans, 1998.

du Rand, J. A. "The New Jerusalem as Pinnacle of Salvation: Text (Rev 21:1—22:5) and Intertext." *Neotestamentica* 32 (2004) 275–302.

Durham, John I. "The King as 'Messiah' in the Psalms." *Review & Expositor* 81.3 (1984) 425.

Duvall, J. Scott, and J. Daniel Hays. *God's Relational Presence: The Cohesive Center of Biblical Theology*. Grand Rapids: Baker Academic, 2019.

Earwood, Greg C. "Psalm 46." *Review and Expositor* 86 (1989) 79–86.

Eaton, John. *The Psalms: A Historical and Spiritual Commentary*. London: Bloomsbury, 2003.

Eddinger, Terry. "Analysis of Isaiah 40:1–11." *Bulletin for Biblical Research* 9 (1999) 119–35.

Edersheim, Alfred. *The Temple: Its Ministry and Services as They Were at the Time of Jesus Christ*. London: James Clarke, 1959.

Edwards, James R. *The Gospel According to Mark*. Pillar New Testament Commentary. Grand Rapids: Eerdmans, 2002.

Eichler, Raanan. *The Ark and the Cherubim*. Tübingen: Mohr Siebeck, 2021.

Ellingworth, Paul. *The Epistle to the Hebrews: A Commentary on the Greek Text*. New International Greek Testament Commentary. Grand Rapids: Eerdmans, 1993.

Ellison, S. D. "Old Testament Hope: Psalms 2, the Psalter, and the Anointed One." *Themelios* 46 (2021) 534–45.

Emerton, J. A. "A Neglected Solution of a Problem in Psalm 76:11." *Vetus Testamentum* 24 (1974) 136–46.

Erickson, Matthew J. "The New Jerusalem Is No Heaven." *Word & World* 40 (2020) 172–79.
Fanning, Buist M., III. *Revelation*. Zondervan Exegetical Commentary on the New Testament. Grand Rapids: HarperCollins, 2020.
Fee, Gordon D. *Paul, the Spirit, and the People of God*. Grand Rapids: Baker Academic, 1996.
Fetherholf, Christina. "The Body for a Temple, a Temple for a Body: An Examination of Bodily Metaphors in 1 Corinthians." *Proceedings* 30 (2010) 88–106.
Fung, Ronald Y. K. *The Epistle to the Galatians*. New International Commentary on the New Testament. Grand Rapids: Eerdmans, 1988.
Gallusz, Laszlo. *The Throne Motif in the Book of Revelation*. London: Bloomsbury, 2013.
Garland, David E. *1 Corinthians*. Baker Exegetical Commentary on the New Testament. Grand Rapids: Baker Academic, 2003.
Garrett, Duane A. *Hosea, Joel*. New American Commentary 19A. Nashville: Broadman & Holman, 1997.
Gerstenberger, Erhard S. "Psalm 69: Complaint and Confession." *The Covenant Quarterly* 55.2 (1997) 12.
Gladd, Benjamin L., et al. *Making All Things New: Inaugurated Eschatology for the Life of the Church*. Grand Rapids: Baker Academic, 2016.
Gillingham, Susan. "Jewish and Christian Approaches to Suffering in the Reception of Psalm 137." *Old Testament Essays* 32 (2019) 444–63.
Goldingay, John. *The Book of Jeremiah*. New International Commentary on the Old Testament. Grand Rapids: Eerdmans, 2021.
———. *The Message of Isaiah 40–55*. London: Bloomsbury, 2005.
———. *Old Testament Theology: Israel's Faith*. Westmont, IL: InterVarsity, 2006.
———. *Old Testament Theology: Israel's Gospel*. Westmont, IL: InterVarsity, 2003.
———. *Old Testament Theology: Israel's Life*. Downers Grove, IL: InterVarsity, 2009.
———. *The Theology of the Book of Isaiah*. Downers Grove, IL: IVP Academic, 2014.
———. *The Theology of Jeremiah: The Book, the Man, the Message*. Downers Grove, IL: InterVarsity, 2021.
Goldingay, John, and David Payne. *Isaiah 40–55*. International Critical Commentary. London: Bloomsbury, 2007.
Goldingay, John, and Tremper Longman, III. *Psalms*. Baker Commentary on the Old Testament Wisdom and Psalms. 3 vols. Grand Rapids: Baker Academic, 2007.
Gordis, Robert. "Psalm 9–10: A Textual and Exegetical Study." *The Jewish Quarterly Review* 48 (1957) 104–22.
Goswell, Gregory. "Forgiveness and the New Covenant of Jeremiah 31." *Zeitschrift für die Alttestamentliche Wissenschaft* 134 (2022) 370–77.
Goulder, Michael. "David and Yahweh in Psalms 23 and 24." *Journal for the Study of the Old Testament* 30 (2006) 463–73.
Green, Joel B. *The Gospel of Luke*. New International Commentary on the New Testament. Grand Rapids: Eerdmans, 1997.
Grindheim, Sigurd. *The Letter to the Hebrews*. Pillar New Testament Commentary. Grand Rapids: Eerdmans, 2023.
Groenewald, Alphonso. "Psalm 69:36 in the Light of the Zion-Tradition." *Old Testament Essays* 21 (2008) 358–72.
———. "The Transformation of the City of Zion: From Decadence to Justice and Prophetic Hope (1:1–2:5)." *Theological Studies* 71 (2016) 1–5.

Grogan, Geoffrey W. *Psalms*. Two Horizons Commentary. Grand Rapids: Eerdmans, 2008.

Gundry, Robert H. "In My Father's House There Are Many Μοναι (John 14:2)." *Zeitschrift für die Neutestamentliche Wissenschaft* 53 (1967) 68–72.

———. "The New Jerusalem: People as Place, Not Place for People." *Novum Testamentum* 29 (1987) 254–64.

Gunn, George A. "Psalm 2 and the Reign of the Messiah." *Bibliotheca Sacra* 169 (2012) 427–42.

Guthrie, George H. *Hebrews*. NIV Application Commentary. Grand Rapids: Zondervan, 1998.

———. "Hebrews' Use of the Old Testament: Recent Trends in Research." *Currents in Biblical Research* 1 (2003) 271–94.

———. "The Tree and the Temple: Echoes of a New Ingathering and Renewed Exile (Mark 11:12–21)." *New Testament Studies* 68 (2022) 26–37.

Hafemann, Scott. "The 'Temple of the Spirit' as the Inaugural Fulfillment of the New Covenant Within the Corinthian Correspondence." *Ex Auditu* 12 (1996) 29–42.

Hamilton, James M., Jr. *God's Glory in Salvation Through Judgment: A Biblical Theology*. Wheaton, IL: Crossway, 2010.

Hamilton, Victor P. *Exodus: An Exegetical Commentary*. Grand Rapids: Baker Academic, 2011.

Harman, Allen M. "The Setting and Interpretation of Psalm 126." *The Reformed Theological Review* 44 (1985) 74–80.

Harris, R. Laird, et al., eds. *Theological Wordbook of the Old Testament*. Chicago: Moody, 1999.

Hays, Rebecca W. Poe. "Sing Me a Parable of Zion: Isaiah's Vineyard (5:1–7) and Its Relationship to the 'Daughter Zion' Tradition." *Journal of Biblical Literature* 135 (2016) 743–61.

Henderson, Ruth. *Second Temple Songs of Zion*. Boston: De Gruyter, 2014.

Hess, Richard D., and Gordon J. Wenham, eds. *Zion: City of Our God*. Grand Rapids: Eerdmans, 1999.

Holmyard, Harold R., III. "Does Isaiah 33:23 Address Israel or Israel's Enemy?" *Bibliotheca Sacra* 152 (1995) 273–78.

Hong, Koog Pyoung. "Isaiah 33 Between Literature and Performance." *Ephemerides Theologicae Lovanienses* 95 (2019) 119–34.

Hoppe, Leslie J. *Isaiah*. New Collegeville Bible Commentary. Collegeville, MN: Liturgical Press, 2012.

Hossfeld, Frank-Lothar, and Erich Zenger. *Psalms 3: A Commentary on Psalms 101–50*. Minneapolis: Fortress, 2005.

Hubbard, David A. *Joel and Amos*. Downers Grove, IL: InterVarsity, 2009.

Huey, F. B. *Jeremiah, Lamentations*. New American Commentary 16. Nashville: Broadman & Holman, 1993.

Hughes, R. Kent. *Genesis: Beginning and Blessing*. Wheaton, IL: Crossway, 2004.

Human, Dirk J. "Psalm 132 and Its Compositional Contexts." *Scriptura* 116 (2017) 75–92.

Hunter, Alastair G. *Psalms: Remembering Zion*. Florence: Taylor & Francis, 1999.

Johnson, Dennis E. *Perfect Priest for Weary Pilgrims: A Theology of Hebrews*. Wheaton, IL: Crossway, 2024.

Johnson, Luke T. *Hebrews: A Commentary*. Louisville: Presbyterian, 2006.

Johnson, Nathan C. "Rendering David a Servant in *Psalm of Solomon* 17:21." *Journal for the Study of Pseudepigrapha* 26 (2017) 235–50.

Joseph, Simon J. *Jesus and the Temple: The Crucifixion in Its Jewish Context.* Society for New Testament Studies Monograph Series 165. Cambridge: Cambridge University Press, 2016.

———. *Jesus, the Essenes, and Christian Origins.* Waco, TX: Baylor University Press, 2018.

Kaiser, Walter, Jr., and Tiberius Rata. *Walking the Ancient Paths: A Commentary on Jeremiah.* Bellingham, WA: Lexham Press, 2019.

Keener, Craig S. *The Gospel of John.* Grand Rapids: Baker Academic, 2010.

———. *Romans.* New Covenant Commentary. Eugene, OR: Cascade, 2009.

Keown, Gerald, et al. *Jeremiah 26–52.* Word Biblical Commentary 27. Grand Rapids: HarperCollins, 2016.

Kerr, Alan. *The Temple of Jesus' Body: The Temple Theme in the Gospel of John.* London: Bloomsbury, 2002.

Kibbe, Michael. *Godly Fear or Ungodly Failure?* Boston: Walter de Gruyter, 2016.

Kirk, J. R. Daniel. "Time for Figs, Temple Destruction, and Houses of Prayer in Mark 11:12–25." *Catholic Biblical Quarterly* 74 (2012) 509–27.

Koester, Craig R. *Revelation and the End of All Things.* Grand Rapids: Eerdmans, 2018.

———. *Revelation: A New Translation with Introduction and Commentary.* New Haven, CT: Yale University Press, 2014.

———. *Symbolism in the Fourth Gospel: Meaning, Mystery, Community.* Minneapolis: 1517 Media, 2003.

Köstenberger, Andreas J. *John.* Baker Exegetical Commentary on the New Testament. Grand Rapids: Baker Academic, 2004.

Kruze, Heinz. "Psalm 132 and the Royal Zion Festival." *Vetus Testamentum* 33 (1983) 279–97.

Laato, Antti. *The Origin of Israelite Zion Theology.* London: Bloomsbury, 2018.

———. "Psalm 132 and the Development of the Jerusalemite/Israelite Royal Ideology." *Catholic Biblical Quarterly* 54 (1992) 49–66.

Ladd, George E. *The Gospel of the Kingdom: Scriptural Studies in the Kingdom of God.* Grand Rapids: Eerdmans, 1959.

Lalleman, Hetty. *Jeremiah and Lamentations.* Tyndale Old Testament Commentaries. Downers Grove, IL: InterVarsity, 2013.

Lam, Joseph. "Psalm 2 and the Disinheritance of Earthly Rulers: New Light from the Ugaritic Legal Text RS 94.2168." *Vetus Testamentum* 64 (2014) 34–46.

Lane, William L. *Hebrews 9–13.* Word Biblical Commentary 47B. Grand Rapids: HarperCollins, 2015.

Lee, Aquila H. I. *From Messiah to Preexistent Son: Jesus' Self-Consciousness and Early Christian Exegesis of Messianic Psalms.* Tübingen: Mohr Siebeck, 2019.

Levenson, Jon D. *Sinai and Zion: An Entry into the Jewish Bible.* New York: HarperOne, 1985.

Lister, J. Ryan. *The Presence of God: Its Place in the Storyline of Scripture and the Story of Our Lives.* Wheaton, IL: Crossway, 2015.

Lohse, Eduard, and Georg Fohrer. "Σιών, Ἰερουσαλήμ, Ἱεροσόλυμα, Ἱεροσολυμίτης." In *Theological Dictionary of the New Testament*, edited by Gerhard Kittel and Gerhard Friedrich, 7:292–338. Grand Rapids: Eerdmans, 1964–76.

Long, D. Stephen. *Hebrews.* Belief: A Theological Commentary on the Bible. Louisville: Presbyterian, 2011.

Longman, Tremper, III. *Psalms: An Introduction and Commentary.* Downers Grove, IL: InterVarsity, 2014.

Lund, Oystein. *Way Metaphors and Way Topics in Isaiah 40–55.* Tübingen: Mohr Siebeck, 2008.

Luther, Martin. *Commentary on Galatians.* Edited by Phillip S. Watson. Oak Harbor, WA: Logos Research Systems, 1997.

Lynch, Matthew J. "Zion's Warrior and the Nations: Isaiah 59:15b—63:6 in Isaiah's Zion Traditions." *The Catholic Biblical Quarterly* 70 (2008) 244–63.

Maier, Christl. "Psalm 87 as a Reappraisal of the Zion Tradition and Its Reception in Galatians 4:26." *Catholic Bible Quarterly* 69 (2007) 473–86.

Mandolfo, Carleen. *Daughter Zion Talks Back to the Prophets: A Dialogic Theology of the Book of Lamentations.* Atlanta: Society of Biblical Literature, 2007.

Mann, Thomas. *Divine Presence and Guidance in Israelite Traditions: The Typology of Exaltation.* Baltimore: Johns Hopkins University Press, 1977.

Marshall, I. Howard. *The Gospel of Luke: A Commentary on the Greek Text.* New International Greek Testament Commentary. Exeter, UK: Paternoster, 1978.

Marshall, I. Howard, and David Peterson, eds. *Witness to the Gospel: The Theology of Acts.* Grand Rapids: Eerdmans, 1998.

Martin, Oren, and D. A. Carson. *Bound for the Promised Land: The Land Promise in God's Redemptive Plan.* Downers Grove, IL: InterVarsity, 2015.

Mason, Eric. *"You Are a Priest Forever": Second Temple Jewish Messianism and the Priestly Christology of the Epistle to the Hebrews.* London: Brill, 2008.

Mathews, Kenneth A. *Genesis 1–11:26.* The New American Commentary 1A. Nashville: Broadman & Holman, 1996.

Matthews, Victor H., et al. *The IVP Bible Background Commentary: Old Testament.* Accessed using Logos Bible Software. Downers Grove, IL: InterVarsity, 2000.

McCruden, Kevin B. "The Eloquent Blood of Jesus: The Neglected Theme of the Fidelity of Jesus in Hebrews 12:24." *The Catholic Bible Quarterly* 75 (2013) 504–20.

Merrill, Eugene. *Everlasting Dominion: A Theology of the Old Testament.* Nashville: Broadman & Holman, 2006.

Miller, Robert D. "The Zion Hymns as Instruments of Power." *Ancient Near Eastern Studies* 47 (2010) 218–40.

Mitchell, David C. *The Message of the Psalter: An Eschatological Programme in the Books of Psalms.* London: Bloomsbury, 1997.

Moberly, R. W. *Old Testament Theology: Reading the Hebrew Bible as Christian Scripture.* Grand Rapids: Baker Academic, 2013.

Moore, Nicholas J. "He Saw Heaven Opened: Heavenly Temple and Universal Mission in Luke-Acts." *New Testament Studies* 68 (2022) 38–51.

Morales, Michael. *Who Shall Ascend the Mountain of the Lord: A Biblical Theology of the Book of Leviticus.* Downers Grove, IL: InterVarsity, 2015.

Morris, Leon. *The Epistle to the Romans.* Pillar New Testament Commentary. Grand Rapids: Eerdmans, 1988.

———. *The Gospel According to Matthew.* Pillar New Testament Commentary. Grand Rapids: Eerdmans, 1992.

Motyer, J. Alec. *Isaiah.* Downers Grove, IL: InterVarsity, 2009.

Mounce, Robert H. *Romans*. New American Commentary 27. Nashville: Broadman & Holman, 1995.

Mowinckel, Sigmund. *Psalm Studies*. 2 Vols. Translated by Mark Biddle. Atlanta: Society of Biblical Literature, 2010.

Nolland, John. *The Gospel of Matthew: A Commentary on the Greek Text*. New International Greek Testament Commentary. Grand Rapids: Eerdmans, 2005.

Noonan, Benjamin J. "Zion's Foundation: The Meaning of בֹּחַן in Isaiah 28:16." *Zeitschrift für die Alttestamentliche Wissenschaft* 125 (2013) 314–19.

O'Brien, Peter T. *The Letter to the Hebrews*. Pillar New Testament Commentary. Grand Rapids: Eerdmans, 2010.

Ollenburger, Ben. *Zion, the City of the Great King*. London: Bloomsbury, 1987.

Osborne, Grant R. *Matthew*. Zondervan Exegetical Commentary. Grand Rapids: HarperCollins, 2010.

———. *Revelation*. Baker Exegetical Commentary on the New Testament. Grand Rapids: Baker Academic, 2002.

Oswalt, John N. *The Book of Isaiah: Chapters 1–39*. New International Commentary on the Old Testament. Grand Rapids: Eerdmans, 1986.

———. *Isaiah*. NIV Application Commentary. Grand Rapids: HarperCollins, 2003.

Padilla, Osvaldo. *The Acts of the Apostles: Interpretation, History and Theology*. Downers Grove: InterVarsity, 2016.

Pennington, Jonathan T., and Sean M. McDonough, eds. *Cosmology and New Testament Theology*. London: Bloomsbury, 2008.

Perez-Gondar, Diego. "The New Jerusalem as Mother: Intertextuality Among Ps 87:5, Gal 4:26, and 4 Ezra 10:7–10." *Biblica* 101 (2020) 543–61.

Perrin, Nicholas. *Jesus the Temple*. Grand Rapids: Baker Academic, 2010.

Peterson, David G. *Hebrews: An Introduction and Commentary*. Westmont, IL: InterVarsity, 2020.

Pierce, Timothy M. *Enthroned on Our Praise: An Old Testament Theology of Worship*. Nashville: Broadman & Holman, 2008.

Piotrowski, Nicholas G. "One Spirit, One Body, One Temple: Paul's Corporate Temple Language in 1 Corinthians 6." *Journal for the Evangelical Theological Society* 65 (2022) 733–52.

Porter, Stanley E. *The Messiah in the Old and New Testaments*. Grand Rapids: Eerdmans, 2007.

Poulson, Frederik. *Representing Zion: Judgment and Salvation in the Old Testament*. New York: Routledge, 2015.

Preuss, Horst. *Old Testament Theology*. 2 vols. Louisville: Presbyterian, 1996.

Raabe, Paul. "Christ and the Nations: Isaiah's Gentile Oracles." *Concordia* 39 (2013) 25–33.

Roberts, J. J. M. "The Davidic Origin of the Zion Tradition." *Journal of Biblical Literature* 92 (1977) 329–44.

———. "The End of War in the Zion Tradition: The Imperialistic Background of an Old Testament Vision of World Wide Peace." *Horizons in Biblical Theology* 26 (2004) 2–22.

———. "Yahweh's Foundation in Zion (Isa 28:16)." *Journal of Biblical Literature* 106 (1987) 27–45.

Rohde, Michael. “Observations on the Songs of Ascents: A Discussion About the So-Called Zion-Theology of Psalms 120–34.” *Zeitschrift für die Alttestamentliche Wissenschaft* 126 (2014) 24–42.

Rohland, Edzard. “Die Bedeutung der Erwählungstraditionen Israels für die Eschatologie der Alttestamentlichen Propheten.” PhD diss., Heidelberg University, 1956.

Rooke, Deborah W. “Urban Planning According to Ezekiel: The Shape of the Restored Jerusalem.” In *The City in the Hebrew Bible*, edited by James K. Aitken and Hilary F. Marlow, 123–43. London: Bloomsbury, 2018.

Sawyer. John F. A. “Daughter of Zion and Servant of the Lord in Isaiah: A Comparison.” *Journal for the Study of the Old Testament* 44 (1989) 89–107.

Schäder, Jo-Mari. “Understanding (the Lack of) Space in Psalm 47:6 in Light of Its Neighboring Psalms: A Spatial Reading of Psalms 46–48.” *Old Testament Essays* 23 (2010) 129–60.

Schenck, Kenneth L. *Cosmology and Eschatology in Hebrews: The Settings of the Sacrifice*. Cambridge: Cambridge University Press, 2007.

Schmid, Konrad, and Peter Altmann. *Is There Theology in the Hebrew Bible?* Philadelphia: PSU Press, 2015.

Schnittjer, Gary E. *Old Testament Use of Old Testament: A Book-by-Book Guide*. Grand Rapids: HarperCollins, 2021.

Schreiner, David B. “The Election and Divine Choice of Zion/Jerusalem.” *Journal for the Evangelical Study of the Old Testament* 1 (2012) 147–66.

Schreiner, Thomas R. *The Joy of Hearing: A Theology of Revelation*. Wheaton, IL: Crossway, 2021.

———. *The King in His Beauty: A Biblical Theology of the Old and New Testaments*. Grand Rapids: Baker Academic, 2013.

———. *Revelation*. Baker Exegetical Commentary on the New Testament. Grand Rapids: Baker Academic, 2024.

———. *Romans*. Baker Exegetical Commentary on the New Testament. Grand Rapids: Baker, 1998.

Schreiner, Thomas R., and Clinton E. Arnold. *Galatians*. Zondervan Exegetical Commentary on the New Testament. Grand Rapids: Zondervan, 2010.

Schürer, Emil. *A History of the Jewish People in the Time of Jesus Christ, First Division*. Edinburgh: T&T Clark, 1890.

Seitz, Christopher R. *Zion's Final Destiny: The Development of the Book of Isaiah*. Minneapolis: Fortress, 1991.

Segal, Benjamin J. “Psalm 126: Of Dreams, Prayer, and Fulfillment.” *CCAR Journal: A Reform Jewish Quarterly* 55 (2008) 50–58.

Seufert, Matthew. “Reading Isaiah 40:1–11 in Light of Isaiah 36–37.” *Journal of the Evangelical Theological Society* 58 (2015) 269–81.

Shead, Andrew. *A Mouth Full of Fire: The Word of God in the Words of Jeremiah*. Downers Grove, IL: InterVarsity, 2012.

Siegal, Elitzur A. “The Hebrew-Based Traditions in Galatians 4:21–31.” *Early Christianity* 10 (2019) 404–31.

Simango, Daniel. “A Comprehensive Reading of Psalm 137.” *Old Testament Essays* 31 (2018) 217–42.

Slabbert, Martin J. “Coping in a Harsh Reality: The Concept of the ‘Enemy’ in the Composition of Psalms 9 and 10.” *Theological Studies* 71 (2015) 1–5.

Son, Kiwoong. *Zion Symbolism in Hebrews: Hebrews 12:18–24 as a Hermeneutical Key to the Epistle.* Milton Keynes, UK: Paternoster, 2005.

Smith, Billy K., and Franklin S. Page. *Amos, Obadiah, Jonah.* New American Commentary 19B. Nashville: Broadman & Holman, 1995.

Smith, Gary V. *Isaiah 1–39.* New American Commentary 15A. Nashville: Broadman & Holman, 2007.

———. *Isaiah 40–66.* New American Commentary 15B. Nashville: Broadman & Holman, 2009.

Smith, James E. *The Minor Prophets.* Joplin, MO: College Press, 1994.

———. *The Wisdom Literature and Psalms.* Joplin, MO: College Press, 1996.

Smith, Ralph L. *Micah-Malachi.* Word Biblical Commentary 32. Waco, TX: Word, 1984.

Snook, Lee E. "Interpreting the Book of Isaiah: Yahweh's Changeless Purpose in the Changing History of Zion." *Word & World* 3 (1983) 448–61.

Stein, Robert H. *Jesus the Messiah: A Survey of the Life of Christ.* Downers Grove, IL: InterVarsity, 1996.

Steiner, Till M. "Perceived and Narrated Space in Psalm 48." *Old Testament Essays* 25 (2012) 685–704.

———. "Spatial Theory and Theology in Psalms 46–48." In *The Psalter as Witness: Theology, Poetry, and Genre*, edited by W. Dennis Tucker Jr. and W. H. Bellinger Jr., 63–74. Waco, TX: Baylor University Press, 2017.

Stevenson, Gregory. *Power and Place: Temple and Identity in the Book of Revelation.* Boston: Walter de Gruyter, 2001.

Sumpter, Philip. "The Coherence of Psalm 24." *Journal for the Study of the Old Testament* 39 (2014) 31–54.

Sweeney, Marvin A. *1–2 Samuel.* New Cambridge Bible Commentary. Cambridge: Cambridge University Press, 2023.

Tabb, Brian J. *All Things New: Revelation as Canonical Capstone.* Downers Grove, IL: InterVarsity, 2019.

Tate, Marvin and David Hubbard. *Psalms 51–100.* Word Biblical Commentary 20. Grand Rapids: HarperCollins, 2015.

Thiselton, Anthony C. *The First Epistle to the Corinthians: A Commentary on the Greek Text.* New International Greek Testament Commentary. Grand Rapids: Eerdmans, 2000.

Thompson, J. A. *The Book of Jeremiah.* New International Commentary on the Old Testament. Grand Rapids: Eerdmans, 2014.

Thompson, James W. *Hebrews.* Paideia Commentaries on the New Testament. Grand Rapids: Baker Academic, 2008.

Thompson, John L. *Genesis 1–11.* Reformation Commentary on Scripture 1. Downers Grove, IL: InterVarsity, 2012.

Tiemeyer, Lena-Sofia. *For the Comfort of Zion: The Geographical and Theological Location of Isaiah 40–55.* Boston: Brill, 2010.

van Wolde, Ellen. "Psalm 102:12–23: Qualifications Rather Than Actions." *The Bible Translator* 70 (2019) 207–22.

von Rad, Gerhard. *Old Testament Theology.* 2 vols. New York: Harper & Row, 1957.

Waltke, Bruce K. "Ask of Me, My Son: Exposition of Psalm 2." *Crux* 43 (2007) 2–19.

Watts, John D. *Isaiah 1–33.* Word Biblical Commentary 24. Nashville: Thomas Nelson, 1985.

———. *Isaiah 34–66.* Vol. 25, Word Biblical Commentary. Waco, TX: Word, 1987.

Webb, Barry G. *Five Festal Garments: Christian Reflections on the Song of Songs, Ruth, Lamentations, Ecclesiastes, Esther.* Downers Grove, IL: InterVarsity, 2000.

———. *The Message of Isaiah: On Eagles' Wings.* Downers Grove, IL: InterVarsity, 1996.

———. *The Message of Zechariah: Your Kingdom Come.* Downers Grove, IL: InterVarsity, 2003.

Wegner, Paul D. *Isaiah.* Downers Grove, IL: InterVarsity, 2021.

Weinert, Francis D. "The Meaning of the Temple in Luke-Acts." *Biblical Theology Bulletin* 11 (1981) 85–89.

Weiser, Artur. *Psalms.* Old Testament Library. Louisville: Presbyterian, 1962.

Wenell, Karen J. "Contested Temple Space and Visionary Kingdom Space in Mark 11–12." *Biblical Interpretation* 15 (2007) 323–37.

Wenham, Gordan, and James D. G. Dunn. *Genesis.* Eerdmans Commentary on the Bible. Grand Rapids: Eerdmans, 2019.

Wesselschmidt, Quentin F., ed. *Psalms 51–150.* Ancient Christian Commentary on Scripture 8. Downers Grove, IL: IVP Academic, 2007.

Westermann, Claus. *Isaiah 40–66.* Louisville: Westminster John Knox, 1969.

Whiston, William. *The Works of Flavius Josephus.* Philadelphia: John E. Potter, 1895.

Whiting, Mark J. "Psalms 1 and 2 as a Hermeneutical Lens for Reading the Psalter." *Evangelical Quarterly* 85 (2013) 246–62.

Whybray, R. Norman, and M. Patrick Graham. *Reading the Psalms as a Book.* London: Bloomsbury, 1996.

Wildberger, Hans. "Die Völkerwallfahrt zum Zion, Jes. II 1–5." *Vetus Testamentum* 7 (1957) 62–81.

Wilk, Janusz. "The Pilgrimage to Jerusalem as Depicted in Psalm 122." *Ruch Biblijny Liturgiczny* 71 (2018) 293–303.

Williamson, H. G. M. *Isaiah 1–5.* International Critical Commentary. London: Bloomsbury, 2006.

Willis, Timothy M. "I Will Remember Their Sins No More: Jeremiah 31, the New Covenant, and the Forgiveness of Sins." *Restoration Quarterly* 53 (2011) 1–15.

Willitts, Joel. "Matthew and Psalms of Solomon's Messianism: A Comparative Study in First-Century Messianology." *Bulletin for Biblical Research* 22 (2012) 27–50.

Wilson, Ian D. "Yahweh's Consciousness: Isaiah 40–48 and Ancient Judean Historical Thought." *Vetus Testamentum* 66 (2016) 646–61.

Witherington, Ben, III. *Isaiah Old and New: Exegesis, Intertextuality, and Hermeneutics.* Minneapolis: Fortress, 2017.

Witt, Andrew. "Hearing Psalm 102 Within the Context of the Hebrew Psalter." *Vetus Testamentum* 62 (2012) 582–602.

Wolverton, Wallace. "The Meaning of Zion in the Psalms." *Anglican Theological Review* 47 (1965) 16–33.

Woodhouse, John, and R. Kent Hughes. *1 Kings: Power, Politics, and the Hope of the World.* Wheaton, IL: Crossway, 2018.

Wright, N. T. *Paul and His Recent Interpreters.* Minneapolis: Fortress, 2015.

www.ingramcontent.com/pod-product-compliance
Lightning Source LLC
LaVergne TN
LVHW050634100826
845148LV00011B/1864

* 9 7 9 8 3 8 5 2 5 4 6 6 8 *